Optimistic Nihilism

Optimistic Nihilism

A Psychologist's Personal Story
& (Biased) Professional Appraisal
of Shedding Religion

David Landers, Ph.D.

IM Print Publishing
Austin

Thank you for purchasing this book!
A portion of royalties will be donated to hunger charities.

Feel free to communicate with the author at
facebook.com/OptimisticNihilism
Twitter: @Opti_Nihilist

Personal stories from David's clinical practice herein have been used with
permission and/or thoroughly disguised to protect the confidentiality of
the persons involved.

**General cover concept by Matthew Arnold, cargocollective.com/mattarnold
Other graphics and consulting by Lance Myers, lancefever.com
and Egan Jones, eganjones.com**

First Edition; first printing
ISBN 13: 978-0692440780
ISBN 10: 069244078X

IM Print Publishing, P.O. Box 93066, Austin, TX 78709

*For my mom, whose hard life
was not a test, experiment, or example.*

Annihilation has no terrors for me, because I have already
tried it before I was born—a hundred million years—and I
have suffered more in an hour, in this life, than I remember
to have suffered in the whole hundred million years put
together. There was a peace, a serenity, an absence of all
sense of responsibility, an absence of worry, an absence of
care, grief, perplexity; and the presence of a deep content
and unbroken satisfaction in that hundred million years of
holiday which I look back upon with a tender longing and
with a grateful desire to resume, when the opportunity
comes.

— Mark Twain

When I consider the brief span of my life, swallowed up in
the eternity before and behind it, the small space that I fill,
or even see, engulfed in the infinite immensity of spaces
which I know not, and which know not me, I am afraid . . .
I marvel that people are not seized with despair at such a
miserable condition.

— French mathematician/philosopher Blaise Pascal
(born 1623)

Contents

Introduction

I'VE WRITTEN THIS BOOK largely in response to modern popular books on atheism, such as Richard Dawkins's *The God Delusion* and Christopher Hitchens's *God is Not Great*. Although I agree with the vast majority of the sentiments presented in these works, I find the authors' tones unnecessarily condescending and hostile towards believers.

If we modern atheists truly want our message to be heard, we need to rein in the vicious and degrading attacks. Hostility never convinced anyone of anything; it's only engaging for the people who are already on your side. Anyway, everyone should know by now that faith, by definition, is exempt from logical argument. We'll make a lot more progress if we can just calm down and live by example. (Not to mention, our hostility suggests that *we* are insecure, which we should also examine.)

So, my book employs a different approach, being a more personal and (hopefully) poignant read. As I share how I ventured from being a very devoted, God-fearing child to a profoundly atheistic adult, you'll see that I was miserable as a Christian—on the brink of suicide at times—but have been much more functional and content since converting to atheism. Now, if you don't enjoy autobiography so much, don't be discouraged: A clinical psychologist by trade, I'm able to tell my story with frequent interjections of psychological discussion, the stuff that everyone likes to read about, such as mental illness, drug addiction, and even violence.

Although not degreed in philosophy I've studied it informally for much of my life, so I'll also include input from the masters, from Lucretius to the band Suicidal Tendencies. Be aware that I've tried to keep the psychological and philosophical discourse intellectual and provocative while accessible to—and perhaps even fun for—the lay reader. I want my book to appeal to Richard Dawkins and his disciples, but also to high school students and such who are only just beginning to ask questions about spirituality.

Chapter 1 sets the stage for the rest of the book, being a casual conversation about contacting reality and being honest about it, potentially always. As far as religion is concerned, I believe that we actually all know the truth deep down (that it's the product of humans, not divinity), the more interesting issue regarding how much of that truth each of us is willing—or able—to endure.

In chapters 2 through 4 I'll disclose how my home life as a devoted Christian child was fraught with turmoil and even abuse, leading to dangerous substance addiction as a teen and onward to significant mental illness as a young adult.

In chapter 5, I'll walk you through the philosophy, history, and science that I found in college that slowly whittled away my faith. Since becoming a full-blown atheist, studying psychological defense mechanisms (chapter 6) has helped me understand why humans feel that they need religion. This cemented my newfound atheistic position, but also has helped me to become compassionate towards those who remain faithful. Understanding evolution (chapter 7) has contributed as well simply by making so much sense. Evolution really is beautiful, the more you understand it. In fact, many of us atheists find a godless creation much more fascinating and precious than one created by any deity.

Chapter 8 is the most Dawkins-esque chapter of the book, as we discuss the toxicity of religion. I try to keep it civilized, but arguably violate my own proposition that we drop the hostility. It's hard to not get angry, and I'll explain why.

Chapter 9 takes it all up a notch, more so than many popular modern atheist writers seem to want to venture, by openly and frankly exploring nihilism. *Nihilism,* as used in this book, is the position that there is no objective purpose to or transcendence from our lives beyond that endowed by evolution: that is, making and raising babies. However, I'll argue that this perspective doesn't have to entail chronic despair. On the contrary, I will explain (as have others) that such a nihilistic perspective may ironically be the one that honors reality the most. It helps us to be present in every moment and to be sensitive to the existence of others, as well as to the universe at large, much more than an authoritarian commandment ever could.

Chapter 10 is a more personal snapshot of myself at the time of this writing. I'm asking readers to spend some time in the mind of a self-described nihilist and see what it's like. It's probably not what most people would expect.

Chapter 11 winds it all down with some relatively explicit advice on how all of us—atheists and believers alike—can approach living in a more wholesome manner, based on some of the principles we'll have discussed throughout this book.

Finally, I've included an appendix that complements the self-help feel of chapter 11 but does not discuss spirituality directly at all. Here, I present the often-ignored but exceedingly invaluable topic of *emotional validation.* Emotional validation is the interpersonal dynamic in which we attend to and acknowledge the inner experiences of others, especially those of our growing children but also those of the adults in our lives. Comprehending these dynamics should enrich your life, regardless of how spiritual you are. If nothing else, it may help explain why a psychologist like myself is so obsessed with being in touch with reality.

CHAPTER 1

Ignorance and Bliss

The great boon of repression is that it makes it possible to live decisively in an overwhelmingly miraculous and incomprehensible world, a world so full of beauty, majesty, and terror that if animals perceived it all they would be paralyzed to act.

— Philosophical anthropologist Ernest Becker,
The Denial of Death

ON THE FIRST DAY of my *Introduction to Forensic Psychology* class each semester, I enjoy beginning to dispel the common misconceptions of the field for my students. Indeed, the notion of *forensic psychologist* tends to conjure fantastic and dramatic scenes: a charismatic criminal profiler donning night-vision goggles, bursting in on the serial killer "dancing around his room in a pair of his mommy's panties, singing show tunes and rubbing himself with peanut butter."[1]

---

1 Brad Pitt's character Detective David Mills in the movie *Seven*. The quote is from a draft of the script by Andrew Walker dated August 8, 1994 as retrieved from http://www.dailyscript.com/scripts/seven_production.html. In the actual movie, Mills imagines it's the killer's "grandma's" panties, but he doesn't mention the show tunes. I would have gone with grandma's as well, but kept the show tunes. The movie citation is Kopelson, A., Carlyle, P. (Producers), & Fincher, D. (Director). (1995). *Seven* [Motion picture]. U.S.: New Line Cinema.

As I have to explain to my students, Hollywood has greatly sen-
sationalized the field; it's not like this at all. In fact, *criminal profiler* is
somewhat of a mythical profession. Last I heard, even the FBI has
had, at most, about a dozen profilers working at a time.[2] Turns out,
most are not even psychologists: They're police officers or FBI field
agents who have worked their way up the ranks in their respective
institutions. And the punchline is that research suggests that they're
not particularly helpful. Although they tend to contribute to investi-
gations, they can rarely claim most of the credit for actually solving
them. Critics will go further, pointing out that criminal profiles can
even impede progress—or worse—by focusing investigators' efforts
in the wrong direction. Infamous failures include the D.C. Sniper
(who virtually no one expected was African-American) and the 1996
Olympic Centennial Park bomber in Atlanta (which led to falsely
accused Richard Jewel's picture being posted all over the world as
the prime suspect). Due to documented inaccuracies such as these,
expert testimony regarding criminal profiles is not likely to be allowed in many courtrooms.

"But, Class, don't be disappointed!" Back on Earth, doing *real*
forensic work as a psychologist is very exciting. I don't get to arrest
serial killers, but I do get to do competency-to-stand-trial and insanity evaluations on real criminals—a small minority of whom have
killed before, some perhaps even serially.

To perform my duties, I get to be a psychologist, a lawyer, and a
detective—all rolled up in one. The psychologist meets the defendant face-to-face and uses his training to nail down the right diagnosis and to comment on competency or insanity, whichever the case
may be. Of course, sometimes the right diagnosis is *malingering*, that
is, the defendant is trying to act crazy when he isn't. Alternatively—and perhaps even more challenging and interesting—the defendant may be *dissimulating*, that is, trying to act *well* when he's actu-

---

2 These perspectives on profiling are from the textbook I use in my class: Fulero,
S. & Wrightsman, L. (2009). *Forensic psychology* (3rd ed.). Belmont, CA:
Wadsworth. Other forensic psych texts that I've perused share similar sentiments.

ally mentally ill. This is a lot more common than you might suspect! People with psychosis typically don't want others to know about it. When someone starts spouting off all about their hallucinations and paranoia in the first few minutes of a meeting, I'm naturally suspicious.

Besides the psychologist, the lawyer element has to know the law, which often provides its own definitions of psychological constructs, whether "insanity," "dangerousness to self or others," or "sexually violent predator." Reading the law can be engaging, especially if you have an obsessive personality like mine. In the law, every *and* and every *or* counts, sometimes punctuation alone leading to heated debate regarding the original intent behind the law in question.

And finally, the detective part gets to pore over police reports and other records, which rarely disappoint. If you like gore, sure, sometimes you end up with crime scene photos, in all their blatant, Technicolor cruelty. With the increasing accessibility of video, criminals are more often recording their crimes. Sometimes it's as mild as a school yard vendetta, but other times it's torture, the kind of shit you might see in a Rob Zombie movie. I honestly don't care for the hard stuff much myself anymore and have basically stopped looking, unless it's clearly relevant to the evaluation at hand. It rarely is.

I suspect that many of my colleagues find this work rewarding because they feel that they're contributing to some greater good for society. However, I'm not ashamed to admit I'm a bit more selfish, appreciating the work more for the compelling personal experiences it provides. I often describe forensic evaluation as a very "existential" enterprise, in that it provokes a lot of introspection and contemplation, which is what really gets me up in the morning. Although traumatic at times, the work has also helped me mature in a healthy way by putting things in perspective, the little things over here and the important stuff over there. I've never felt as thankful as I have on any one of the hundreds of occasions while driving away from a jail or psychiatric hospital having just completed a psychological evaluation. I'm so thankful because I've got my *sanity* and I'm *free*. You know, the basics. Now, there's something less gratifying about feeling good when it comes at someone else's expense. But, back on the other hand, there's also no denying that sunlight feels about as good as can be once you've been deprived of it for a few hours, surrounded by insanity, stink, and injustice.

Confidentiality restrictions prevent me from discussing my own cases in much detail, but I can discuss those that are declassified. One of the most provocative in all of forensic psychology is that of Alvin Bernard Ford. In my class, we talk about him at the end of the course because that's when we cover the death penalty. However, for my book, it makes for a better beginning. So, go brush your teeth, put on your jammies, and get ready for bed, and I'll tell you his story.[3]

Alvin was attending high school in Florida during the late 1960s when public school desegregation in the South was in full swing in the wake of the Civil Rights Act of 1964. His high school, Lincoln, was converted into a middle school, so he and other black students were transferred to Palmetto High to be a part of this momentous chapter of American history. School staff say that Alvin took it all in stride; besides a period of what appeared to be traditional senioritis, he was "a good student . . . from a nice family." He seemed to handle integration relatively well, as he "wanted you to know he was black but he didn't push it."

No doubt, Alvin's high school résumé was a lot more distinguished than mine: Vice President of the Science Club, Vice President of Future Farmers of America, a member of Future Business Leaders of America—and he showed a cow at the county fair! Alvin played basketball and was a linebacker on an 8-2 football team, his coach

---

3 Adapted from the following: Two separate stories from the *Sarasota Herald-Tribune* by White, D. (1984, July 21), "Decade of uncertainty darkens case of Alvin Ford: Former Palmetto man waits on death row" and "Slain officer's memory is inspiration to department"; also, Ford v. Wainwright, 477 U.S. 399 (1986). I found the newspaper articles via Google News.

describing him as "hard-nosed, very aggressive . . . One of our best players. First string. Very reliable." Alvin's senior yearbook photo shows a handsome young man who just seems to exude athleticism. He looks like the kind of black guy that a white kid like me always wanted to be friends with, in hopes that some of his cool would somehow make me cool by association.

After high school, Alvin tinkered with the idea of college but ended up working instead, first at a Red Lobster. While still legally a juvenile, he was caught (along with some accomplices) stealing $3,000 worth of automotive supplies from a moving company. As often the case for such a first offense, adjudication was deferred and he was placed on probation. I've never come across any speculation about the psychological dynamics behind the decline in Alvin's behavior, but I have to wonder if it was the earliest manifestations of what would later be full-blown schizophrenia.

In any event, Alvin later worked at another restaurant in Gainesville where he became assistant manager. However, it was apparently too much responsibility and he lost the job. Ironically, he next landed a position as a guard at a state prison, very near the same facility where he would eventually be imprisoned for the rest of his own life. Completing another twist, Alvin lost that job in the early 1970s because he was arrested on suspicion of having robbed the same Red Lobster where he worked after high school. He allegedly forced the manager at gunpoint to open the safe, leaving with $4,000. However, the case was dropped because of dubious eyewitness testimony. For reasons that seem unclear, Alvin couldn't keep steady employment thereafter, and suspicions are that he turned to dealing drugs. Again, I speculate that his mind wasn't quite right.

What is more clear is that on July 21, 1974, twenty-year-old Alvin and three accomplices attempted to rob a different Red Lobster from where he had previously worked, this one in Fort Lauderdale. The whole thing went down in broad daylight, the robbers wearing stocking masks like something out of one of the myriad television police dramas of the time. During the robbery, a couple of potential witnesses escaped, so Alvin's accomplices bailed. Alvin lingered and was the last to leave, perhaps not quite as willing to give up as the others.

Officer Dimitri Ilyankoff was the first officer to arrive on the scene, and he did so alone. He was a 15-year veteran of the police force, "quiet, soft-spoken and [he] loved to fish . . . Next to his family, he loved the water most."

When Alvin and Officer Ilyankoff surprised one another at the back door of the restaurant, the latter was armed with only a clipboard. Alvin shot him twice in the abdomen. A witness who had been watching through the slatted door of the closet in which she was hiding testified that Alvin ran to the officer's car but the keys weren't there. He returned to Ilyankoff, who was wounded but in the process of radioing for help, and demanded the keys. Once he acquired them, he took Officer Ilyankoff's own revolver, pressed it behind his ear, and executed him. Ilyankoff was the first officer murdered while on duty in Fort Lauderdale since the force was founded way back in 1911. His wife would later hold a private memorial service and spread his ashes at sea from his boat.

At Alvin's trial in 1975, the judge described him as a "human animal that does not deserve to live in the company of civilized man," and he was indeed sentenced to death by a jury. He attempted a few appeals over the years, routine as far as I know, except that on one occasion his execution was delayed less than 15 hours before he was to be electrocuted to death. At any rate, each of the routine appeals ultimately failed.

While on death row, Alvin had initially been functioning well, all things considered. However, after some time, he became "uncooperative, threatened to 'kill me some crackers (guards),' had been found in possession of homemade weapons, [and] smashed his black-and-white television." He eventually demanded that his remaining appeals be terminated and that he be executed. The state was willing to oblige, but Alvin got another stay, again less than 15 hours before the moment of truth—but this time it wasn't routine.

This time, his defense was arguing that Alvin *was not mentally fit to be executed*, and the associated arguments would ascend the judicial ladder, all the way to the Supreme Court of the United States.

It was revealed that behind all of the hostility was a bizarre web of psychotic delusion. In the early 1980s, after hearing of a Ku Klux Klan rally in nearby Jacksonville, Alvin had come to believe that the organization was conspiring with others to somehow force him to commit suicide. He felt that the guards in his prison were involved, and that they had been killing people and burying their bodies in the prison walls. According to the United States Supreme Court syllabus of his case,

> he began to believe that his women relatives were being tortured and sexually abused somewhere in the prison . . . The hostage delusion took firm hold and expanded, until Ford was reporting that 135 of his friends and family were being held hostage in the prison, and that only he could help them. By 'day 287' of the 'hostage crisis,' the list of hostages had expanded to include 'senators, Senator Kennedy, and many other leaders.' . . . Ford appeared to assume authority for ending the 'crisis,' claiming to have fired a number of prison officials. He began to refer to himself as 'Pope John Paul, III,' and reported having appointed nine new justices to the Florida Supreme Court.

Particularly relevant for his legal situation, Alvin apparently no longer believed he could be executed: "I know there is some sort of death penalty, but I'm free to go whenever I want, because it would be illegal and the executioner would be executed . . . I can't be executed because of the landmark case. I won. *Ford v. State* will prevent executions all over." (*Ford v. State* was Alvin's earlier routine appeal, which he lost.) Record has it that Alvin also felt he was immune because "he owned the prisons and could control the Governor through mind waves."

Alvin's case opens an unfathomable can of worms; it probably deserves a whole book unto itself (apparently there is one, but I have to admit I haven't read it). We could talk about the *diathesis-stress model* of psychopathology, the well-accepted notion that individuals may carry genes that predispose them to a mental illness such as schizophrenia, but the illness lies dormant unless a traumatic stressor (such as sexual abuse, homelessness, and of course, imprisonment) arouses it.[4] We could talk about psychosis and the different types of delusions, at which point we'd have to investigate the fascinating relationship between grandiosity and paranoia, which kinda seem mutually exclusive at first glance but often go hand-in-hand. We could devote significant time to discuss whether Alvin was feigning his illness. Certainly, some folks suspected he was, but most, including the justices of the United States Supreme Court, believed it was real. Based on what I've read, I concur. Some folks can fake psychosis quite well for a few minutes, maybe even hours, but not for months or years. Not like that. As I tell my students, often the most difficult part of interacting with a malingering defendant is not busting out laughing at their poor attempts to act crazy.

Cases such as this also raise all sorts of ethical issues, some quite nuanced. One of my favorites regards the psychiatrists who prescribe the medications for insane death-row inmates such as Alvin Ford. That is, the psychiatrist's Hippocratic Oath says something about "I will keep [the sick] from harm and injustice." Not even considering the "injustice" part, is it right to treat a delusional patient, if successful treatment necessarily means he is to be put to death?

These issues are all wonderfully provocative, but the one that I am most compelled to consider is the following: What would I prefer if I found myself in a situation like Alvin's? *Would I keep the delusion*

---

4 In my practice, I observe that imprisonment is indeed one of the more common predisposing events to psychosis. Solitary confinement and/or rape while there seem to raise the probability of the illness emerging, from which some inmates never recover. After you've met enough of these patients, you really start to feel that our prison system is inherently cruel and unusual, at least for some inmates.

that I'm in control and that I'm going to survive, or would I take the treatment, exit the delusion, and face the reality of my execution? Let's simplify, and assume there's no physical pain either way. What I'm interested in is the mental aspect, the *awareness* of impending annihilation—or not—all else being equal. And all you have to do to venture to the other side is take a pill, *Matrix*-style.

When teaching various psychology courses over time, I've conducted informal polls of my students regarding what they would prefer in a situation similar to Alvin Ford's. About two-thirds to three-fourths have preferred the delusion, at least when queried on the fly. Although my classes have not exactly comprised a random sample of the population at large, their position corroborates my hunch that most Americans prefer the delusion over the truth.

Well, Class, you're out of luck: The United States Supreme Court ruled that it would be cruel and unusual to execute Alvin in his delusional state. Paradoxically, however, one rationale provided is that executing the delusional "simply offends humanity," partially because we have an obligation to "protect the condemned from fear and pain without comfort of understanding." Legally, at least in the context of execution, appreciating when and why one is about to die is regarded as the more humane option.

Otherwise, to address those cases in which the convict is simply so delusional that "fear and pain" are not likely to be at issue, the Court included another rationale to postpone executions: In these cases, execution would now have "questionable retributive value." Of course, it's not all about treating the convict humanely. We do want him to suffer, but only for the right reasons.

There was one specific rationale that may be easier to digest: Executing the insane does not permit him to properly prepare for death, such as by seeking atonement. Alvin Ford seems to be an exquisite example: He thinks he's the Pope, that he's the one who has the authority to forgive others!

I'm not sure if this makes me smart or stupid, but I see the situation more like the Supreme Court than like the majority of my students. Not just the prepare-for-death issue, but the other issues of humane treatment as well, however grotesque and twisted the situation is overall. That is, I have always had the opinion that I'd want the pill, if given a choice. It's a reflexive position over which I really don't even have to deliberate. I feel like I want to know if I'm dying, and why. Give me the pill, remove my delusion, so that I can die lucid. In my gut, knowing the *truth* simply trumps *peace of mind*. I need to be in touch with reality as much as possible, regardless of how much it hurts.

In the highly recommended *The Wall*, Jean-Paul Sartre's character Pablo apparently feels similarly. He's just been sentenced to death by firing squad, to take place at dawn only hours away. In the interim, he's falling in and out of sleep in his holding cell:

> Perhaps I lived through my execution twenty times; once I even thought it was for good: I must have slept a minute. They were dragging me to the wall and I was struggling; I was asking for mercy. I woke up with a start and looked at the Belgian: I was afraid I might have cried out in my sleep. But he was stroking his moustache, he hadn't noticed anything. If I had wanted to, I think I could have slept a while; I had been awake for 48 hours. I was at the end of my rope. But I didn't want to lose two hours of life: they would come and wake me up at dawn, I would follow them, stupefied with sleep and I would have croaked without so much as an "Oof!"; I didn't want that, I didn't want to die like an animal, I wanted to understand.[5]

It's a pretty passage to me, obviously horrifying at the same time.

Now, in an effort to be as open-minded as possible, I'm forced to entertain the notion that maybe the pain or true realization of dying will change my mind. Perhaps I'll want the delusion, when push

---

5 Kaufmann, W. (Ed.). (2004). *Existentialism from Dostoevsky to Sartre* (p. 292). New York: Plume.

comes to shove. David Ulin quoted much maligned celebrity atheist Christopher Hitchens in the *Los Angeles Times*, in a memoir of the latter's death in 2011:

> "Before I was diagnosed with esophageal cancer a year and a half ago," [Christopher] observed in his final column for Vanity Fair, "I rather jauntily told the readers of my memoirs that when faced with extinction I wanted to be fully conscious and awake, in order to 'do' death in the active and not the passive sense . . . However, one thing that grave illness does is to make you examine familiar principles and seemingly reliable sayings. And there's one that I find I am not saying with quite the same conviction as I once used to: In particular, I have slightly stopped issuing the announcement that "Whatever doesn't kill me makes me stronger."[6]

I chose to open this book with Alvin's story because it is such a wonderful metaphor for religiosity. In a sense, we are all like Alvin Ford, each facing our imminent mortality and with a choice whether to acknowledge it. Alvin can take a pill to face his while we can join a religion to deny ours.

Although it will be difficult to conjure a scenario more provocative than Alvin's, it can still be engaging and enlightening to contemplate the dilemma of acknowledging reality in other contexts as well. Back here on Earth—specifically, on bar stools at happy hour, I recently ended up chatting it up with a medical student who was completing her residency in a hospital emergency room. She was visibly unsettled when she told me a story about a young man not

---

6 Ulin, D. (2011, December 17). Christopher Hitchens' first loyalty was to the truth. *Los Angeles Times*. Retrieved from http://articles.latimes.com/2011/dec/17/entertainment/la-et-1217-christopher-hitchens-20111217

far past adolescence who died on her shift due to a poisoning of sorts. His was not a peaceful death. It was very dramatic, with hollering and flailing and other dying behavior, the likes of which I had never heard or even seen in a movie, Hollywood or otherwise. The closest thing that comes to mind is a vague memory of a cartoon of Bugs Bunny having a heart attack, or I suppose he had been faking one.

The resident was emphatic when describing the climax of her story: When surviving loved ones approached hospital staff, they insisted that the supervisor tell them that the young man didn't suffer. The doctor was happy to oblige, reporting that he passed calmly like most of us fantasize about, without as much as a chest-grab. "Thank you," as if Doctor Soandso was the messiah saving souls.

During a staff debriefing, doctors and doctors-to-be explored the Hippocratic Oath, again, the one about not doing harm. Supporters apparently argue, "What's the point of causing more suffering in this situation, when soothing is so readily available (for the survivors, that is)?"

Of course, this is a personal opinion, a value judgement not necessarily shared by all medical professionals. For the record, I personally doubted the doctor's choice, despite the circumstances, and wonder whether it was right to lie to the survivors, in the Grandest Scheme of the Cosmos. I can imagine myself responding to an order like "Tell me he died peacefully" with something more akin to "I'm so sorry, but I can't," and cross the subsequent bridges accordingly. Admittedly, I am speculating. At the moment of truth, and given a history of working in the war zone that is an ER, I might pull a Christopher Hitchens and tone it down even more.

Worth noting, other professionals on record have publicly condemned the notion of doctors lying to patients, at least in other contexts. I recently came across an article explaining that prescribing placebos is becoming increasingly popular in Germany, even advocated by the German Medical Association under certain

circumstances.[7] The article was largely about the ethics of the practice (scientists do know that placebos can be effective at times; that
part is hardly debatable). Apparently, the American and British
medical authorities regard the deception as unethical. More specifically, a professor of medicine at Harvard condemns the practice,
adding "That's what I call lying . . . It would be unacceptable in the
US [where] we have a commitment to transparency . . . The Ger-
mans seem to be saying that it's OK to lie a little." For argument's
sake, I know of at least one American ER doctor who believes it's
okay to lie a little, too.

Personally, I've learned from experience that I simply can't do
it. I have to tell the truth, and may even be a bit obsessed with doing so. I had to tell my roommate in college, Roman, who has been
one of my closest friends since age 16, that I believe he was the one
who accidentally killed our cat. It was an absolutely horrific experience. After a night of University of Texas-sized keggers, he had
driven home and, in a moment of frivolity and rambunctiousness,
parked his car in the front yard. Our cat, "Dog," was nowhere to be
seen the next morning, until finally Roman found her, mortally
wounded, lying in the grass not far from where his car was still
parked. It physically hurts me to type this story even now, more
than twenty years later.

Roman was in tears, panicking like I had never seen him before
or since. He somehow picked Dog up, put her in a cardboard box,
and rushed her to the vet, but she succumbed. We hadn't talked
about it much for a while, until Roman finally asked me months
(was it years?) later, very calmly but directly, during some other
beer and/or pot buzz we were sharing, if I thought it was him. He
was so solemn; I'm not exactly sure what he was hoping I would
say. He might have been like that poisoned kid's loved ones, begging for me to lie to him, or maybe he really needed to know the

7 Associated Press. (2011, April 1). German medical group pushes placebos. *Globe Newspaper Company*. Retrieved from http://www.boston.com/news/world/europe/articles/2011/04/01/german_medical_group_pushes_placebos/

truth. Either way, I had to tell him. I said, calmly and without condemnation, "I think maybe you did." He just kinda looked down and didn't say much. I don't remember if I said anything else or just left it at that.

Somehow, I simply felt it was wrong to lie about a Truth that was so serious, about an event that was so significant to our lives. Telling the truth seemed more important than averting suffering. Maybe suffering shouldn't be avoided at all costs. Maybe if we would just face the horrors of our lives they wouldn't be as horrible as we anticipate. And even if they are, maybe they should simply be respected and experienced as the horrors that they are.

I suspect many readers have difficulty with this position, at least regarding some of the examples so far. But I also suspect everyone has a point at which the painful truth is preferred. Consider if your spouse or mate was cheating on you, like having an affair with someone at his or her office. Would you rather know, or would you rather live your life, and maybe even go to your grave, ignorant? It's interesting: Romantic cheating is something that we're usually more interested in knowing about. With cheating, we can't tolerate—well, being cheated. Here, we are not merely out of touch with reality; someone to whom we're emotionally attached is intentionally deceiving us, and we won't be the object of that. Sure, we'll deceive ourselves till the cows come home. As long as we're in control of the deception, it's okay.

That said, we mustn't forget Landers's First Law of Psychology: "It depends; exceptions abound." Ask Elvis:

Honey, you lied when you said you loved me.
And I had no cause to doubt you.
But I'd rather go on hearing your lies,
Than go on living without you.[8]

---

8 Turk, R. & Handman, L. (1926). Are you lonesome tonight? [Recorded by E. Presley]. [Vinyl record single]. New York: RCA Victor. (1960).

Coming down even a little closer to Earth, let's acknowledge that we have to choose to be honest (or not) almost every day. And when I say "be honest," I'm talking about both *to ourselves* as well as *to others*.

At the time of this writing, it's 2010 and I recently returned from a jaunt to San Antonio with some friends to see defied, pioneer heavy metal band Iron Maiden. Now, I was never a true "Maidenite," but had become intrigued as a kid, ironically, when I first heard them on this Christian anti-rock sermon my parents had given me on cassette tape. The preacher guy played a few samples to present the blatant satanic messages from the band's infamous album *The Number of the Beast*. I, too, was shocked and even a little scared—but also a bit titillated. It would actually be one of the first albums I ever bought. I remember listening to it, literally in turmoil, rocking out but at the same time stressing over my soul.

By the time high school rolled around, I was a pretty faithful wannabe Maidenite. I had most of their albums and knew most of the words to the songs therein, but I had never seen them live. Roman and I had this pastime in high school where we would sit in the parked car, roll up the windows, smoke a joint, and blare whatever Iron Maiden we had over the stereo. We called it, aptly, *The Iron Maiden Experience*. Sometimes, we would invite Maiden virgins to join us, in hopes to convert them to our Club. We actually did impress a couple of folks, I think. As you can imagine, this rich history made going to see them, finally at the age of 40, a momentous occasion. Perhaps I would finally earn the right to call myself a true Maidenite. If nothing else, I was finally gonna buy a fucking t-shirt with their raging skeletal mascot, Eddie, on it!

To set the bar even higher, the Paladia cable music station had recently been airing *Flight 666: The Movie*, this fantastic documentary about the band's world tour in 2008. It gave me chills—I couldn't wait to see how the show would be live, finally! So me, Roman, "Wally," and our one true Maidenite friend, "Big Mike" DeLeon, all piled into my tiny Nissan Sentra, clown-style, and made the eighty miles to San Antonio. We were literally giddy, with an Iron Maiden classic mega-mix blaring over the stereo the whole way, leaving the faintest trail of cannabis exhaust through the Texas Hill Country in our wake. The slightest hitch was when we got there, Mike seemed a little uncomfortable, being the only Hispanic in the Alamodome, but otherwise . . . *it was perfect.* (And that's a joke about no Hispanics being there.)

Oddly, the band opened with a song I hadn't heard before. A slight letdown, but I was still riding the wave of energy and excitement that got me there. After that, they played another unfamiliar, slightly disappointing song. Uh oh: My buzz was starting to take a hit. Then another. With each unfamiliar, slightly disappointing song, I could feel my wave slowly dissipating, until it hit me kinda hard: They're not gonna play any classics! This is one of those damned, fucking Here's-our-New-Album tours, Like It or Lump It. Shit fuck hell damn!

How *dare* they deprive me of the profound experience of reminiscence I paid to have! And it wasn't just me: The tension in the stadium felt thick. I could tell that many other people were equally disappointed, but trying to behave as if otherwise. I'm not sure how many—maybe even a majority, but I could feel it, regardless. It was salient as people started sitting down way too early. The crowd had noticeably (granted, not dramatically) thinned before the show was over. It was truly dull, and at least a bit depressing.

Afterwards, wiping the remnants of our beer/pot buzzes away at a nearby Taco Cabana before we hit the road again, I took the floor. I was nervous but my irritation egged me on, so that I emphatically proclaimed this was *"the biggest disappointment of my adult life."* Sure, I was using hyperbole to make a point, but the show really did suck. This was bad, and I wanted to be the one to admit it, goddamnit.

The reaction of my friends was palpable. They had seemed disappointed before, too, but no one had said so aloud. After my proclamation, everyone seemed to shift from private disappointment to a more overt, public depression, joining me. No one repeated my hyperbole, but neither did anyone contest it, at least not convincingly.

And then I felt bad. Should I have kept my mouth shut? I felt like they felt worse after I spoke, because by doing so it somehow let them see through their defenses and realize that the show was indeed lame. (The psychological principle of *cognitive dissonance* predicts that the more money one spends on his Iron Maiden ticket, the more difficult it becomes to admit he didn't like the show— ours were $50 each!) Had I not said what I did, each would have been much less in touch with the depressing reality.

Roman later confessed that another friend of ours, Jennifer, had actually warned him earlier that the show sucked; she had been to opening night just twenty-four hours before in Dallas. He hadn't wanted to say anything, afraid it might ruin the show for us. On the contrary, now I was irritated *at him* for not warning me.

No, I don't think we must tell the truth always. Trust me, I have a few secrets about myself, family, and friends that I would never offer, and would refuse to disclose even if confronted directly. Aside from secrets *per se,* I've simply had ill feelings at times towards some of my loved ones that I'd rather them never know about. And, for some reason that I don't fully understand, I feel it's relatively appropriate to lie to children sometimes. Helping a kid cope with and learn about death via "doggie heaven" and the like doesn't necessarily feel like a sin to me. I can't guarantee that I'll use doggie heaven myself if I ever have kids, but I certainly see the value in not risking overloading children with the brutal truth, lest we traumatize them. I'm just not so sure about adults. Perhaps facing the brutal truth is part of growing up. Freud thought so (I'm saving his quote on the topic for later.)

Back on the original hand, I kinda wonder how high the risk is—we haven't tested being honest with kids very much. However, in the wonderfully engaging documentary *The Nature of Existence*, Roger Nygard interviews some kid, Chloe, who has apparently been raised atheistic by her parents.[9] At least she has been permitted atheism by them. She looks about twelve or thirteen years old at the time of the interview, but her poise and confidence are almost unsettling. She definitely does not seem traumatized or deranged. If anything, she's a little cocky about her position, just like so many grown-up atheists. She asserts with an almost-devious smile, all the more peculiar because there are braces in it, "There is no afterlife . . . there's no heaven, no hell—you die. Boom! Dead." Later in the program she adds, with precocious wisdom, "I think truth is what we're all really searching for, isn't it? Even though sometimes it's more fun to search for it than actually find it." Amen, you little brat.

Austrian philosopher Kurt Baier may have argued that there's less risk in raising a kid atheist than Christian. It seems there's less to lose if the kid grows up atheist, because she can always convert to Christianity later. On the other hand, once raised a believer,

> when the implications of the scientific world picture begin to sink in, when we come to have doubts about the existence of God and another life, we are bitterly disappointed. For if there is no afterlife, then all we are left is our earthly life which we have come to regard as a necessary evil, the painful fee of admission to the land of eternal bliss.[10]

9 Nygard, R., Tarantino, P. (Producers), & Nygard, R. (Director). (2010). *The nature of existence*. U.S.: Walking Shadows.

10 Baier, K. (2008). The meaning of life. In E. D. Klemke & S. M. Cahn (Eds.), *The meaning of life: A reader* (3rd ed., p. 106). New York: Oxford University Press.

I hope by now you're asking yourself what you would prefer in each of the instances above, and others like them. Many such scenarios are worth contemplating from both sides, you as the one telling the lie and you as the one being deceived.

Is it acceptable to be a party pooper and tell your friends when you had a terrible time at the show you've fantasized about for decades? Alternatively, are you willing to hear your friend declare he had a terrible time? Would you mind taking a pill that works, even if it's not really a medication? Could you prescribe one, if you were a doctor? Would you lie to your roommate so that he could come to believe that he did not accidentally kill his cat after a keg party? Would you want to be deceived if you accidentally killed your cat? Do you need to know if your lover is cheating on you? Could you cheat? If a loved one recently passed, and suffered a great deal while doing so, would you rather know how it happened, or be lied to about it? Again, if you were a doctor, could you lie about it? And most importantly, at your execution, would you rather understand what's about to transpire, or instead believe that you're the Pope who's the one controlling the switch?

Most of my respective preferences are pretty obvious for me. I have few regrets about disparaging the Iron Maiden show, although I have to admit that the experience didn't feel good or bring us together. I *could have* faked it, and I bet everyone would have bought in and the ensuing mood would have been different. But it would have been fictitious. A false representation of reality, which feels somehow unacceptable—bordering on *obscene*—to me.

Honestly, I wasn't sure at the time if telling Roman about the cat was the right thing to do, but now, having done it, it feels right. Wake up—this is important! While writing this book, I asked him about the experience, twenty years later, and he told me that he did indeed want to know the truth, *that he asked me in the first place be-*

cause he thought I'd tell it. If you're reading between the lines (you better be!), you'd be correct to suspect that this whole experience ultimately brought us together, rather than pushed us apart. My guess is that the truth has the capacity to bring people together like this much more than telling lies does. And even if that's not always the case, even if lies are just as good sometimes or even better, I still feel like lies are wrong, *almost* always.

Now, Elvis Presley, you were one of the first celebrities I ever adored, but screw you: I would be *destroyed* to find out that I had been engaged in romance under false pretenses. No thanks; I don't want any part of that. I don't even want my girlfriend to lie to me when I ask her, "How are you doing?" If your day sucks, it's okay to tell me. And that doesn't just go for girlfriends; it goes for regular friends as well and even strangers, if they're up to it. Let me see your reality, so I can *know* and try to say something kind accordingly, instead of tricking me into disregarding it via small-talk. Of course, it's your prerogative, but at least be aware that you don't have to hold back on my account.

And Doctor, I don't want you to lie to me, either. It hurts to think of my loved ones suffering, but I'd rather know the truth. Sure, you can spare me the gory details, but don't make up shit out of concern for *my* feelings. This is not about me. If you feel it's important to cater to me at this time, realize that *I believe it's more respectful to the deceased and his or her dying experience if I comprehend the reality of how it transpired.* And not only do I need to know how it happened, I need to know *why* it happened. If it was a drug overdose, I need to know if it was accidental or intentional. This helps me construct the reality and respond appropriately, which I believe honors that dead person's experience, regardless of how brutal the reality is.

Curiously, for me, the most ambiguous of the scenarios we've been discussing is the placebo. No, I couldn't lie to a patient about it, out of respect for her autonomy, but I don't think I'd be too upset to learn that a doctor had lied to me about it. It's interesting to contemplate how this latter situation may be different from the others. At first glance, it seems to be the least *emotionally laden* of the scenarios. There's less, if any, emotional betrayal when given a placebo. In each of the other instances we've discussed, the lie prevents the deceived person from experiencing the appropriate emotions that are due to the cosmos.

CHAPTER 2

Fear Itself

There is no terror in a bang, only in anticipation of it.

— Alfred Hitchcock

BACK IN THE FALL OF 1990, I was still living at home with my parents at the getting-too-old-for-this age of twenty. One Sunday evening, after an extraordinary road-trip bender the likes of something out of *Fear and Loathing in Las Vegas,* I retired to my room to watch TV so that I could detox and start dreading work in the morning. "Retiring" at the time meant watching Operation Desert Storm, while my parents did the same in the living room.

I can still remember lying on my bed watching Patriot missiles and M-1 tanks and night-goggle vision and all, which aroused one of my peculiar old childhood fears: *being drafted.* The anxiety of the thought forced me into the present moment, as anxiety can do, so that my senses seemed to become a bit more acute and I became a little too conscious of my body. My heart felt gross inside my chest, all full of blood and squeezing according to some biological hocus-pocus that I didn't understand. The thought of being so out of control of the process made me feel vulnerable, unsure of why my heart must necessarily keep beating.

The human circulatory system is too complicated; there are so many places where something can go wrong. Things can clog and

26

electrical signals can get out of whack. Some hearts just stop beating altogether. What does it feel like when the heart fails? Does it feel differently depending on how it fails? Why am I thinking like this? Perhaps my brain knows my heart is about to stop, and these are the last thoughts of a dying man. As my anxiety spiraled out of control, the beat became even more salient, and harder and faster. More biological and out of my control. I panicked.

Suddenly and viciously, I was completely certain that I was going to collapse and die. Equally certain was that I wasn't going to die, but that I was losing my mind. Regardless of what was happening—and despite this being the first time for it to transpire —there was an eerie feeling of familiarity, as if this had always been a part of me, my destiny, and that it would always be like this, for whatever eternity is for me. It was so surreal: Perhaps I had already died, and this was my hell?

I formulated an unfathomable goal, to just stand up and get to the living room where my parents were so they could help me, just in case I wasn't actually dead yet. Every movement I made was done with utter terror, as if my continued existence somehow depended on every thought and muscle contraction. I've never felt so much "in the moment." But this wasn't Zen or Nirvana; it was the opposite, a quintessential suffering of cosmic proportions. Transcendent, but hellish.

Miraculously, I made it to the living room, in a daze, and announced to my parents bluntly, "Something's wrong with me." The words came out surprisingly calmly, given the horror I was feeling inside. The rest is a bit of a blur. I recall my mother acting strangely and seeming upset herself. Did she leave the room? Months later, if not years, she would finally tell me that my announcement made *her* have a panic attack, because she knew right away what was happening and what was in store for me. That was the first time I ever learned of my mother's panic disorder. Since then, I've always supposed that she panicked that night because a great fear of hers had been confirmed, that she had some role in passing panic to me.

Even if true, I don't hold any sort of grudge. My mother was a sweet lady but just wasn't comfortable expressing it.

She also told me later that she gave me one of her Valiums but I honestly don't remember that. What I do remember, however, is sitting on the couch while my parents continued to watch Desert Storm (or was it just my dad?), afraid to be alone in the event I went crazy again or died again and needed help. Inexplicably, I did calm down on the couch, even became sleepy, and eventually went to bed. Now that I think about it, I must have taken something. I calmed down too well, given what had transpired.

I went to work the next day at my cubicle, cheap-tie office job at the Blockbuster Video distribution center, feeling almost normal, but also with this strange sense that an ominous seal had been broken. Sure enough, that night, Monday, it happened again—same Bat Time, same Bat Channel. And it happened again Tuesday evening as well. I went to the doctor on Wednesday, and got some Valium of my own, my first real prescription ever. But oh, there would be more. So many more.

I was to take 5-10 milligrams every four hours, which I did. It worked pretty well; although it made me a little groggy, it dramatically reduced the number of panic attacks I was having. I still had a few, but they were different, truncated, like if you took a 10-minute panic and compressed it into 30 seconds. I'd be totally incapacitated but it would pass so quickly that no one could tell. I remember it happening one time while I was driving. As far as I know, I didn't swerve or anything but I remember feeling like it had been dangerous. Anyway, regardless of how much the Valium did help overall, the doctor told me I couldn't take it for more than a month because of its addictive potential.

My doctor, a general practitioner I picked somewhat randomly from my insurance referral list, was ultimately not qualified to handle my case. After my month of Valium vacation, he had me come in to discuss the next phase of my treatment. He mentioned that he had just returned from some conference on bipolar disorder, and he quizzed me regarding the symptoms that he had apparently just learned about:

"Do your thoughts race sometimes?"

"Uh, yeah, I guess . . . especially when I'm panicking."

"Are you moody?"

"Hell yeah, Doc—-that's the story of my life! I'm kinda down a lot, but sometimes I just feel great, for no reason, out of the blue."

And that's all it took: I was now a bipolar patient! I actually remember feeling somewhat soothed being diagnosed as manic depressive, because my education up to that point (comprised of a couple of community college general psychology courses and Jimi Hendrix's song on the topic) had taught me that it was a serious condition, and my condition definitely felt serious. I felt validated, and assured that I'd be receiving significant attention as a result. Alas, over the years, after much more education, including face-to-face interaction with *real* bipolar patients, I'd learn he was so incredibly wrong and that bipolar disorder is commonly misdiagnosed as such by armies of unqualified professionals like him.[1]

The punchline about my doctor is that not only did he misdiagnose me, but he also gave me the wrong medication for my misdiagnosed condition! I got Mellaril—an old antipsychotic medication for schizophrenia. It's not really for bipolar disorder. Which I never had.

---

1 Most of the people I meet in my practice who think they have bipolar disorder actually have a more traditional moodiness/anger problem, related to a personality disturbance or some degree of trauma. But doctors like the bipolar diagnosis because insurance companies readily pay for the treatment; patients like it because it readily qualifies them for disability benefits. So, no one's complaining. To make matters worse, the meds kinda work, falsely validating the diagnosis (heroin would also reduce their anger but it doesn't mean it's diagnostic or appropriate). Some of the drugs for bipolar actually have abuse potential, so some folks don't even take them, instead selling them on the street to supplement their government checks. Similar dysfunctional dynamics popularized ADHD before bipolar, and autism since. We need to be much more careful, so that disorder "awareness" does not become disorder hysteria.

And I can tell you from experience it doesn't work for panic, either. Instead, it made me more depressed than I had ever felt in my life. I remember telling a therapist later that I would have killed myself during that time but I was so apathetic I just didn't have the energy to do it. I remember not being able to eat, because everything was dirt and clay in my mouth. And I started panicking daily again, off the Valium. I called my doctor and he was kinda short with me, and told me to double the Mellaril. That didn't help, either.

The only good advice that he gave me was to find a therapist. I had already learned in my community college psych courses that meds are a band-aid, not a panacea, and that therapy would be necessary to make legitimate, enduring improvements. I first visited some clinic in Dallas that was supposed to specialize in anxiety disorders. I was in really, really, bad shape the day I went for my intake interview. It was around Christmas of 1990, the worst I have ever felt in my life. I had been taking the new dose of Mellaril, and to boot, I was sick with the flu. I remember being so disoriented from my anxiety and the medication that I wasn't even sure if I was physically ill at the time, even though I was visibly shaking with the chills. So, I kept my appointment, on a dreary and rainy Texas winter evening. I remember being so nervous and shaky that I could hardly talk. The lady who did my intake was really sweet and sensitive, kinda grandmotherly, but she apparently didn't have the authority to tweak my meds or intervene otherwise. She called someone else whom I never got to see, a Wizard of Oz of sorts, and almost seemed to be pleading with him or her when stating that "I have this young man here, and *he is really anxious*, and needs to see someone." I was sitting there, shivering, excited about the prospect of something changing, but I was denied a visit with The Wizard for the time being. I remember sitting in the car in the parking lot afterwards, trying to conjure the energy and courage to drive home, and feeling scared in a new way because the notion of suicide was starting to feel like a legitimate option for the first time.

And it wouldn't stop raining, and my windshield wipers sucked. As with my first panic attack, there was this layer of creepy feeling that this was my *destiny*, that I had somehow known, all my life, that all of this would come to pass and that these were The Moments of Truth, unfolding according to some cruel prophesy.

I reluctantly called the anxiety clinic later in the week to discuss the next move, but the lady with whom I spoke broke the camel's back. Inconceivably, she seemed insensitive, apparently not appreciating the gravity of what was happening to me. While talking about counseling, she told me something to the effect of "You don't know how to live! You have no self-esteem." I was so puzzled by her tone because she sounded critical and confrontational, the last thing in the world I needed at the time. Defensively, I said, "No, I'm actually very confident," referring to my abilities as a functioning citizen, not quite appreciating the difference between self-esteem and confidence at the time. She corrected me, pointing out that the two are distinct, but again her tone was abrasive and condescending. I didn't like where this was heading, so I didn't sign up for that shit. And fuck you, bitch, for talking to me like that when I was damn near ready to die.

I continued in despair like this for a few more weeks, trudging through my job, pushing pencils over TPS reports with the hope of a slave or prisoner of war, until my appointment with a psychiatrist finally arrived. It was at the infamous Timberlawn, a private psychiatric hospital in Dallas. The place was somewhat legendary and had always been so dark and mysterious to me, like a haunted house on the hill where children had been murdered and eaten—or worse. I had heard that there were people there who cut themselves on purpose, a notion about which I was so horrified but kinda intrigued.

Well, it turned out that the place was very bright, clean, and nice. Even better, my doctor was not frightening in the least, but somewhat angelic, especially in the wake of the previous professionals before him. I remember him well, decades later, a Jewish fellow with afro-ishy hair; he reminded me of Ron Silver as Alan Dershowitz in *Reversal of Fortune*. He was calm and his voice was really soothing, slightly effeminate but not over-the-top. He wasn't the least bit confrontational or insensitive like all those other fuckers. When I told him I was taking Mellaril, he laughed ever so slightly and just said, "Let's stop that." I immediately felt a tremendous sense of relief, knowing I was in better hands. He put me on imipramine, a popular antidepressant at the time used for treating anxiety disorders. He also gave me some more Valium, but just a few for emergencies. Okay, this all sounds much more reasonable. First glimmer of hope in weeks, since around Thanksgiving.

My favorite moment during the interview was how he asked me, tenderly but matter-of-factly, "Are you suicidal?" I paused, feeling embarrassed, but was so moved by the whole experience of being asked for the first time that I felt obliged to be open and honest. I looked down, avoiding his gaze, and said, "yes." I didn't cry, but part of me wanted to. His reaction was brilliant, in that he didn't really react much at all, and he just quizzed me a bit more, a quiz that I myself have now given hundreds of times since: "I can tell you're really upset and having a hard time, and I'm sorry . . . Now, lots of people *feel* suicidal from time to time. But I need you to tell me: Do you have *intentions* to harm yourself—are you in danger?" Energized by the whole interaction, I responded, truthfully again, "no."

Unfortunately, Dr. Dershowitz would be the only skilled professional with whom I would interact for some time. We got my meds in order, but I continued to have panic attacks. They were definitely not as frequent as before, happening about twice a week instead of daily, but they remained just as frightening. Plus, during the down time, I was often worried about the next one that could happen at any moment. I had some agoraphobia as well, but it was kinda backwards from the traditional: Instead of having a fear of public spaces, I was more afraid of being alone because if I really did have a heart attack no one would be around to save me. So, for example, driving in the country was a reliable context for panic. But I couldn't win: There was also a significant social component, in that I was also afraid that if I shit my pants or had a seizure in public the associated humiliation could almost be as bad as dying or going insane. Another cruel paradox was that drinking a few beers made me feel normal, even good, so that I was truly immune to panic when buzzed. Alas, a hangover was another one of the most dependable prompts for an attack. It's true what they say about things going up having to come back down.

Disenchanted with the experience at the anxiety clinic, I figured I'd try just contacting a psychologist directly. Again, I turned to the PPO list for my insurance company and found a guy who was close to home. My sense was that he was particularly successful, but our therapy was pretty much a bust. We just talked, which of course was nice and maybe helpful on some level, but I don't feel that we connected in a meaningful way, nor did we address the panic directly enough. Oddly, the conversation I most vividly recall is me telling him—sincerely, I wasn't trying to be tacky or anything—about a recent blow job that led to the best orgasm I had ever had. My therapist suggested that perhaps it was so good because this gal was able to make me relax more than I had during previous sexual encounters, so I wasn't worried about performance. That made a lot of sense to me, and I think he was right. But it didn't help my panic attacks at all.

I moved to Austin that fall, in 1991, to start school at the University of Texas. That was the most exciting time of my life, getting away from home for the first time, reuniting with my friends who had made the exodus from Dallas to Austin before me, and becoming immersed among young, vibrant, beautiful, and open-minded people like I never had before. I recall walking around that campus, literally, with a big grin on my face as if I was the luckiest person alive. It was perfect.

Except I was still panicking. I soon signed up for a therapist at the university counseling center and was assigned to a youngish, Hispanic psychiatrist-in-training who was apparently doing his residency or something. He kinda reminded me of how I might eventually be as a therapist, his suit obviously cheap and his tie askew, seeming slightly unsure of himself but smart and compassionate nonetheless. Indeed, we connected better than anyone since Dr. Dershowitz at Timberlawn. But this wasn't enough, either. We conversed meaningfully, but again didn't address the panic as directly as necessary. The attacks kept coming, even at school sometimes, so that I had to leave class every now and then because I'd start freaking out that I was gonna shit or piss my pants or throw-up or pass-out or something. I never did. I was actually doing really well at school, making straight As almost every semester. I loved studying, and would bust my ass doing so at least four nights a week. On the weekends, though, we partied like rock stars. Rock stars who really loved beer and pot. There didn't seem to be any hard drugs in Austin back then, the good ol' days. I hadn't even heard of any white, powdery substances since I left Dallas.

Summers turned into falls, and falls into springs (there is no legitimate winter in south-central Texas). Imipramine was switched to Paxil, and John Mackovich—praise the Holy Name of Jesus—gave way to Mack Brown.

At some point, I learned that the psychology department (my major) had a professor, Dr. Michael Telch, who was apparently some sort of guru on panic disorder and was running a progressive treatment laboratory that was allegedly producing results that were virtually unheard of in psychology, some estimates of success being greater than ninety percent. Dr. Telch had been a graduate student of the venerable Dr. Barlow at Stanford, a name with which I was already familiar so early in my psychology education. I contacted the lab and signed my ass up.

Because the treatment was part of a research program there

were both treatment and control groups; I was randomly assigned to a group that was obviously some sort of control. Mine was a group therapy format, about 10 panic-ers altogether, very open-ended, where we basically just talked about whatever we wanted, but of course anxiety was often center stage. Our group leader was a really good listener, and really pretty. I enjoyed going to those meetings. All the patients were sweet people; no one was the least bit obnoxious. Everyone was self-conscious and sensitive, apparently to a fault. But if the world was more like my group, there would be no war, that's for sure.

When that didn't work (as it wasn't expected to), the same group was provided the experimental treatment, which was supposed to work. It was a cognitive-behavioral exposure therapy, analogous to what might be used to treat, for example, a specific phobia of spiders. The idea is not new, the bottom line being that if you face your fear—in increasingly manageable doses as supervised by a therapist—the fear will eventually lose its steam. Over 300 years ago, philosopher John Locke described the process of what is now called *systematic desensitization* (although I suspect he wasn't the first, either):

> Your child shrieks, and runs away at the sight of a Frog; Let another catch it, and lay it down at a good distance from him: At first accustom him to look upon it; When he can do that, then come nearer to it, and see it leap without Emotion; then to touch it lightly when it is held fast in another's hand; and so on, till he can come to handle it as confidently as a Butter-fly, or a Sparrow. By the same way any other vain Terrors may be remov'd; if Care be taken, that you go not too fast, and push not the Child on to a new degree of assurance, till he be thoroughly confirm'd in the former.[2]

---

2   As quoted in: Hergenhahn, B. R. (2001). *An introduction to the history of psychology* (4th ed., p. 119). Belmont, CA: Wadsworth. The original work is Locke, J. (1693). *Some thoughts concerning education*. London: Printed for A. & J. Churchill.

And so, through the longest run-on sentence of the Enlightenment, Locke captured the essence of anxiety treatments that we use regularly today.

Seriously, this really is how we do it. If you are afraid of spiders, we find something spider-like that you can handle, something that arouses your anxiety to about a 4 or 5 on a 10-point scale. For some—no kidding—this might be simply saying the word "spider." Once you have confirm'd your assurance of that task so that your fear decreases to a 1 or a 2, we raise the bar and find some other 4-5 stimulus to get used to, which might now be a cartoon drawing of a spider. We keep doing this until you're ready to hold a dead spider or even be in the room with a live one.

If you have a fear of contamination we do the same thing but switch dirt for the spider. If it's speaking in public, you give me a speech and we work up from there. Such exposure therapy is also part of treatment for trauma (you telling your story of victimization is one potentially feared stimulus to engage). Exposure can even be used in treating personality disorders. For example, a narcissist may become accustomed to failure if exposed to it in manageable doses and processed with a skilled therapist. Of course, some exposures are trickier than others because the feared stimulus is not readily accessible, but there are options. For example, with a fear of flying some of the exposure can be done via virtual reality. And so on.

With panic, much of the exposure involves provoking peculiar physical and psychological sensations. Leading theories assert that people who suffer from attacks are sensitive to *internal cues*, that is, bodily sensations that trigger a "false alarm" that the person is in danger, thereby activating his "fight or flight" response unnecessarily. Such internal cues include dizziness, heart palpitations, and shortness of breath. So, we practiced becoming accustomed to spinning in chairs, jogging in place, and breathing through a straw (not at the same time, at least at the beginning). For some patients, the primary trigger for panic is *depersonalization*—the strange feeling that one is not himself, as if he is stuck in some sort of waking dream. To approximate such experiences we were instructed to stare into a mirror. Turns out that staring into a mirror for 10-15 minutes can create some very peculiar subjective experiences. No kidding: I hallucinated, and it wasn't trivial. In fact, one time when doing this away from the lab as "homework," I panicked and had to call someone to calm me down. The other very interesting exercise that might surprise you is that we breathed from a bag of carbon dioxide. Apparently, many patients are "chronic hyperventilators"; perhaps due to chronic, low-grade anxiety, they don't breathe as deeply as normal and instead do so in a choppy, shallow manner. Breathing as such disrupts the proper ratio of oxygen to carbon dioxide in the body which can contribute to uneasy feelings leading to panic. All that hippie crap about taking slow, deep breaths to relax isn't just annoying mumbo-jumbo; there's a medical explanation for why that feels good.

Well, as clever as all this may sound, I was part of the 2-5% or whatever who didn't respond to the treatment and kept panicking just as before. Fortunately, for ethical reasons, I was not shoved out the door but provided a graduate student therapist-in-training instead so we could keep on truckin'. My therapist and her supervisors must have thought I needed a lot of help, because we began with twice-a-week, one-and-a-half-hour sessions.

Jessica and I connected very well and would ultimately cure my panic. We continued the exposure therapy at first but it didn't seem to help, again. I suppose she just needed to see for herself. But we talked about everything, much deeper than I had with my previous therapists. I dove in headfirst, caution to the wind, not hiding anything. I told her about how there had never been any affection in my home, that the only self-esteem I got from adults came from teachers at school. I told her about how hard I was spanked as a kid, and how I was forced to sit at the kitchen table for what seemed like hours because I was too "finicky" and food I couldn't eat would not go to waste. I told her about all the drugs I had done. We talked about sex and masturbation and fantasies. I told her about the time when I was a little kid and found a baby blue jay wandering alone in the middle of the street. I didn't know what to do because I had been told you weren't supposed to touch baby birds or their moms might reject them. I ran inside to tell my parents but couldn't get any help. When I ran back outside to do something, it was too late: It was a blue pancake, the car that had run it over being nowhere in sight. I told Jessica how I was *crushed*, *destroyed*, because I had made a bad decision and wasn't able to save the baby by myself. All I fucking had to do was corral it out of the street without ever touching it. It would have been so easy.

And we talked about my deteriorating faith. I had grown up in a very God-fearing home: Although the emphasis was on the fear, I had always had a legitimate, functional relationship with Him. Even in college, despite not having been to church in years (outside of weddings and funerals), God had remained central to my life and identity. But it was college education that chipped away at my faith, and as doubt began to overtake me I was starting to feel "bitterly disappointed" just as predicted by Kurt Baier cited in chapter 1 of this book. I remember Jessica attempting to soothe my existential distress by noting that "there are different degrees of belief." This felt like another challenge to my "black-and-white," "all-or-nothing" thinking problems at the time, as she was trying to argue that one can believe without believing 100%. But I couldn't buy into it. Once the seal broke on my doubt, there would be no stopping it, just some delays.

One day, while talking as such (I honestly don't recall the specific topic; it could have been anything from God to masturbation), I had a full-blown panic attack right there in that little, windowless, almost-claustrophobic excuse for a therapy room. I remember feeling it coming on: I began to feel unreal, a little too present in the present moment. And then a sense of doom, as if something catastrophic beyond my imagination might occur soon, like the sun might explode and annihilate all of existence. My ears buzzed a little and my vision became grainy. It was hard to speak, but I managed, "I'm starting to have one now."

Like Dr. Dershowitz, her reaction was remarkably calm; she might have even have smiled, just a little, and not inappropriately. She took my hand gently but it wasn't soothing as one might predict. Instead, it added to the discomfort but, classic David Landers, I didn't dare say this out loud for fear that it might make *her* uncomfortable. Then, the panic washed over me, that tidal wave of doom and tension and incoherence for the thousandth time—no, this was actually the first time *this* had ever happened. But then it passed, like it had a thousand times before.

About a month later, I noticed—surprisingly casually—that I hadn't had a panic attack since that evening in therapy. It was 1995, and this was the longest I had gone without an attack since it all started in 1990. And then it became clear to me why it finally stopped, that we had previously been missing a critical trigger, the one to which I needed exposure therapy, my Locke's Frog: *publicity*. That is, I had kept my anxiety too private until then, as I had been so terrified of others seeing it and appreciating how defective I was. By finally having a panic attack with someone, and telling her about it as it unfolded, and her being present with me throughout the whole thing, from beginning to end and beyond, that incredible, indescribable force had finally lost its—well, *force*. I didn't panic again for many more months, and only about three more times ever. And these were only on isolated, peculiar occasions, that is, when accidentally smoking too much pot. These never led to a legitimate relapse.

Surprisingly, once my panic was cured my emotional life really didn't improve dramatically otherwise. Honestly, I barely noticed a difference, at least in the immediate aftermath. That said, I had been changing in other ways aside from panic reduction; most significantly, as I alluded to moments ago and will detail later, it was during those years of therapy with Jessica that I also gave up God and became an atheist. Now that I think about it, finding atheism and losing panic were approximately coincidental. I suspect some readers would like me to decisively proclaim that dumping religion cured me of panic, but I don't recall feeling a clear connection, at least at the time. On the other hand, in retrospect, it's hard to argue that those two momentous developments weren't related, at least to a degree. In any event, what I do recall is that I stayed in therapy for quite some time after both religion and panic left me because there was still plenty of other crud to work through regardless.

I suppose the reason my emotional life didn't improve much otherwise once the panic left is because my anxiety was actually much older and deeper than what became evident that Sunday evening watching Desert Storm. Panic—while a very salient manifestation of my distress—was only the tip of some other iceberg.

CHAPTER 3

Growing Up with God

He who spares his rod hates his son, But he who loves him
disciplines him diligently.

— Proverbs 13:24 (NASB)

MY PARENTS OFTEN REMARKED about having been saved by the Lord
around the time I was born (ironic, now that I think about it). They
always gave the impression that this was some sort of dramatic
event, but—as with most issues in the Landers family—they never
discussed it openly. Over the years, I gathered that their pre-
Christian days included, at worst, some degree of alcohol consumption, but I suspect it was nothing compared to how much I'd
drink when I was the same age. Rumor has it they met in a bar, a
notion about which they always seemed embarrassed but that I
somehow found endearing.

For as long as I can remember, we had been attending a First
Assembly of God in northeastern Dallas at this modern and imposing TV-evangelical-looking structure. Some of my earliest childhood memories are set in or around that building. I can literally
remember, albeit vaguely, being in a crib at the church nursery
while my parents were engaged in some other church function.
When I was old enough, I started Sunday school. And when I
wasn't quite old enough, my parents started making me go to Big

People Church. I was restless and didn't understand much, but I didn't dare complain openly, for fear of bringing judgement from my parents, or worse, from Above.

Ours was a very Pentecostal production, with regular laying-on-of-hands and speaking-in-tongues. I got to see it all up close, occasionally some grown-up speaking in tongues while standing right next to me—my own father, no less, who was a frequent flyer. I'd sneak a peek at his face, careful not to look too long, like you might when negotiating a solar eclipse. It was frightening to me at times, but I was mostly in awe. Still am, in a way. I obviously don't believe in Jesus any more, but I still think that shit's real, whatever it is.

As a family, we were entrenched in that church. For most of my life growing up, both of my parents actually worked there, my mom as a teacher in the day care and my dad as the maintenance man/groundskeeper. Because Dad needed to be available in case of any sort of crisis, he was essentially obliged to be there at almost every service, twice on Sunday and once on Wednesday. He wasn't too keen on going alone, so typically we all went. But that's not the only reason we did. My dad was a quintessential Man of the House, a bit puritanical, the kind of dad who might quote Old Testament scripture in casual conversation or when lecturing us. Now, he wasn't exactly *Carrie*'s mother from the Stephen King story, but no kid of his was going to sit at home and watch TV while he and everyone else were at church. Mom was a less assertive believer. She seemed as faithful but not as devoted; I suspect we would've stayed home with the TV if she had been in charge. Instead, we had our own personal pew space, informally reserved on account of our almost perfect attendance over the years, sitting in the same spot, conspicuously missing if we weren't there.

I remember feeling so upset some Sunday afternoons, packing up the weekend early to get ready for another freaking church service on Sunday evening, only having been home from Sunday school for just a few hours. Those were the days before cable television, and it always seemed that the best TV shows for the entire week were on Sunday night, like *Mutual of Omaha's Wild Kingdom*. Instead of being a joy, that theme music for *The Wonderful World of Disney* was often a cue that it was time to get up from the living room carpet and clean up for church. It always felt cruel and unusual to have to trade in Mickey Mouse for some grown-up church service that I really didn't have the capacity to follow in a meaningful way. I never understood why I couldn't just have my private relationship with God and skip it. The public relationship, at that big scary building around all those adults, would never do the private one any justice anyway. I was a lonely, distressed kid; God was sometimes the best company I had, and quite often the *only* comfort I had. I spoke to Him daily, and prayed more formally every night before sleeping, diligently and methodically thanking him for the blessings and asking forgiveness for the sins of that day. Praying like this was not negotiable: I wouldn't go to sleep without it. As I prayed, I'd feel a calm come over me. He was listening and I felt safe and no longer alone. Life wasn't great, but it was tolerable with prayer.

There was something wrong with our church anyway, manifested as this cycle of conflict between different factions of the congregation that peaked every few years. The first time happened when I was too young to be privy to goings-on, and too young to figure it out myself. All I know is that some contingent of the congregation had "run off" Pastor Salter, a man I always saw as intimidatingly angelic. His replacement, Pastor Brach, was also railroaded out a few years later. After that, representatives from the national First Assembly of God ruling body or whatever stepped in and somehow supervised the hiring of the next pastor. It was so weird: Each week a different preacher was on the pulpit, essentially auditioning, each quite distinct from the rest. Some were hard-core fire-and-brimstone motherfuckers, while others were calm and soothing. Fortunately, we ended up with Pastor McCoy, one of the sweetest human beings I have ever encountered, hands-down. His entire family seemed so pure, to truly embody the essence of Christianity, the way you really expect it to be but is rarely realized. They were all glowing with joy, and it always seemed so real. Still does today, in retrospect, despite my evolved cynicism since.

In any event, being in my early teens, I was now old enough to understand what was transpiring when even our sweet Pastor McCoy and his family were excommunicated (I'm running out of verbs here!). The problem with the McCoys was that the old-timers wanted a more traditional, preachy sermon, instead of this younger, more progressive man who liked the idea, for example, of incorporating a drum set into the musical portions of the service. I remember it getting nasty, people arguing loudly in the halls after church sometimes. Sure enough, my dad and our family friends were in the middle of it all, on the pro-McCoy side. I remember spying from afar, worried that it was going to come to blows, but it never did.

Back at home, things were rough for me, and always had been. Don't get too excited: I don't have a dramatic horror story to tell, nothing like David Pelzer's of *A Child Called It* fame, whose mother allegedly starved him and assaulted him and tried to make him eat vomit and feces. My problem was a lot less dramatic, a lot more commonplace. My problem was that I was an anxious and sensitive kid, and neither of my parents was affectionate or otherwise accommodating. You'll see, I was doomed nevertheless.

There *used to* be a debate in psychology regarding whether our personalities and psychological symptoms and strengths come from nature (that is, our genes) or nurture (that is, our upbringing). I say "used to" because there's not much of a debate today: We know it's both. Of course, genes and upbringing interact in complex ways, so many questions remain regarding the relative roles of each. And of course it depends on the condition in question. Some mental health issues may be determined almost entirely by genes (for example, some intellectual disabilities), while others, by definition, require an experience (for example, trauma). However, most development occurs on the middle ground, in that our genes form the foundations upon which life experiences have their impact. Sometimes the genes provide a strong foundation of strength and resiliency, but at other times a shaky one of sensitivity and susceptibility. Even with trauma, one person's bad day could be another person's life-changing calamity, depending on their respective inborn temperaments.

I haven't had the privilege of genetic testing, but I get the sense that less-than-optimal genes have been running in my family. I couldn't help but notice growing up that my mother's mother, my Mamaw, was an exceptionally anxious woman, with the kind of anxiety that just seemed psychiatric as opposed to psychological—that is, more natured than nurtured. For as long as I can remember, even when I was really too young to appreciate what clinical anxiety was, she always seemed so nervous, her voice quivering when she talked and her hands shaking when she chain-smoked. On rare occasions, my mother did violate the apparent Landers Policy of Secrecy and disclosed a few tidbits that confirmed some of my suspicions, such as that Mamaw had once spent some time in a state hospital for a "nervous breakdown" of some sort. Keep in mind that back in those days, "nervous breakdown" could mean anything from full-on psychotic to just pestering your husband too much. But a few more tidbits over the years suggested something legitimate, something about a profound fear of spiders that bordered on delusional . . . and something about a fear of intruders in the home, so that one of my mother's duties as a little girl was to search the house upon returning from the grocery store or whatever, to look under the beds and in the closets to make sure someone hadn't snuck in while they were gone. That's what I mean by psychiatric and genetic, not psychological and learned, if that makes any sense. My mom got some of those anxious genes, and so did I. I can almost feel them in me sometimes, manifest as extreme self-consciousness that can smell a little like paranoia. Often when I hear laughter in public, especially when I'm alone, I reflexively assume it's directed at me, and might even do a scan to make sure my zipper's up. When taking my turn in line at the post office or ATM I can *almost* hear the disdainful thoughts of the impatient people behind me, wanting me to hurry; at times I've kinda felt an impulse to turn around and tell them to fuck off, but never have.

As you might expect, Mamaw wasn't well equipped to be the best mother. On other rare occasions, my mom made vague allusions about physical abuse in the home, the real thing, Pelzerarian. She talked, very little, about long days waiting desperately for her fireman father to get home so it would be safe again. I think one of the kids may have even had to go the hospital once, or at least should have. That apparently changed things, alerting my grandfather to what was going on while he was at work fighting fires, and he put a stop to it. Better late than never, but surely some damage was already done, and it didn't fix everything.

So, even if our genes had been perfect, my own mother obviously hadn't received the best education on how to be an effective parent, so my own nurture got off to a bad start shortly after conception in 1969. In her womb, I was apparently exposed to alcohol and amphetamines on a fairly regular basis. Those were the days before fetal alcohol syndrome had even been formally named, and it was not uncommon to give pregnant moms diet pills so they wouldn't gain weight while pregnant. And "diet pill" in 1970 didn't mean green tea extract or ginseng: They were real amphetamines not a whole lot different from today's methamphetamine. It's probably not a coincidence that those are the two drugs—alcohol and meth—that would later provide me with the most comfortable highs in adolescence and early adulthood. I truly believe that my fetal brain was exposed to these, got a little wired-up to accommodate them, and now feels a little deprived without them (or, alternatively, feels relatively *whole* with them).

I'm quite confident that I didn't get a lot of attention from my parents during infancy. Mom once told me that I was an exceptionally quiet baby, rarely demanding attention. I strongly suspect this suited my parents well, facilitating a policy of "If it ain't broke, don't fix it" when choosing whether to interact with me. Neither of my parents ever had the gift of warmth, but for different reasons. To finish mom's story, I would repeatedly have a peculiar experience during my college years when I would bring a girlfriend or other guest home with me for a holiday. At some point, I'd leave my guest alone with my mom while I went to the bathroom or whatever, my mom always lighting a cigarette as I exited the room. Later, when I was alone again with my guest, she or he would tell me that while I was away my mom unloaded about how she always loved me but was afraid to try to show it when I was little, because her mother hurt her so badly and she was afraid she would somehow do the same, so she just kept her distance. I'm not sure if that's all there was to it, but it is validating to know that she knew *something* was wrong. And it makes me really sad to think about all of this, not just for my own sake but also for that of my mother's, and her mother's, and so on.

My father's problem was simply egocentrism, but a caricature of the same that we all have. My mother would often joke about it, his conversations often being obscenely one-sided. It really was remarkable—a recurring joke from an animated sitcom featuring Homer Simpson or Peter Griffin—how my dad would demand that you listen when he spoke but he would reflexively drift off when it was your turn. Of course, it's not funny when you're a baby, learning about reality and forming a sense of identity and self-esteem. Through education and experience, I feel that this is one of the most underrated parenting skills one can have: simply paying attention to your kids. Many psychologists (including this one) believe that there is no free trial period. Even the littlest of babies is noticing how and to what degree his parents are interested in him, and he's forming ideas about his identity as a being and his value and role in the world. His little brain is growing very rapidly, making relatively permanent connections, all in the context of getting attention—or not.

Worth noting, I don't really recall ever *feeling* neglected. My only memories are of perceiving emotional solitude as normal, perhaps even preferred. Was that preference natured or nurtured? Does an independent baby have leave-me-alone genes that allow, or even provoke, parents to keep their distance? Or is it more nurture: Has the baby simply learned *very* early on that there's no use trying? At any rate, Mom did describe one exception where I demanded attention, that I would go ape-shit whenever my diaper was dirty. I remain a bit obsessive-compulsive about cleanliness and order today, and have to entertain that my diaper fits were more about nature than nurture, because it's difficult to imagine how I could have *learned* that response so early. On the other hand, we can't forget Landers's Second Law of Psychology: "You never know."

I don't remember anything about wearing diapers, but I do remember *fear* being an integral part of my childhood experience, along with solitude. Regardless of how it all came about, I was such a scared little kid, just like my chain-smoking grandma, tense most of the time in general but also cursed by myriad irrational phobias. I threw the cliché tantrum on Santa's lap during my preschool years, and another on the first day of kindergarten. I was terrified of elevators and even escalators. I was afraid of heights in general and amusement park rides in particular. I was scared of water. I couldn't put my head under water, whether at the pool or even in the bathtub. In fact, for some time, I couldn't even put my head under a running faucet. During my early bathing career, my mother had to rinse shampoo out of my hair like they do at a salon, except she would use a cup. Getting water in my eyes made me think I was gonna drown. Swimming pools during summer were never fun for me. For most of my childhood, it was a humiliating chore, until I finally became comfortable swimming in my early teens. I'm not sure how that happened; the fear just dissipated, just like most of the others.

There's more. I was deathly afraid of blood, always having a fit if I saw any coming out of me, in any capacity. Drops, even. More dramatically, I was terrified of anything that resembled a medical procedure. But just like I had never really been cut or never nearly drowned, I never really suffered any medical invasions, only vaccinations and such. One of my earliest memories is of my dad, a doctor, and several nurses wrestling with me so that I could get some kind of shot in my butt. I was screaming bloody murder, seriously, like it was the end of the world. I also have the vaguest memory of problems getting my polio vaccine. Yes, that's the one where there isn't even a shot to take: All you had to do was eat a sugar cube. I remember waiting in line for that, and I remember being afraid, but I don't remember anyone trying to comfort me. I certainly don't recall anyone explaining that there was no shot. Who knows, maybe they did and I just didn't believe them (which would be interesting in itself). My clearest memory of the whole ordeal is that some time afterwards I was told that I was "the only kid who cried" there.

Most of the emotional dysfunction at home would probably best be characterized as emotional neglect, but sometimes it felt more like emotional abuse. I vividly recall one evening, ten years old, when my dad and I were watching our gigantic, full-of-mysterious-tubes television and *Burnt Offerings* came on. It's this creepy horror movie starring Karen Black and Oliver Reed about a family staying in a haunted house, à la *The Amityville Horror*. It was so fucking scary; I was too young to be watching it.

One scene was particularly frightening, in which Oliver Reed—who was somehow quite imposing by default, somehow reminiscent of my own dad—momentarily became possessed by a house spirit and attempted to drown his son in the pool. It probably didn't help that the boy, played by Lee Montgomery, was named

David. I became overcome with fear in a way that I had not experienced exactly before or since, and I just started to *weep*, lying there on the living room shag.

Unsure of what was happening and what to do, I slowly looked up to my dad as he sat in his Scary Dad Loungy Chair. His reaction to my panic was precisely antithetical to what I needed—perhaps more than ever before in my life. When he realized I was crying and groveling for help, he appeared *frustrated*, maybe even *mad*. At the very least, he was quite inconvenienced and disappointed. He responded by saying one thing, while kinda shaking his head and sighing: *"You're such a pussy."*

I did what I could: I *retreated*, at least emotionally. Physically, I just continued to lie there, watching that movie and soaking in the trauma. I remember feeling deeply unsettled by the whole experience, like something broke, something that wasn't going to be easy to fix.

Perhaps adding to the confusion and disorientation of it all, I never felt bitter toward my dad for how he treated me—just detached, estranged. Maybe I wasn't bitter because I always knew that it wasn't his fault, just like my mother's distance from me wasn't her fault, either. For Dad, there was something about a physically abusive stepfather, a "drunk" who used to hit my sweet Granny, maybe even in front of my dad. And something about my dad threatening to kill him if he didn't stop. That's really about all I know, except maybe his stepdad died young (from alcoholism, maybe cirrhosis?).

Regardless of how forgiving I am to my father, incidents like the *Burnt Offerings* one messed me up, setting me up for others, like the Stratego calamity. Someone had given me the Milton Bradley board game for my birthday or Christmas when I was still a pre-teen. I hadn't planned to actually play the game with anyone, preferring to just tinker informally, alone, with the board and all the neat little parts that came with it. I opened it all up and was strangely captivated by the orderly rows of the 80-something game pieces, half red, half blue, all bright and laced with gold pictures of bombs, flags, and various soldiers. In my excitement, I dumped the pieces out onto the floor. But as I began to study them more closely, it struck me that I would never be able to put them back in the holder exactly the way they had come because I had not studied them carefully enough while housed. Inexplicably, I became so upset at this that I began hitting myself in the face with my fists. I didn't hurt myself badly; I don't recall bleeding or leaving any marks. But I hated myself for screwing that up forever. I knew it could never be returned to the peculiar order in which it came, and I knew I couldn't tell anybody about my distress because they wouldn't understand and couldn't help anyway. If I was a pussy for crying at a horror movie or at a polio vaccine, what on Earth would be the meaning of *this*?

As far as physical contact goes, most of it in my family growing up had been what most psychologists today would call violent, that is, my dad whuppin' me and/or my brother real good. I can't say I never did anything wrong, but these spankings were clearly excessive. At least I know that now. At the time, I was relatively confused about them.

It would often start with Dad lecturing me about some transgression, usually a pretty mild one. Mischief, or a lie, not exactly a little white one, but neither a big black one. This would snowball, sometimes all on its own, without any input from me whatsoever. His blood pressure would rise, face turning red, veins growing on his forehead. He'd start yelling at me and then something would click, the decision to strike. He'd say something like, "I tell you what, I'm gonna tan your hide. C'mere to me . . ."

He'd approach me in what felt like a charge and I'd crumble to the floor in fear. I'd start bawling before my dad even touched me, because he was so big and scary looking and I knew what was about to happen. When I was younger I'd literally beg, "DADDY! PLEASE DON'T!" He'd grab me by the arm, and hold me up, and strike my ass with his gigantic open hand, seemingly as hard as he could, but he would always deny that afterwards. I couldn't manage a strike-count, but it often seemed to go on until he got tired, but I'm supposing it would be around 10 strikes that simply felt like forever. Sometimes, he'd use a belt. I have vague memories of having to pull my pants down to get ready for some of those. Sometimes, me and brother would both get spankings, and for some reason I was usually second. This added a whole new layer of trauma to the whole experience, having to watch my brother get his, waiting for mine. Sometimes I'd have this ridiculously irrational hope that I would somehow be granted amnesty by the time he was done with my brother. My brother was older and tougher than me, so he would require more work before he threw in the towel and started crying. I can remember seeing the moments when my brother succumbed, the transition between angry defiance and pitiful, painful subjugation.

I can't deny it: I clearly was the "pussy" of the two, screaming bloody murder during mine. My mom told me once afterwards that if I didn't stop hollering so much the neighbors were gonna hear. She seemed somewhat confused about my wailing, implying—whether she meant to or not—that my spankings weren't so bad and that I was overreacting. More routinely, dad would invalidate the experience by apologizing afterwards and stating the clichés, such as "I do this because I love you" and "This hurts me more than it does you." But it was hard to feel the love in that beating, and equally difficult to see how it could have hurt him more than me. He would also explain how he didn't hit me as hard as he could. Reflecting on this today, I don't think that's true. I think he deceived himself into *believing* that he had been pulling punches because he was unconsciously aware, deep down, that he had lost control and he felt bad about it.

A couple of times, Dad would hug me after a spanking, which, outside of the context of the beating I just took, would have appeared sincere. But, given the context, it felt remarkably inappropriate. It's difficult to find the right word, but I want to call it *obscene*. Touching me like that, following a beating like that, had the slightest tinge of what I imagine sexual abuse must feel like. I never felt invested in those hugs. I just wanted them to be over, just like the spankings before them. On top of it all, I also recall feeling confused and guilty about *those* feelings: How can a son reject his dad's best hug, regardless of the context? And those really were his best hugs; I don't recall being hugged much otherwise throughout my life. I don't think me and my mom hugged until I was 21, visiting from college, and I initiated those.

Once, after me and my brother had been spanked for arguing (seriously, we hadn't been physically fighting, although I think we had said some hateful things that my dad overheard), my dad made us hug. I love my brother, and love hugging him today, but there was something obscene about this order as well. We had just been infuriated at each other, for which we had then been physically overwhelmed and hit by Dad, and now we were being forced to embrace each other. I remember we were both in our pajamas, as this had all transpired at the breakfast table. Both of our pajamas were more like veils, very thin because they were cheap to begin with and were now old and worn; we might as well had been naked. To this day, I still remember how confused I felt hugging him, like on some level I really did care for my brother and was sorry, but the way I was literally being forced to show it was perverse.

In any event, my spankings largely spoiled any chance of me and my father having a meaningful relationship. Outside of confusion, my most salient reaction was *anger*. I remember thinking that you'll be sorry. I hated you, at times, and wanted to physically harm you, and definitely would have, if I had had the capacity. That's probably not what you were after.

Anyway, the hatred always dissipated, but a compelling disinterest always endured, akin to the taste aversion that comes after a vicious bout of food poisoning. And just like a taste aversion, it can last a long time, forever even.

All that said, I honestly don't feel like I hold a grudge today. This part of my book is not about getting revenge on my dad, that's for sure. In fact, I've been tormented at times over how or even whether to publish all of this, because I feel sorry for him. I'm only doing it to vent a little of my own pain, to spend some time on the anti-corporal punishment soapbox, and—for the sake of the rest of this book—to show that having God in one's home doesn't necessarily guarantee a good home. Spankings sure didn't help my relationship with Him, either. I also felt anger towards God after a good whuppin', so much so that on a couple of occasions I broke down again once I was alone, shooting my finger to the Heavens, yelling "FUCK YOU!" to God, tears flowing down my face. I fantasized about taking my anger out on His House, vandalizing the sign out front so that instead of reading "First Assembly of God," it would say "First Ass of doG" or simply "FAG."

I finally did experience healthy human contact when I was about twelve or thirteen years old, at Christian summer camp. Camp was unexpectedly fun that year. I spent a lot of time on the miniature golf course, where I had become a force with which to be reckoned. That was also the first time in my life that I realized that there's something worthwhile about playing horseshoes. I never liked competitive games so much, win or lose, but horseshoes really resonated well with me, and still does.

In the evenings, following dinner, there were more serious, church-like events. As with regular church back home, I went somewhat begrudgingly, but I don't think much more than anyone else. Sure, I'd rather have been back on the putt-putt course or chunking horseshoes, but I also had enough faith and conviction to not gripe too much on the way to the chapel.

One night's meeting was particularly serious and momentous, a younger person's version of what often went down at Big Church on Sunday evenings back in Dallas. As my father and other major church figures would often remark, "the Holy Spirit descended" on us, so much so that it eventually became clear there would be no sermon—only worshipping. We were getting down that night, praising the Lord full throttle.

It never felt creepy. No one ever whipped out a snake and started dancing with it or anything like that. Instead, we were just singing songs and holding our hands up, like you see on television advertisements for gospel albums. However, this was less dramatic. There was no soft-filter lens on the camera; everything was acutely distinct. The ambiance was generally pleasant, but there was also a sense of something awesome in the air. It was so serious, no laughing matter. I can't fathom someone being irreverent at a time like that, not even George Carlin, if he had been there.

After some time, in a relative lull, the leader of the event asked if anyone in the audience was ready to come forward and be saved. Until that moment I had assumed I was already saved because I had believed in Christ all my life and always prayed to Him so well. However, it became as clear as anything had ever become clear before that I had actually been lacking something, and that *this* was my Time. It would be some kind of unpardonable sin to pass it up. I might as well have been standing in the open door of a crashing, burning airplane, parachute on, helmet, goggles, the works. Gotta jump, buddy!

Scared to death but knowing what I had to do, I abandoned my inconspicuous seat among the pews and headed down to the altar, joining the handful of other folks who hadn't dawdled as much as I had. With increasing confidence, I got down on my knees and put my hands back in the air, but higher this time.

It felt like I was on a stage, the volume of everyone's worshipping around me and the overall intensity of the experience now blaring. I was still scared and not sure where it was all headed, but it felt big, wherever it was. Along with the fear was a seemingly inconsistent sense of *security*, because I was hardly in control: Something else, something bigger than me, was guiding me through those peculiar motions. It was scary, but *right*, in the cosmic sense. I was at the center of the entire universe.

Then, I felt someone next to me. It was Patsy, my mother's oldest friend from all the way back from her high school; she was a chaperone. Right away, I could tell she knew exactly what was happening inside me, but she still asked, "Are you ready to receive the Lord?" I nodded. With a reassuring authority, clearly from experience, she knelt down beside me, to my left, and put her right hand on my shoulder, and that's when all Heaven broke loose.

Magic went into me from her hand; I felt something electric, but calm and soothing. I exploded into tears, hands in the air the whole time, feeling some of the most profound emotions I ever had in my entire life. Something was touching my hands, too—that whole gesture finally made perfect sense to me. You surrender, and then you are touched; He holds you. I knew that I was Forgiven, all was well, and I was finally Saved, for real. It all made such wonderful sense, profoundly, unambiguously. That was the hardest I had ever cried, outside of being spanked. The popular hymn would resonate for some time to come:

Shackled by a heavy burden,
'Neath a load of guilt and shame.
Then the hand of Jesus touched me,
And now I am no longer the same.

He touched me; Oh, He touched me,
And oh the joy that floods my soul!
Something happened and now I know,
He touched me and made me whole.[1]

---

1 Gaither, B. (1963). He touched me. [Recorded by The Bill Gaither Trio]. On *He touched me.* [Vinyl record]. Nashville: Heart Warming Records. Many sources indicate that Bill's wife, Gloria, also helped write the song.

Indeed, my relationship with God had suddenly matured and reached new heights. I was no longer a painting of a kid in his pajamas praying at the side of his bed. I was now the real thing, like the grown-ups of whom I used to be in awe. I could raise my own hands in grown-up church now, and was even qualified to "testify," if the Holy Spirit ever moved me as such. If nothing else, I'm going to Heaven. Praise him.

Patsy must have told my parents about what happened, because shortly after camp was over and I returned home my dad approached me to talk about it. I remember it pretty clearly, him saying, so seriously, "I hear you were filled with the Holy Spirit." I was kinda shy about it, like I wanted to keep it private, just like everything else. But I was apparently in the club now, wise. It was exciting, but also a little frightening, as the bar of responsibility had been raised higher. There was no turning back.

It took years—decades, even—before I realized that it wasn't a spirit that had touched me that evening. It was just Patsy.

Enthused by my experience at camp, I became determined to read the entire Bible, to become a serious student and realize my new-found status as an adult Christian. I picked up my New American Standard version one day and started reading from The Beginning.

Inconceivably, however, in the wake of my salvation, I immediately found the Bible disorienting and frustrating. Don't jump ahead: I don't recall *doubting* during that fledgling period, but I clearly recall feeling quite *confused* right off the bat.

Not far past the front cover, God tells Adam not to eat from the "the tree of the knowledge of good and evil . . . for in the day that you eat from it you shall surely die."[2] Further down the same page,

---

2 Genesis 2:17. All Bible quotes in this book are from the *New American Standard Bible, Reference Edition*. (1975). Chicago: Moody Press.

however, Satan assures Eve that she won't really die, but instead her eyes will be opened, like God's, so that she can appreciate the difference between good and evil, as implied by the tantalizing tree's name. And the damnedest thing happens: She *doesn't* die that day as God promised, but instead her eyes are opened, as Satan predicted! What an unfathomably bizarre way to begin the Bible: God doesn't tell the truth, but Satan does? I can tell this isn't going to be easy. One doesn't simply *read* the Bible—it's work! Or maybe art, which I've never been too good at.

I'm being too rigid. Perhaps a "day" is not to be taken literally: Perhaps Eve would die later, in a God-day, which could be years. That makes some sense, as it fits with the notion that the earth also wasn't created in six "days," as we now know via science. This is tricky, though, because a "day" was defined in Genesis 1, with the sun going up and down, which sounds like the same "day" of today. But maybe the issue is not about time at all. Maybe when God said, "you shall surely die," he meant it figuratively, like it's *your innocence* that will perish. Or maybe he wasn't being figurative at all: Maybe He just changed his mind about killing Eve.

A little further on, Genesis 3:22 seems to offer some explanation but it just creates more bewilderment while doing so. God says that Adam, because he ate from the tree of the knowledge of good and evil, has now "become like one of Us," presumably the angels and whatnot. God seems nervous and goes on to suggest that if Adam were to now eat from the tree of life he would achieve eternal life and—it doesn't say explicitly—but the implication is that he would become another God or something?! God is so unsettled by the prospect that he banishes Adam from the Garden and installs an angel guard with a flaming sword at the gate to prevent the peculiar, ill-defined catastrophe. This is all so weird—no one has ever mentioned this stuff in Sunday school! And what a baffling scenario to create in the first place, these excruciatingly tempting trees with such profound influence on the nature of existence.

Soon thereafter, Adam and Eve's children, Cain and Abel, have a conflict because God is not happy with Cain's sacrifice to him. The whole notion of sacrifice is kinda odd as well, especially at the beginning of time when you have the whole Earth at your disposal. It seems like you'd need to slaughter an entire species or burn down a whole forest to make it count. Anyway, Cain is so upset that he kills Abel. Then God banishes Cain to some other land, called Nod, where Cain finds a wife. Huh? There's another land with people in it?

Okay, this is obviously not just about "literal" versus "figurative" statements anymore—apparently, you also have to read between the lines. Unequivocally, I see, the Bible demands speculation outside of what is explicitly stated. In the case of Cain, there must have been some sort of activity outside of Eden, not yet discussed in the Bible. Perhaps there were other Gardens of Eden throughout the world, and Genesis only told the story of one such place. Making this maneuver in the first book set a precedent that would be necessary quite often throughout the rest of the Bible. No problem, though, I see how it works. I'll keep reading.

But then Genesis 6:6 makes the peculiar assertion that the "the Lord was sorry that He had made man on the earth, and He was grieved in His heart." This seems to corroborate the suspicion that the earlier chapters had raised, that God was actually kinda human. He apparently doesn't really know the future and is essentially flying by the seat of his pants like the rest of us. He could apparently make mistakes and even have regret about them. When it said that man was created in God's image, they weren't joking!

So God decides to destroy humankind. Here we go again. I was no nautical engineer, but I had perused enough *National Geographic* magazines to know there was no way that two of every animal could fit on Noah's ark. They give the dimensions—I looked up a "cubit"—that vessel's just too small. It probably wouldn't have provided enough space to house the fauna of Madagascar, not to mention its flora.

Alright, well, like Cain, the story of Noah must have just been one such story. There had to be other arks throughout the world, like one for Kenya, one for Vietnam, and probably a couple for Brazil. My suspicion gained momentum when I looked up Mount Ararat in our encyclopedias and learned it's really not that tall, in the grand scheme of things. So, there must have been something on the order of fifty other peaks across the world that were not flooded, either, that could have landed the other arks. Yes, there must have been multiple arks, because it also seems unlikely that Noah and his family were the *only* humans who had earned the right to stay alive. And, of course, if there were not other arks, Noah's family would have to engage in all sorts of gory incest in order to repopulate the world. And we learn later that incest ain't gonna fly. That's one topic upon which God and Darwin agree!

As a young Christian learning the Word, I'm still feeling okay despite these obstacles in Genesis. But I am somewhat nagged by the demand that I have to augment the information in the Bible in order to make the Bible work. It's not that I expected the authors to state *everything* clearly, but it's just bothersome that I'm being granted liberty—or, more accurately, *required*—to figure out so much on my own. I may have been prepubescent but I was old enough to have a sense of the perils of *subjectivity* (although I didn't know that specific word at the time). Subjective interpretation is fine in some contexts, like studying a painting, but it's risky in others, like law and morality and issues of eternal life. A guide can't be *too* subjective, otherwise it's useless—why have a guide at all? I guess the trick is learning where to draw the line. This must be what "spiritual growth" is all about.

Nevertheless, I petered out somewhere in Exodus, not long after I got confused again when God killed what must have been thousands of apparently innocent little boys in order to get Pharaoh to bend to his Will. That simply defied any sort of rationale I could possibly conjure. Fuck this; I'm skipping to the New Testament. I had dabbled there enough already to know that it would be much more palatable. It even seems to give us permission to discard much of the Old Testament, with all of its confusion and boredom. For example, 1

Timothy 1:4 says not "to pay attention to myths and endless gene-
alogies, which give rise to mere speculation rather than furthering
the administration of God which is by faith." Besides the paradoxes
and tedium of the Old Testament, I had been getting the vibe that the
New Testament was simply more relevant and useful in modern
times because Jesus had somehow changed things.

But, damn it, turning all those pages to find the New Testament,
now I'm bothered by the very fact that there's even a distinction between "Old" and "New" testaments, and that there was some sort of
transformation between them. God was supposed to be perfect—but
how can something perfect *change*, that is, improve? He *must not*
have been perfect, then. In addition to creating man in the first place,
God made another mistake: He had been too strict on him during
Old Testament days. Jesus got him to lighten up.

And although "old," that testament *is clearly bigger* than the new
one. How much of it has truly expired? How do I know what to discard and what to keep? Is it all there just to show how much better
Jesus made things? It couldn't be that, because the Ten Commandments are in there, along with the 23rd Psalm, as well as the part
about God making humans in his own image, all of which are still
very popular today.

And I can't understand why I get to exist in New Testament,
post-Jesus days, and am therefore able to reap the benefits of Jesus'
first coming. It feels unfair to me, reminiscent of what I now know is
called *survivor guilt* in the context of trauma. Why do I get to live in
the kinder times, and basically do what I want, as long as I truly feel
sorry and ask for forgiveness later (which I always did, being a very
guilt-ridden little boy), while millions of people before me had to
constantly walk on eggshells, lest they get covered in boils, plagued
by frogs, or turned into salt? That was another frustrating story for
me: I bet Lot and his family wished that God was being figurative
when he told them not to look back upon Sodom and Gomorra.

Well, the New Testament was much more engaging and easy to
read than the Old, as advertised. Unfortunately, it also had plenty of

contradictions and head-scratchers of its own.

Matthew 18:3 tells us we need to be like children to enter the Kingdom of Heaven, but right down the street at 1 Corinthians 13:11 the suggestion is to grow up. John 3:16 says all I have to do is believe in Him to be saved, but Matthew 19:24 adds an alarming caveat: If I'm financially wealthy, the odds are greatly reduced, comparable to those of getting a camel through the eye of a needle! Speaking of which, his "only begotten" son? Why does everyone emphasize that part like it's so important? Was God himself somehow limited to having just one son?

Ephesians 6:5 makes some troubling statements that slaves should obey their masters, with "fear and trembling." I had learned about Abraham Lincoln and Harriet Tubman in regular school, and their whole take on slavery made a lot more sense to me. This seriously raised the question of whether the Bible is truly timeless, as all the pastors of my church had always proclaimed. It's wrong here, hands-down. That slavery part was clearly written for people of a time and place where slavery was acceptable, but we all know now that it isn't. I had seen *Roots* and knew all about the life of American slave Kunta Kinte: That shit was fucked up! I hadn't thought about it at the time, but later I would begin to wonder: Has the Bible actually fostered violence and oppression at times? Maybe slavery was acceptable such an inconceivably short time ago—in this country—because the Bible said it was.

Similarly, 1 Corinthians 14:34-35 tells us that women aren't supposed to speak at church, but instead "if they desire to learn anything, let them ask their own husbands at home." But some of the most respected people in *my* church are women! And some of them don't merely speak at church, some of them *speak in tongues*, allegedly compelled by the Holy Spirit. Indeed, it was a woman who touched me and catalyzed my salvation, and got me here in the first place. What gives? Something is happening at my church that seems miraculous, but the Bible is suggesting that it shouldn't be happening at all. Are those women sinning? Are the men sinning by listening? Are we not a real church? What if we *are* wrong about our version of Christianity, like the Baptists and others might argue?

I suspect I could go on like this for quite some time, if I hadn't simply given up my quest to read the Bible altogether. I have to admit: I really haven't read most of it.

But it's not all my fault! The contradictions, ambiguities, and confusions made it so that I wasn't finding the Bible a useful part of my quest. On the contrary, it was becoming a bit of an obstacle. Sure, sometimes it could be comforting, such as when it suggests that I will inherit the earth someday, me being meek. But I began to doubt even the comforting statements such as this. What exactly does "inherit the earth" mean? How do I know the author wasn't simply being figurative again? Even worse, how do I know the statements I find comforting won't expire someday, like those oppressing women, slaves, and homosexuals—and those condoning harsh corporal punishment, such as hitting your child with a stick? Heck, maybe the meek *have already* inherited the earth, figuratively or something, and from now on they would be trampled by capitalism and other bullies. I'm completely disoriented. Going in circles. I'm done with this Book.

Fine; I would still be a Christian, I just wouldn't be a *Bible-reading* Christian. I needed to loosen up. Just because all these claims about the Bible being holy and whatnot have now become dubious, by no means does that have to imply that *God* and *Jesus* are not real. Apparently, man was just not very good at writing about them. I had been learning elsewhere that we simply cannot fully comprehend the Lord. Perhaps poor Bible-writing was just another manifestation of that.

The good news was that loosening my grip on the Bible was not always a bad thing. It also afforded the ability to question—if not disregard—some of the scarier stuff that I didn't want to believe was true anyway. For example, perhaps the Apocalypse and hell are not quite as tormenting as suggested by avid Bible readers. Now that was a nice thought, because I couldn't be so childish to assume that everyone I know and love is going to make it to Heaven. Maybe hell is really just more of a limbo, a nothing, but just described as fire and brimstone to scare people, or because the authors really didn't know and that had been their best guess . . . or perhaps they were describing Hell figuratively.

Overall, regardless of how much I had to recalibrate my reverence for the Bible, I honestly didn't undergo any fundamental spiritual changes otherwise. Most importantly, I felt just as moral as ever, because my beliefs in God, eternal life, and how to get to the latter were steadfast. I continued to go to church (although I had no choice to skip it anyway), and I still had spiritual moments, both in the pew and elsewhere.

Most reliably, I continued to find comfort through prayer. Regardless of the injustice suffered by Lot's wife or American slaves just a few generations ago, God was listening to me, helping me, comforting me. Some version of heaven still awaited after this "necessary evil" of my life, and that's all that really mattered.

Well, despite all that good stuff, I started experimenting with drugs and by my mid-late teens was using fairly steadily.

I suspect some agnostic and atheist readers would like for me to argue that the spiritual turmoil I've been discussing thus far drove me to drug use, but I honestly can't do that, at least with certainty. Some hardline Christians might even suggest that drugs were God's mechanism to smite me for not being able to consume his Word, or for telling him to fuck off after a spanking. Of course I can't agree to that, either. All I can say with certainty is that having Jesus in my life, or at least my relatively Bible-free version of him, sure didn't keep me from drug use.

And mine got pretty bad, too. I went crazy a couple of times, and I think I might have even have died once.

Not Necessarily Stoned, but Beautiful

I have absolutely no pleasure in the stimulants in which I sometimes so madly indulge. It has not been in the pursuit of pleasure that I have perilled life and reputation and reason. It has been the desperate attempt to escape from torturing memories, from a sense of insupportable loneliness, and a dread of some strange impending doom.

— Edgar Allan Poe

Some of us look for the Way in opium and some in God, some of us in whiskey and some in love. It's all the same Way and it leads no whither.

— Somerset Maugham, *The Painted Veil*

REMINISCENT OF HOW I DISCOVERED IRON MAIDEN, I was turned on to drugs in very ironic fashion. When I was young, like in early elementary school even, my dad bought some *World Book Encyclopedias* from a door-to-door salesman. Like some kind of almost-autistic kid, I became a bit addicted to these and would spend large parts of many days in self-imposed seclusion poring over them. I was enthralled by everything they had to offer, whether it be astronomy, kings of England, snakes, ships, or now-defunct nations, like Upper Volta. I was so young when I first began this habit that I wasn't able to read well or interpret some of the mathematical figures. However, instead of feeling discouraged, this only added to my sense of awe.

One day when I was in the fourth or fifth grade, I was browsing the *L* volume and settled on the entry for "literature." It included pictures of specific books in order to provide examples of the types available—fairy tale, history, and so on. As an example of an educational book, it depicted the cover of one called *What You Should Know about Drugs*. The letters on the front were all spaced-out 70s psychedelic; it was apparently about drug abuse and users. I was drawn to it and somewhat frustrated that I couldn't reach into the *L* encyclopedia and open it. At the time, I was only interested in drugs academically and quite frightened of the notion of actually using them. But I wanted to see what that book had to say.

And I'd be damned: My library at Alex Sanger Elementary school had it—and it did not disappoint. Of course, there were respective chapters on marijuana and alcohol. Those were worthwhile, but nothing compared to the one on, say, heroin. What could possibly motivate someone to do a drug that could so readily kill you? But I mostly wanted to read about the even weirder shit, the stuff I had hardly even heard of.

So it was the chapter on LSD that really grabbed me. I can still remember it clearly, thirty-some-odd years later, especially the subjective accounts of people's acid trips—one guy told a story about doing it at school! He described how sitting in class, presumably under fully lighted conditions, he began to perceive that the tiles in the floor became wavy and eventually morphed so that seaweed grew up from them. When his teacher came into the room and sat down, flames came up around him and then out of his head. When the flames started heading towards the kid, it was a little too intense so he excused himself from the class.[1]

---

1 Gorodetzky, C. W. & Christian, S. T. (1970). *What you should know about drugs* (p. 50). New York: Harcourt Brace Jovanovich.

Reminiscent of hearing *The Number of the Beast* for the first time, my fear was again tinged with titillation. Before I finished that chapter I had an epiphany of sorts, perhaps the first epiphany I ever had: I was going to do LSD some day! Not soon—no, I would have to be more grown up. But there was no way in hell someone was gonna have an experience like that without me. I wanted to trip, and I was certain that I was going to eventually.

But of course I didn't start with LSD; I started with weed.[2] My brother was three years older than me and had already started smoking with some neighborhood hooligans, making it just a matter of time before I would have my opportunity. I was real nervous at first and my brother was not very enthusiastic about letting me do it, apparently because he felt some duty to keep me clean. Nevertheless, we broke the seal during the summer of 1982 and I have to say it was a riot about which I have no regrets. That was one of the best summers ever. One of the hooligans had cable TV, which was not terribly common at the time. We sat around all summer long, getting high and watching MTV and rated-R movies, most significantly, the ubiquitous classic *Fast Times at Ridgemont High*. Yes, I learned about sex from Phoebe Cates, Judge Reinhold, and Jennifer Jason Leigh. Despite the horror this thought might bring to many parents, looking back on it now, I don't think it was unhealthy and it was about as good a way to be exposed to sex as any other. Judge Reinhold taught me that masturbation was nothing to be ashamed of; in fact, it could be funny! And Jennifer Jason Leigh's sexual adventures—which culminated in settling down with the wholesome dork—made me consider, early on, that looks and popularity are not everything. Really, that was a great movie

---

2 No, I'm not a big fan of the *gateway drug* hypothesis. I suspect many people have been like me, destined to do hard drugs regardless but starting with pot simply because it's the most readily available. I've known a lot of stoners in my time, and the vast, vast majority of them have not used harder drugs, at least chronically.

for me at the time. And of course, the young cast was one of the greatest ever, hands-down.

I eventually did do LSD, at sixteen, a seasoned stoner by the time and a pretty good drinker as well. I had been talking to my experienced friend Chris about it for a while in preparation, our conversations feeling more like some sort of spiritual consultation than anything else. At the time, Chris worked (actually, lived) at Theater Gallery in Deep Ellum, the most punk venue in the punk scene in Dallas in the 1980s and early 1990s. One night I had made arrangements to spend the night out in hopes to make it to my first big show there, Bad Brains. As fate would have it, the show was sold out and Chris couldn't sneak me in, given the significance of the event and my status as a mere wannabe. However, he was able to score some LSD, so we decided I would do that instead once the show was over and Chris was relieved. He would be my sober "guide," something that was highly recommended among the more responsible acid-using crowd. The stuff that we were doing in Dallas in the late 80s always came on little pieces of paper, about a quarter-inch square. My first had a relatively boring graphic, just alternating orange and blue stripes. Except mine was just orange stripes, because it had accidentally had been through this guy Brian's washing machine and the blue had washed away. I think Brian just gave it to us, or maybe it was $5. We didn't even know if it was going to work.

I waited around outside for the show to end and for Chris to be free, smoking and drinking out in the streets, but not as much as usual because I didn't want to pollute the adventure to come. We went back to Chris's house some time after midnight and I finally swallowed it. I had an experience that would become very familiar, although the first time was the best, in ways.

For the first 30 to 45 minutes, nothing happened except natural giddiness and nervousness about what was to come—and, in this case, if anything was going to happen at all, given the washing machine factor. However, after about an hour something salient and novel did come over me, although its quality was somewhat unexpected: a discombobulated feeling of numbness and stupidity. I wasn't discouraged, though, as my guide informed me this would be transient. As with most of the LSD experience, the feeling is difficult to describe but I somehow felt like my brain was purging, doing the neural equivalent of a colon cleanse to get rid of the old and to prepare for the new.

Sure enough, the numbness only lasted for a few minutes until it was replaced by the opposite and more compelling and enduring sensation: My mind became extraordinarily *clear*, centered and lucid, in the present moment, eventually to a degree that was far beyond what I had ever experienced before during any sort of non-LSD consciousness—including being born again at camp years before. As intensely spiritual as that experience had been, it was still an event that occurred on Earth, an event that could be adequately conveyed in words, whereas LSD was otherworldly, very far from describable. A real writer, Aldous Huxley, came closest to capturing the profundity of psychedelia with words:

"There seems to be plenty of it," was all I would answer, when the investigator asked me to say what I felt about time. Plenty of it, but exactly how much was entirely irrelevant. I could, of course, have looked at my watch; but my watch, I knew, was in another universe. My experience had been, was still, of an indefinite duration or alternatively of a perpetual present made up of one continually changing apocalypse.[3]

---

3 Huxley, A. (1954). *The doors of perception* (p. 21). New York: Harper & Row. Huxley actually took mescaline, a drug whose effects are very similar to those of LSD.

"Popping" was the best I could ever come up with, to describe this sensation that each moment was inexplicably more profound than the last, despite being perfectly convinced that the last was as incredible as a moment could be. But now I prefer "a perpetual present made up of one continually changing apocalypse."

As dramatic as these transitions were, I felt surprisingly comfortable during them. Any previous concerns about having a "bad trip" felt so remote, grossly unfounded, utterly ridiculous. Bad trips were off in some other universe, with Huxley's watch. Clearly, *this* consciousness was the right one; the other one that I had been in for 16 years was the one of which to be leery. I would always use derivatives of the word *rapture* to attempt to describe the feeling, and was so overcome with it that I just sat there, mouth agape, looking around at the room, myself, and at Chris, speechless except able to utter an occasional "Wow . . ." or "Dude . . ." Everything looked so amazing and beautiful, and it all felt so . . . rapturous. Chris was smiling the whole time, because he knew. He would occasionally ask me, "Isn't tripping cool?" And I would just say something, slowly, like, "I had no idea . . ." Indeed, no amount of book reading or interviewing seasoned users had prepared me for *this*.

Similar to the rapturous feelings and sensations of enhanced consciousness, the visual hallucinations on LSD felt surprisingly comfortable, *ego-syntonic*, as some psychologists say—that is, a part of me, not alien or intrusive. The most simple scene on LSD, Chris's living room even, was much more beautiful than anything I had seen in real life otherwise, whether landscapes, beaches, mountains, titties, whatever. Everything within eyesight—the floor, the rug on it, the walls, pictures, vases, and knickknacks—was more resolved, every color was brighter and more saturated, so much so that many colors seemed like they had never been perceived before. Every surface was literally vibrating, but comfortably, with a life that I had never noticed before but that had obviously been there all along. The longer I looked at anything the more alive and hypnotic it became, relatively expansive surfaces such as walls, floors, and ceilings being particularly vibrant tapestries for hallucination. At first glance, such a surface might be merely emitting an aura or shimmering, but if I held my gaze it would suddenly come alive and begin swirling, waving, and melting, somehow depending on its actual physical traits on Earth. Regardless, it was mesmerizing, beautiful, and as real-looking as real could be. There was not even the slightest sense of intoxication—although I never forgot I was on a drug. But it was hard to imagine how anything would look the same again once it was over. I'm forced to borrow from Huxley again: "I was seeing what Adam had seen on the morning of his creation—the miracle, moment by moment, of naked existence . . . 'This is how one ought to see, how things really are.' And yet there were reservations. For if one always saw like this, one would never want to do anything else."[4]

Evident without any provocation whatsoever were what we all called "tracers," that is, the smeared afterimage of anything that moved across your visual field. Whenever Chris walked in front of me, from one side to the other, he would leave a continuous trail of himself that could grow to several feet long, then once he stopped, it would catch up to him and be absorbed with such salience that I could almost feel or hear it smacking his reality. With a lit cigarette in a dark room we could readily create what looked like ribbon dancing or time-lapse photographs of kids waving sparklers on the Fourth of July.

Chris did a great job at being my guide, usurping Patsy, you know, the woman who had taken me on my relatively measly spiritual adventure at camp previously. He kept showing me stuff that I might enjoy, like album art, books, trinkets, and rocks. Eventually, once he became convinced I was comfortable, he raised the bar a little. He told me that in order to *really* see what LSD can do, you have to sit still and stare at something so that it has time to mani-

---

4 Ibid., p. 17; 34-35.

fest. He suggested I stare at my hand. It didn't sound like a strange request at all at the time; in fact, it sounded like a great idea. So I sat down, him right next to me, and I just stared at my hand, palm facing me, fingers fanned out comfortably.

After a few seconds, the skin on my hand began to undulate, to pulsate, as if something were inside it, moving and wanting out. Again, it wasn't scary at all—just mesmerizing. The undulations gave way to melting, my skin a river of wax running down my wrist and out of sight, but a fantastic, M.C. Escher-type perpetual melting so that there was always more hand to come, never any blood, muscle or bone. Over time, this gave way to more idiosyncratic hallucinations, so that eventually five little eyeballs formed, one on each of the most distal joints of my five fingers, you know, where your fingerprints are. Each looked like the eye on the back of a dollar bill, just an eye, looking at me, but they were *alive*, each blinking at its own pace, independent from the others, and each seemed to have its own little expression or personality even. I was completely enthralled by this scene, like I have never been enthralled before, and for some reason it was *funny*. I just giggled at the magnificence of it all. Then, each eye morphed further, so that they were no longer eyes but some other living shapes—my fingertips became little clams, like those barnacles that attach to garbage in the Gulf. As the eyes that had been blinking before, the clams were snapping, little mouths that didn't make any noise, and each continued to have its own personality of sorts. I kept giggling; I must have had the most wonderful smile on my face.

Later, when I was "peaking," the hallucinations would come much more readily, requiring less staring to get them going. I remember us going into the kitchen because Chris wanted to see if I'd like to try some food. While he was digging through the fridge, I perused the little dining/bill-writing table in the corner and found an 8 x 10 piece of paper, only it was filled with a magnificent design, akin to an oriental rug—curly, ornate, symmetric with paisleys, but the detail was so fine I couldn't begin to speculate how it was drawn. I studied it, soaked it in while Chris kept digging through the fridge. The picture looked unworldly, like it must have been printed by alien technology, but I realized I had taken a drug and of course it wasn't from outer space. Still, I asked Chris, incredulously, "Dude, where did you get this?" He looked at me, incredulous himself—I think he thought for a moment I was joking—and said, "That's a blank sheet of paper." And apparently it was. I put it down kinda abruptly, startled. Good news is, that was the most unsettled I became all night, those few seconds.

Turns out, food is kinda gross when you're tripping. I can imagine someone converting to vegetarianism after the experience. Some things, like oranges and orange juice, are orgasmic, but meat is just gross on LSD, reminiscent of how it's depicted in a Jan Svankmeyer film (I bet that dude is "experienced"). And you're not horny, either. I loved to touch things on acid, but never wanted to touch another person, especially their goo. People look ugly, usually, but in a comical way, not necessarily frightening. They're all bulbous and meaty and start to melt if you look at them too long. And your own skin feels kinda grimy; all things considered, the last thing on your mind is sex. You're way, way beyond it when on LSD. It becomes a trivial thing, something that lesser beings do because they don't have *this*.

Eventually, when the sun was about to start coming up, Chris felt comfortable enough to leave me unsupervised and decided to go to sleep. We both got into his big bed, slumber party-style. He told me not to leave the room because his folks would be getting up soon, and he fell fast asleep. I just lay there and kept having the time of my life. I took a hand-held mirror with me to bed and just stared into it. My face, like my hand earlier, began to look kinda peculiar, as if it wasn't mine anymore, like I was wearing a mask but it was part of me at the same time. Then, in what was now a well-lit room, as clear as day, that mask (my face) began to distort. My upper lip became a huge harelip, grotesque but hilarious. I had to strain to not laugh out loud and wake Chris, but I was literally shaking with stifled laughter as my harelip kept growing, proceeding up to my nose, then through it and beyond, all the way between my eyes and up behind my longish hair. My eyes began to crawl about my face similarly until the face in the mirror became wholly unrecognizable as a face. I shook my head and it started over.

The hallucinations finally began to dwindle and I could tell that I was coming back to the world, which was an experience in itself. I had been so far away that I had kinda forgotten what regular reality was like. I guess that's why they call it "tripping." Despite how profound it had all been, I had had my fill and was ready to be back, back in the world of obligation, worry, and pretension. It's strange: LSD may be the only drug that can truly be satisfying, where you sincerely feel that you've had enough.

On the other hand, there was also a slight sense of *sadness*, because this had clearly been the most captivating eight hours or so of my life. I'm a bit embarrassed to admit it, but yeah, there was a feeling of revelation, as if LSD had been waiting for me all this time and that it was my new best friend. It was the most marvelous thing that had ever happened to anyone, and resonated with me perfectly like nothing else before or since.

Important to note, even though LSD made my salvation at church summer camp years before pale in comparison, it didn't diminish the value of that previous experience. At least for the time being, the glory of tripping existed in parallel—not in lieu of—the glory of Jesus. If anything, the net effect of having taken LSD only raised the bar of my expectations of heaven. If God would allow me to have the psychedelic experience on Earth for five ridiculous dollars, via *200 millionths of a gram* of a drug derived from a fungus that grows on rye, of all things, imagine what must await me after death! Certainly, heaven would ultimately make even LSD pale in comparison.

Despite being so smitten, I only tripped about thirty times over the next three years or so. It just didn't feel like something that should be summoned frivolously. I respected it, even revered it, the way boy scouts are taught to respect the wild, like bears and rapid rivers and freezing mountainsides. These things are beautiful and magnificent but you gotta behold them cautiously or they can turn on you and even destroy you.

Alas, I eventually became reckless and broke the cardinal rule of tripping: I took some acid impulsively, and sure enough had a trip that was as hellish as the first had been wonderful.

Everyone learns in LSD 101 that you don't take it under certain circumstances, like when you're upset, anxious, or depressed—or when you have obligations in the near future. My mistake was that I took it one evening when I knew I had to be home later that same night and there simply wasn't enough time to let it run its course; I was 19 and still had something like a curfew, which was definitely in effect that night. Tripping in my house was just a terrible idea; I might as well be doing it at school or at a job interview—way too risky. If nothing else, my house was just too small, and my room was kinda in the middle of it, a converted den that also served as a bit of a thoroughfare. There were two doors to my room, one on each end, and I couldn't even close them because the window air conditioning unit that cooled the whole house was in my room. There was nowhere for me to hide in my house, a luxury I always envied of my peers.

I had actually tripped the night before, coincidentally with Chris. We had spent the entire day having a great time at the Galleria, one of the fancier shopping malls in Dallas, in the north, Ross Perot part of town. Without having slept that night, the next day I was telling my homeboys about the Galleria experience, which got them excited so that they wanted to trip that evening themselves. So, we went out and got some more acid, including a hit for me, in the stupidity of my sleep deprivation. It was "Saturn," this notoriously "serious" shit with a picture of the planet on it. I think it was around eight o'clock when we "dropped," and I had to be home by two a.m., not negotiable. I don't know what the fuck I was thinking.

After an hour had passed and I didn't feel anything I made another mistake by beginning to hope that it wasn't going to work. I had never tried to trip two days in a row before, but I had read that we build tolerance to hallucinogens very quickly. Maybe I wouldn't get off at all or perhaps if I did it'd be relatively mild. Contrasting the hope that it might not work was a wish that it would hurry up and start, if it was going to happen at all. I had to be home in about five hours—if it starts later versus sooner, I'm gonna be peaking right about the time I have to go home! Fuck.

We got in the car and drove around to do the usual playground circuit, to play on swings and look at the trees and stars and stuff. Tragically, I eventually did begin to get off, a record two hours after I took the acid. And the initial weird, unsettled feelings never gave way to comfort as they had thirty times before.

I started feeling anxious, but decided not to say anything, partially out of simple courtesy: I just didn't want to bring anyone else down. Not entirely irrational, I was kinda afraid that if I told them I was having a bad time it might be contagious and cause someone else to become upset, too.

As the hallucinations started, there was an unpleasant tone that I hadn't experienced before. Things were ugly as they often are on acid, but for the first time it wasn't cartoon-y and comical. Ugly was finally bad. Everywhere we went, everything had this moss growing on it—a damp, greenish-black moss that was thick and disgusting. I didn't want to see it, but it was everywhere, on the ground, on cars, and even on my friends.

Miraculously, over time, the anxiety and tension seemed to level off and maybe even wane. Perhaps getting through a couple of hours without the others noticing increased my confidence; they were clearly having a good time, and I never had any paranoid feelings involving them directly. I was beginning to feel pretty sure I wasn't going to have a bad trip, the kind you read about in the newspaper or hear via urban myth. I had only been close, thank God.

When it was time for the guys to take me home, I actually thought I might be alright. Perhaps once I was alone the pressure of having to keep my freak-out a secret would dissipate and I could just ride out the rest in peace. All I had to do was avoid my parents, which shouldn't be too much to ask. They were almost always asleep this late.

When we got to my house, the lights were indeed out and my folks were apparently asleep, which was a momentous relief. I don't know what the fuck I would have done if they had been awake; probably would have just ran away. There's no way I could have faced either of them like that. The cat would have finally come out of the bag, whatever that would have meant.

I took a piss at the bush where I always did when coming home simply drunk and/or stoned, in order to minimize commotion once I got into our little three-bedroom house. As I looked up into the trees while standing there, the silhouette of branches and leaves against the lighter night sky looked as they always did on LSD: flat and surprisingly symmetric, like those snowflakes you made in elementary school with scissors and construction paper, except much more detailed and the paper was black. Also unlike paper snowflakes, the whole scene was alive, a gigantic kaleidoscope turning in various circular motions. It was beautiful but ominous, because I was definitely tripping, just like I had been the day before at the Galleria, only now I was about to enter my scary-ass home, a place I had never really felt perfectly comfortable, even when sober.

Making it to bed did not go well. The front door was locked, and I didn't have my fucking key. A little panic: If the backdoor is locked, I'm stuck. I'd have to wake someone up to get in, but would probably opt to just stay outside until I either sobered up or one of my parents woke up and came to get me. There was no telling how that would go down, but I'd rather be late and relatively sober than on time and tripping like this. They would know, or the tension would simply be unbearable and I'd have to tell them. At the time, I could fathom this ending up as a trip to the ER somehow. I had to avoid facing them at all costs.

I had to climb our cyclone fence to get into the back yard and to try the back door. As I walked up to it, our 100-plus pound Alaskan malamute, Amber, was there to greet me. She was giddy to see me as you normally like a dog to be, but at the time I couldn't trust her and was even kinda scared, like she might somehow sense how different I was on LSD and maybe not even recognize me. I really had some paranoia that she might attack me as an intruder. I talked to her, and reached out slowly, as if she was some huge dog I was meeting for the first time, not one with which I had snuggled for years. She didn't bite me or anything and instead behaved normally, but I didn't dawdle.

Praise Jesus again, the backdoor was unlocked. However, ours was a noisy backdoor, and it did its worst when I tried to sneak in. But the lights were out, and clearly no one was up. Cool. All I had to do was go about fifteen feet across the kitchen into my converted-den bedroom and jump into bed and act like I had been there for some time. Our house was a pitch-black cave, so there was little concern about anyone seeing how dilated my eyes must have been at this point. I snuck into bed.

I made it! All I had to do now was sit in the dark and sober up. Granted, this could take hours, but it wasn't like I was in jail or the ER.

But I was tripping really hard now; I swear to God it was still getting more intense by the moment. As usual, the air conditioner mounted in my window was loud as fuck and it was freezing cold. And it was so dark. My mind soon started wandering like it had never wandered before. And then . . . unbelievably . . . the goddamned, motherfucking phone rang.

Our phone rarely rang, much less at 3:00 in the morning. Presuming crisis, I was immediately concerned that one of my friends had started freaking out on his acid, too, and had been busted by his parents. It must be one of my friends' parents calling to wake up mine so that they could bust me, too. I had this crazy paranoid thought that the parent would suggest something sinister for punishment, like for my mom to act weird to freak me out, so that the punishment would be appropriate for the crime. You know, the ol' smoking a pack of cigarettes when you get caught smoking for the first time.

I had to get to the phone before anyone else, which was actually a cinch because it was in the kitchen, much closer to me, and I was the only one who was so incredibly awake.

When I answered it, I quietly asked, "Hello?" I was scared shitless like some hot chick in a horror movie about to get murdered. There was just silence, but the other person didn't hang up. I couldn't hear anything. I said, "Hello" one more time, feeling like my voice must be quivering, but I wasn't sure. I hung up the phone gently, so as not to make any more noise, and prayed it wouldn't ring again. I headed back to bed, with only memory for navigation.

Staggering through the darkness—unfuckingbelievably—I suddenly collided with another human being. It was the end of the earth—I totally expected a gigantic knife to land in my chest next— but it was just my mother. She had gotten up to answer the phone and I hadn't noticed. Reflexively, and inexplicably, I said something that sounded magically appropriate, like "Oh my God—you scared the crap out of me! It was a prank call." She just kinda mumbled, apparently not even half conscious, and presumably retreated back into the darkness. I climbed back into bed.

With my anxiety stirred-up like a hornet's nest, my mind quickly became lost again when I was alone in the pitch-black darkness of my room, the air conditioner blaring white noise or something similar. There was nothing else salient to capture the attention of my mad, racing mind, so it turned on itself. Lying there in the darkness, I eventually became profoundly disoriented, but paradoxically hyper-conscious; there was no element of sedation to help me. Eventually, I could no longer hear the air conditioner but instead a cacophony of sounds, and they were loud: simultaneous bells, whistles, sirens, various musical instruments, controlled by mad devils who were trying to make the most horrible sound ever.

Eventually, the bed I was lying on seemed to vanish, leaving me to exist without any sort of tether to Earth. This progressed so that I began to lose my sense of connection with my body as well, which was not pleasant. My sense of my *size* became distorted, like I couldn't tell if I was big or small. Everything was just relative but without a single reference point whatsoever. Eventually, I couldn't feel my body at all, as if it was shapeless, but *I* was somewhere. I was only a consciousness, flitting about the darkness, truly mad, in the way I had always fantasized madness might be. More than fully conscious, but unfathomably uncomfortable, relentless, horrifying.

I had to stimulate myself somehow or I was going to start screaming. I somehow managed to turn on my jam box that was next to my bed and put on the headphones, which were already plugged in, thank God. But when the little red power light came on as I flipped the switch, it wouldn't be still: It immediately took off, in a circular motion, spiraling out and away from its original place in space until it disappeared into the distance. Further alarmed by that, I lay back down, and alas, the noise from the radio wasn't helping. I was so incredibly disoriented—I'm not making this up for dramatic effect—I couldn't comprehend anything I was listening to. When the DJ talked, I couldn't understand the words he or she was saying. When music played, I couldn't tell what kind it was, like country or rap or big band or salsa. At least as afraid as before, I turned it off and took off the headphones.

I entertained the idea of waking my parents and telling them I needed to go to the ER. But I couldn't, not because I was worried about getting into trouble, but because I was paranoid. I was afraid

of what I would see if they were in the light: They might be grotesque, deformed—or even demented and evil. I was afraid they
might lose control and try to hurt me for punishment, and even
wondered if it might not be my parents at all sleeping in that room!

I needed light—I needed to see. The one in my room was too
bright and could wake my parents, so that wasn't an option. I eventually decided to go to the bathroom and pretend I was taking a
shit for a while. I was able to get in there and close the door without incident, and only then did I turn on the light. The brightness
was painful, but so much more comforting than the hell of my
room. As soon as I looked at my face in the mirror, it immediately
became a mask and melted. As intense as this was, it was relatively
familiar and quickly brought me back to Earth—granted, LSD
Earth. There was still something dangerous about hallucinating in
my own home, but at least I could tell once again that I was simply
on drugs. I used to like melting in the mirror.

I sat on the toilet, pants down and all in case someone walked
in and wondered what I was doing. I sat there and observed another familiar and comforting tripping scene, the little black tiles
on the bathroom floor beginning to shimmer and move, realigning
themselves in various patterns never intended by the carpenter
who put them there. Some of them would lean, like little solar pan-
els trying to maximize contact with the sun. Thank you, tiles.

But I couldn't stay. Someone was gonna need to pee themselves, and I couldn't risk another confrontation. I went back to
bed. Realizing that light was the key to sanity, I'd just have to risk
it. I turned on the little black-and-white TV next to my bed but
turned the brightness way down so that I could barely make out
the images on it. That was the trick: It was so much better to have a
visual reference point—I just needed *some* reality, and this would
do. I lay there in bed like that for the rest of the night, watching
very dim *I Love Lucy* episodes and such with the sound off. I apparently fell asleep like that, but I don't know when.

I later woke up to the normal sounds of my folks bustling

around in the kitchen, having coffee and breakfast and whatnot. The world seemed normal, but I wasn't anymore. I was sober, but was very unsettled, in a way that felt kinda permanent. I've often told people, including my therapists over the years, that I felt like something "broke" that night. I even felt *violated*, betrayed by LSD, even though I knew it was my fault. The most magnificent experience I knew had now become the worst experience I had ever had, hands-down. I was lost, in a way.

And it wouldn't be the last time. I obviously couldn't do LSD anymore, but I'd be traumatized by other drugs as well.

Cocaine got me less than a year after my bad LSD trip; I was still about 19. After some other long night of partying, I found myself stranded in Deep Ellum, as everyone else had trickled away home or to late-night breakfast joints and I had missed all the boats while holding out for the best one. Luckily, I eventually ran into a friend from high school, but unluckily he didn't have a ride, either. As the crowds in the streets continued to thin we were starting to get nervous, because the walk home was long and necessarily through one of the more dangerous neighborhoods in Dallas. As hope was dwindling, we finally found a ride to an unrelated high school party that was closer to our neighborhoods to the east.

The party was essentially over by the time we got there, but a salient aura remained from what had transpired earlier, a sea of empty keg cups and niches of improperly disposed cigarette butts. There were only about ten or twelve people left, some uncertain number of whom were crashed throughout this guy's spacious and fancy house; his parents were out of town, presumably very far away. The kid himself was a big-time wrestler at a neighboring high school, one of those overly energetic jocks who liked to party hard and even fight sometimes. Those guys always made me uneasy, as loud macho guys typically did. But they were always nice enough to me, despite the fact that they were athletes and I had salient punk leanings.

After high-fives were done, I and the three or four other people who were still clearly awake went out back to smoke a joint. But this was no ordinary joint: I watched the guy roll it, and it was about half weed and half cocaine. I had never smoked cocaine, but was ready to try. It had been a long night and I still felt edgy and geared up. I remember thinking that this would probably get me off real good, but then I'd finally be able to crash.

We passed that thing around the four of us in the darkish back yard, the porch light bouncing off beer cans and keg cups strewn about. I'll never forget the smell of the joint: It really didn't smell like weed at all, but just synthetic chemicals. It was gross, and tasted bad. I only took a couple of hits or so, but I took big ones, thinking that the more I could get off, the harder I would crash. It was gonna be hard to sleep on the floor at this place. I needed to get really tired.

Sure enough, I started getting fucked up fast, and within moments was having an unexpectedly good time. I felt high, really high—drug high, not pot high—particularly energized and excited. Suddenly, I wasn't worried about crashing anymore. This was gonna be a special fun time, something I hadn't bargained for. The joint disappeared; we all held our positions in the smoking circle, but paired off, everyone talking with a lot more enthusiasm than when we started.

Over time, I kept getting more and more fucked up, beginning to hope that I'd level off but I never did. I eventually had to stop contributing to the conversation altogether, as I became disinterested in talking, and at some point began to find it hard to say anything at all. No worries; I'd just listen for a while.

We went back inside, and I was feeling less and less comfortable, a little lightheaded and weak, some stings of anxiety starting to come over me. We sat down at the dining room table under this very parental-looking chandelier that seemed so out of place after having smoked coke just thirty feet away. We each took a side of the square table, my friend ending up opposite me. He was talking energetically, obviously very high off that joint, too, but definitely having a different experience than I was. I was beginning to feel quite uncomfortable, bordering on scared.

Then I started to hallucinate. My friend suddenly had a broken jaw, his face distended on one side, but it didn't prevent him from talking, and even smiling. Then my hearing began to fail, in that the volume was fine but I could no longer understand what the others were saying. My vision became grainy, remarkably so, like the snow on a TV set, but I could still make out the forms of the others on the screen. Something was definitely wrong, and I was about to freak out, but I had no idea what that meant, or how to approach it. Am I supposed to say something to the others, or just let it happen, whatever it is?

My ears began to ring, loudly enough so that I couldn't even hear the garbled speech of the others anymore. That was it. Reflexively, I stood up and walked out of the dining room and into the living room. I'm not sure if I thought moving around would help, or if it was more of a metaphorical *run*, the flight portion of the fight-or-flight response. But, of course, there was nowhere to run. I remember there was a mirror on the ground, leaning against the wall, presumably because the party had caused it to fall, but it wasn't broken. I could only see my legs in it, Vans skater shoes, white socks, and shorts, but I felt disembodied: Those things didn't quite look like *mine*. This walking around business wasn't helping. In fact, things were getting worse, so I headed back to the Table of Doom. At least there were people over there.

The last thing I remember was my vision tunneling from the edges inward, so that all I could "see" was the back of the dining room chair nearest me; I don't know if anyone was sitting in it. Something else, not me, decided to reach out for it. As I did, the tunnel vision became cliché, darkness closing in on the back of that chair like the end of a Looney Toons cartoon. Everything went black before my hand touched it, but I could still feel the trajectory of my hand reaching in that direction. But instead of making contact when it should have, the chair became a fog and my hand just passed right through it, and then I lost consciousness. That's all, folks.

I often tell people that this unconsciousness felt deeper than when asleep, and was instead more akin to being under general anesthesia during surgery. That sense that you have when you awake from sleep, that you were still existing despite having been asleep, was never there.

I became conscious again, at least a little. I still couldn't see—everything was completely black. I couldn't really hear, either, or at least I couldn't understand what I was hearing, but it was like there was noise. And I couldn't move, but I felt like I was moving—violently, like I was being wrenched around by an extraordinary force, like a shark attack from *Jaws* or a Satan attack from *The Exorcist*. At one point, it felt like something hit me hard in the face. The wrenching went on for just a few seconds, and then I was gone again, super-asleep or in surgery or dead or whatever.

I came to again, only this time everything was almost okay. I could totally see again, and there was no TV snow or broken jaws. I was obviously on the ground, because what I could see were five or six faces above me in a circle, all in shock, a scene from a comedy where I had been knocked out by a blow to the head or groin. The faces were frozen, and so was I. Yes, I was totally paralyzed, but felt surprisingly well, all things considered. I desperately wanted to move so that I could tell them it was over and that I was okay, but couldn't. Then, suddenly, as if my invisible restraints had burst, I popped off the ground, onto my feet and started saying, out loud and repeatedly, "I'm OK! I'm OK!"

And I was. It was the damnedest fucking thing: I was *totally* sober and pretty clear-headed otherwise (which is generally inconsistent with a major seizure, which tends to leave one disoriented in its wake, but I don't believe seizure activity can be ruled-out entirely). I did have a really bad headache, but that was welcome compared to what had been happening. After the initial shock left the room, someone got me some water and aspirin and they put me on the couch. I didn't argue; I was so fucking tired. Indeed, I fell asleep—mission accomplished! Thank you, cocaine.

When I woke up the next morning, I felt tired, disheveled, and broken, very reminiscent of the day following my bad trip on LSD. However, there was much less betrayal this time, I guess because I hadn't had a relationship with cocaine before. And, frankly, this seemed to confirm some sort of suspicion that I may have had all along, that cocaine was gross, unpredictable, and potentially dangerous. Still, the sense of trauma was there again, a general sense that I was less safe than I had been the day prior. I felt uncomfortably mortal, now knowing very intimately what it's like to have my Self be at the mercy of my guts and chemistry and physics. Realize that I still identified as Christian at the time—quite strongly—but I lost that sense that He was necessarily taking care of me. For the first time in my life I began to appreciate that I really had the capacity to put myself in harm's way, that God would not always have my back if I tempted him with my recklessness.

Adding to the uneasiness of it all, I would later learn that while I was unconscious, one of the other party attendees (whom I didn't know beforehand) had proposed that they drag my body to the front yard and call 911, saying that they found me this way. I guess I couldn't have blamed him; what difference would it have made? I'm glad it didn't get that far.

Perhaps the drug to which I felt most addicted, in the traditional sense, was *methamphetamine*. That's right: speed . . . crank . . . *The Devil's Dandruff*.

Like many drugs, meth has been greatly misunderstood by nonusers. The subjective experience is much more about euphoria than velocity. It actually has very little to do with restlessness or the jitters—at least until you start to come down. I've done a lot of drugs, most of the main ones except heroin, and I gotta say the euphoria of meth is the best, next to, of course, aptly named ecstasy. Turns out, the *A* in real ecstasy, MDA, stands for *amphetamine*, the whole awesome word being *methylenedioxyamphetamine*. Yes, they are chemically similar, and meth does feel a lot like ecstasy, just not as intense. Unless you shoot it, from what I've been told, as I never went that far myself.

You might also be surprised with whom I was using. One tends to associate meth with trailer parks in Missouri, with all their mullets and pit bulls and "professional" wrestling. However, the scene in Dallas that also did a lot of speed was comprised of wealthy, talented hair stylists. They were a well-dressed, attractive, hip, sometimes gay community that might charge over $100 or more a haircut, which was very pricey in 1990. They went to the fancy, upscale bars in Dallas and didn't break many laws otherwise.

After the cocaine fiasco, I eased my way into it because I didn't want to risk another overdose or whatever the fuck that was. However, I had learned enough in school and so forth that meth, despite the bad reputation, is actually a lot less toxic than cocaine, at least acutely. It's almost unheard of to overdose on meth, whereas people often die from cocaine. Cocaine can cause heart attacks, strokes, or seizures in susceptible individuals. The main threat from meth, if you overdo it, is becoming temporarily psychotic and acting a fool (which, of course, can also be dangerous).

Besides euphoric, meth made me remarkably confident socially, which I now believe was a large part of why it was so reinforcing for me. I've always been lonely, but nervous about meeting people, especially girls. Meth just turned this upside down. Whereas I was Woody Allen when sober, I was Clark Gable on meth. And it wasn't an illusion: Girls readily gave me their numbers when I was high on the stuff. Sadly, though, I'd rarely call because Woody Allen would set back in before I had the opportunity.

One night, very late, I was so high that I got lost (in my hometown), stuck in one of these weird meth-obsession-things that can happen sometimes, where I refused to do anything but keep trying, only to realize hours later that I had literally been driving around in really big circles and not making any progress. Eventually, I got pulled over by a cop for a tail light or something. It was a woman, and she was real friendly to me, almost strangely so. I swear to God, for a moment I felt like I was in a porno, like she might push me around and make me fuck her in the back seat of her car. In reality, all that happened was that she gave me directions out of there . . . but she was smiling the whole time, having absorbed my infectious friendliness, just like everyone else did when I was high on speed.

That's all great and good, but the reason why meth doesn't work in the long run is because—more than any other drug I've done—the crash is as at least as aversive as the high is wonderful. There is a host of uncomfortable physical symptoms and you become so incredibly anxious, a new kind of anxiety that you haven't experienced before, a profound edginess combined with disorientation and hypervigilance that can morph into paranoia. You can even hallucinate a little, but the tone is more bad-trip than good.

It's hard to pee, and sometimes you leak a little. I'm not sure if it's related, but yeah, your dick shrinks smaller than it has ever been, like when you've been swimming in an arctic ice-fishing hole. It's so dense from the compression that it feels hard as a rock—or, I guess I should say, as a boner. Speaking of which, you can get so horny that it hurts. If you dare masturbate, your dick then becomes huge, now bigger than it's ever been, making you feel like a porn star—a very proud one, at that. I've marveled at the size of mine during these adventures. Sadly, I never had a gal to share it with, so there were no witnesses, and these were the days before camera phones.

But much more compelling than your mind-boggling range of dick size are the anxiety and disorientation. I recall one particularly distressing crash that started at a friend's really cool high-rise apartment in downtown Dallas. Several of us had met there after a night of partying in Deep Ellum; actually, it had been the second consecutive night for some of us, essentially sleep-free heading into day three. We were watching Sunday morning TV, which had been fun until the final remnants of buzz gave way to the first signs of ick. Mine came on exceptionally fast, and I started having these peculiar hallucinations in which I couldn't really tell what we were watching. It was definitely some sort of nature documentary, but precisely which part of nature they were showing wasn't clear. The screen was full of flowing motion, and for a moment I was pretty sure it was a time-lapse sequence of budding flowers. But as I squinted and peered at the screen, my perception suddenly shifted and I could tell that it was instead turbulent ocean waves. The experience was not the least bit pleasant but quite alarming, so I kept it to myself. I was starting to feel physically weak around that time as well, like I might pass out if I wasn't careful. I needed to lie down soon, but I couldn't do it there with so many people around. I had to get out.

I told my friend I was crashing hard, so he gave me the keys to his apartment which was a significant distance but not inaccessible. I staggered to my scooter parked on the street, wondering if I was gonna faint or otherwise fall before I could sit on it. It was sunny, and the world was bustling and loud and full of incredibly sober people, greatly intensifying the unsettling feelings I was having.

I did sit down, and yes, started driving. I was feeling wobbly and like I was leaning more than I possibly could have been, which prompted me to consider pulling over a few times. I decided against it because I didn't want to prolong the suffering any more—I just had to get to a bed, or even a floor, where I could just be alone and freak out in private. It was so goddamn hot wearing that fucking helmet; I felt like I wasn't breathing very well, either.

Amazingly, I did make it, and finally felt some relief when I opened that apartment door. It was quiet and there were plenty of places for me to collapse. My friend wasn't even moved in yet so there was no bed or even a couch, but the carpeted floor would do just fine.

I went to the bathroom to piss. When I unbuttoned my shorts, both those and my boxers just fell to the floor because I had lost a notable amount of weight over the weekend. I'm not exaggerating: You lose enough weight in even 24 hours while on speed that it's visibly apparent. Sometimes your clothes no longer fit as they did when you put them on before you first went out. I took my shirt off to take a closer look in the big ol' mirror in the bathroom, and saw a familiar sight: me, as lean as I had ever been. I can't lie; you look kinda hot, like a competitive swimmer or Calvin Klein model. But there's some creepy stuff going on, too. Your hair and fingernails are noticeably longer than they should be, which seems to corroborate the hunch you've been having that you've aged more like a week than the two or three days that have actually passed. In case you're wondering, don't get any ideas about tinkering with meth to lose some weight. The weight comes back with a vengeance because once the drug is totally gone from your system, you're *very* hungry. Ravenous, like a castaway. That's the best part of recovering from a speed episode, indulging your appetite when it finally comes back, and you realize you're gonna live.

Appreciating my emaciation and such hastened my desire to get my ass to bed. I'll never forget that feeling: I didn't really expect to *sleep*. It was more like I was preparing to *pass-out*, and I just needed to make sure I was lying down when that happened so I wouldn't hit my head or something. I found a comfy looking spot on the floor whereupon to crash and curled up in the only blanket I could find. As I lay there, waiting for unconsciousness, something especially frightening began to happen. I would eventually lose consciousness, but each time I did, I would awaken suddenly, gasping for air, feeling like I had stopped breathing each time. A couple of times I awoke so suddenly and startled that I jumped up off the floor, as if the smoke alarm had gone off, but it hadn't. Strangely, I was so tired and over the whole experience, the fear wasn't even enough to keep me awake. I basically just told myself that I don't care if I die in my sleep, I just want to be unconscious, regardless of the mechanism. This approach somehow calmed me, and I eventually stopped waking up gasping for air.

The next time I woke up, it was dark outside, and I had no idea how much time had passed. But praise Jesus, I felt pretty normal, outside of ravishing hunger—which was reassuring itself, verification that it was all over. I found a quarter somewhere and called my mom from the pay phone down the street, still not knowing for sure what day it was; I assumed it was the same night of the gasping-for-air morning. When mom answered the phone, she wasn't alarmed, confirming my suspicion that a whole other day hadn't passed. Whew.

One more meth story and we'll move on. The incident was particularly momentous because it was the final nail in my serious-drug-use coffin, finally scaring me enough to make me call it quits. It took a delusion—a very pure, classic one that was unlike anything I had ever experienced. It literally lasted only seconds, but was so frightening I can't imagine how I could have endured any more than that.

I had already been awake for about 40 hours, having partied enthusiastically the night before and yet to rest entering the second night. For me, this was a "bender." I could rarely make it all the way through that second night and into the third day, because of shit like this. I was always baffled at my friends who could stay awake on speed for four, five, or even more days at a time. (Which is nothing for someone who shoots it: Serious intravenous users will stay awake for weeks or even months on end, surviving on mere cat naps along the way.)

On the second night of my little bender, I ended up hanging out with some folks who were more like drug buddies than friends, except for one, Dan. I really liked him, but he was so sweet and nurturing that it kinda made me uncomfortable. Paradoxically, he spent a lot of time with some relatively seedier people on the fringes of our larger crowd who just creeped me out. Some of them used heroin, which was a little more than I wanted to be around, and there were also rumors that some of them had a history of sneaky, antisocial behavior to get their drugs at times, which was also just not acceptable in my more intimate circle of friends. I know, methamphetamine ethics. Who would've thunk.[5]

I had run out of speed but happened to have a hit of ecstasy, in a capsule. Dan wanted to get high, too, so we decided to split it but snort it. I remember worrying that this approach would waste the precious nectar but I ended up being surprised at how high it made me.

A bunch of us were sitting around on the carpet, conversing enthusiastically, and someone was rolling a joint. I ended up sitting next to one of the creepy people, this guy who dressed like an 80s metal hair band idiot. He also made me nervous because when I had met him once before he had been smoking heroin. But I was sufficiently high not to care too much, so I engaged him. It didn't work, though. I remember him seeming all grumpy and telling me something to the effect of "Dude, you're bothering me talking about how high you are," as if he was jealous and this was some-how socially inappropriate. I reckon it was, to a junkie who only has pot to smoke.

I turned away, got into the pot circle, and took a few hits. Eerily reminiscent of my cocaine overdose many months prior, the pot

---

5 The term *antisocial* is one of the most misused in all of psychology, not just by laypersons but also by some of my colleagues. *Antisocial* means *against* society: dishonesty, irresponsibility, rule-breaking. If you like to spend a lot of time alone, you are *asocial*. Many antisocial people are actually very social.

smoking had an adverse effect, as I started feeling less high and increasingly uncomfortable. Like before, I got quiet and had no choice but to just see what would happen.

The joint landed in my hand again, and I figured I would take a final hit, just to not be a pussy. It was little, just a token drag, so I could just pass it on. After I did to the person on my right, I looked across the circle to see Dan's creepy girlfriend staring at me. Next to her was this other creepy kid whom I never quite understood but I always got a bad vibe from, and he was staring at me as well. They were staring at me together, not talking, but with clear expressions of anticipation on each of their faces. I started to hallucinate, subtly, but as convincingly as ever. Their faces were kinda bright, their eyes wide, and their mouths turned up at the ends in sinister grins, like the Joker from Batman. *Sinister* was the hallucination. Their faces were the epitome of it, grinning together, in cahoots about something, something about me.

Then it hit me like a freight train: I was absolutely positive that they had poisoned me with the marijuana, which explained why I had begun feeling uncomfortable. They had been watching me, waiting for the poison to hit, and now it was. I had no fucking idea what kind of poison it was—it could make me lose my mind or maybe even kill me—all I was sure of is that I had been poisoned, intentionally and maliciously, for their sinister enjoyment.

I leapt up from the carpet, saying something aloud like "Holy Shit!" and stormed from the room. Dan followed me to investigate, reflexively and with a calm resolve that somehow suggested he knew what I was feeling and that he knew what to do, which soothed me significantly, right off the bat. We ended up alone in the other room, door closed, and I was crying, pretty good, like I hadn't in years. He had some Valium, the most precious asset of the habitual meth user, and gave me one, and it worked as advertised. I calmed down after a while and fell asleep, back on the carpet. For a third and final time, when I eventually awoke I was much, much better, but broken somehow.

And that about ended my meth run; I think I was 20 at the time. In fact, that was about the end of all of my "hard" drug use. I did some things a couple more times over the next few years, as you do when kicking a bad habit, whether it be cigarettes or a girl-friend who isn't working—but that was effectively the end, that night crying on Dan's carpet, absolutely positive that I had been poisoned. The marijuana smoking also slowed to a crawl thereafter, but of course I kept drinking too much for a while, until the panic attacks started.

CHAPTER 5

Candide, Dionysus, and Gravity-Induced Loss of Consciousness

And the day will come, when the mystical generation of Jesus, by the Supreme Being as his father, in the womb of a virgin, will be classed with the fable of the generation of Minerva in the brain of Jupiter.

— Thomas Jefferson, "To John Adams,"
April 11, 1823

AS I SUGGESTED EARLIER, although I first began using drugs around the time my spiritual turmoil began, I honestly can't assume that drugs caused that turmoil (nor that the turmoil caused the drug use).

However, I did have a ground-shaking experience during high school outside of drug use that clearly did change my world-view, in a manner that put my faith on a more slippery slope than the mere chinks acquired during middle school via my labored attempts to study and understand the Bible. As part of an English class assignment—I think it was during my junior or senior year—we were assigned Voltaire's *Candide, or Optimism* (from 1759!).

I had been expecting some boring *Great Expectations* or *Scarlet Letter* tedium, but instead ended up reading the whole thing in just a couple of sittings, laughing all the way. (Granted, it's only about

100 pages, and small ones, too.) I would read it several more times over the years, its message soaking in a little deeper each time.

Voltaire was at issue with Gottfried Leibniz, a philosopher/ mathematician at the time, an optimist who championed the idea that ours is the best of all possible worlds because God would not create an imperfect one. In *Candide*, the philosopher Pangloss (representing Leibniz) has taught everyone in his master's castle not to question the evil in the world, or even to be discouraged by it. The castle inhabitants live by the mantra that everything happens for a reason, which Pangloss has instilled in them well. All of his students roam the earth essentially brainwashed, taking the horrors of their lives in zombie-like stride. Here, the "toothsome" Cunegonde is telling her crush, Candide, about all of the goings-on since they were separated prematurely by disaster:

> I was in bed fast asleep when it pleased heaven to send the Bulgars into our beautiful castle of Thunder-ten-tronckh. They slit the throats of my father and brother, and hacked my mother to pieces. A great big Bulgar, six feet tall, seeing that I had passed out at the sight of all of this, began to rape me. That brought me round. I came to, screamed, struggled, bit him, scratched him. I wanted to tear that big Bulgar's eyes out, little realizing that what was taking place in my father's castle was standard practice.[1]

I don't think there's anything funny about rape, but that's a funny passage. It's funny because the joke isn't about rape. The joke is about people who have become so delirious with optimism, that they—on some level—*excuse* rape and other misfortunes, or have at least become unable to fully acknowledge them for the horrors that they really are. Some people can't completely appreciate the terrors of the world because they have indeed convinced themselves that

---

1 Voltaire. (1990). Candide. In *Candide and other stories* (R. Pearson, Trans.; p. 18). Oxford: Oxford University Press. (Original work published 1759).

this is the best of all possible realities. Misfortune, and even terror, must have a place. God wouldn't have it otherwise.

Before *Candide*, constructs such as *hope* and *optimism* had had some sort of diplomatic immunity; it would have been blasphemous to make fun of those. Sure, I had seen hilarious and grotesque irreverence before, such as Eddie Murphy in *Delirious*, but this was different. Eddie Murphy joked about Michael Jackson, homosexuality, and bitches, but I had never seen anyone make fun of optimism before!

But once Voltaire made me laugh at it, a seal broke; my vision cleared significantly and I felt liberated. Of course, it couldn't possibly always be true that "Everything happens for a reason," despite how assuring it sounds and how everyone nods and smiles when we make such claims. Perhaps this kind of reflexive optimism is a mass hysteria. And perhaps it can even be insensitive and toxic.

My spankings growing up had never felt as if they were for the best, despite how my dad and the Bible always asserted they were. I had always realized they were technically legal, but the bottom line is that they were attacks, assaults, by none other than the adult who was supposed to be the most important person in my life, the person who was supposed to protect me from harm. With post-*Candide* vision, I could finally stop trying to rationalize how my whuppin's must have brought out some good in me. On the contrary, it became easy to see that the most likely experiences they brought about were anger, depression, and estrangement from my father—and later, drug abuse and panic disorder that would almost kill me.

And of course it wasn't difficult to find much more intense suffering in the world than mine. Not even considering the glaring examples of genocide and famine and such, it seemed likely that for many people—perhaps even the majority of people who have ever lived on Earth—life is (or was) very hard, much harder than mine. It really can be unfair, and for many, full of relentless suffer-

ing. For some people at some times, assurances like "Think positive!" or "You can do anything, if you believe!" are unrealistic and
therefore potentially discouraging or even offensive. As I thought
about it carefully, I realized that encouragements like that had often
nagged me, despite having been inspirational on occasion. Finally,
having met someone else who found such imperatives vacuous (at
best), I didn't have to feel so dark about feeling that way. And who
would've guessed: My companion was some French dude from
centuries ago who probably wore one of those ridiculous white
wigs with all the curls and whatnot.

I had always thought my *Candide* experience was somehow unusual, that it was an odd catalyst for any sort of epiphany. At one
point while writing my book I was even wondering if I was being
silly to include this part of my story. Damnedest thing, though, in
2012, over 20 years after I read Voltaire's book the first time, I read
Christopher Hitchens's *God is Not Great*. Christopher didn't think
my experience was unusual at all:

> Their [Pierre Bayle's and Voltaire's] method certainly tended
> to be irreverent and satirical, and no reader clinging to un-
> critical faith could come away from their works without hav-
> ing that faith severely shaken. These same works were the
> best-sellers of their time, and made it impossible for the
> newly literate classes to go on believing in things like the
> literal truth of the biblical stories.[2]

Not only must the literal truth of the biblical stories become suspect, but also the literal truth of the inspirational passages between
them. For example, 1 Corinthians 10:13 asserts that "God . . . will
not allow you to be tempted beyond what you are able . . . to endure." Verses like that simply don't seem to apply to some of the
people I've met more recently while working as a psychologist, like
those who have had auditory hallucinations of the voice of God

---

2 Hitchens, C. (2007). *God is not great* (p. 264). New York: Twelve.

himself ordering them to do evil things. Clearly, some people are tempted beyond what they can endure, beyond what is reasonable and fair.

Heck, some people aren't even graced with temptation! For an obscure but illustrative example, there really is a condition called REM sleep behavior disorder in which people tend to act out their dreams, some of which, of course, are violent. Because of this, some people with the condition have seriously assaulted or even killed their loved ones without even being aware of what they were do-ing. This particular phenomenon is rare, but that's not comforting to the victims, as obscurity rarely is. And as you consider other rare but similar phenomena they begin to accumulate so that *rare* be-comes *occasional*. So occasional that most of our United States have an insanity defense so that one can defend herself by arguing that her mental state (or total lack thereof) prevented her from appreci-ating that what she did was wrong. Again, it's not common, but people do win these at times—*and they should*—because sometimes people truly know not what they do. It seems, then, that the state law of Arkansas can be more realistic and reasonable than the Holy Bible!

Now, you're not gonna win an insanity defense if your primary mental illness is drug addiction, kleptomania, or pedophilia. How-ever, at least in the realm of drug addiction, I have to entertain that some of those folks have also been tempted more than they can en-dure. Personally, I have known an inordinate number of people who have died from using drugs—good, fun, charming, successful, beautiful people even. Similarly, I've met quite a few people who were unable to resist the temptation to commit suicide, some of them just children. I just find it hard to entertain that all of these people are in hell as a result. Once you start to appreciate what the real world is like, *Candide* also starts to seem a lot more realistic and reasonable than the Holy Bible.

Well, despite all my criticism of and frustration with the Bible, I'm actually not discouraging reading it. Even today, my own book complete, I truly believe that the Bible is beautiful and wonderful in places. I just don't believe anymore that it's holy or divinely inspired, and I haven't since I was a kid. Lots of things can be inspirational despite being secular, from the *Tao Te Ching* to Shakespeare to *Calvin and Hobbes.*

As far as I know, no one in my immediate family had ever graduated from college. My maternal grandfather had at least attended some, at Austin College in Sherman, Texas, but apparently didn't graduate; family lore has it that he got distracted by his promising football career or flying fighter planes in World War II. Besides him, my dad sometimes alluded to some leaf on our family tree, way out on a low branch somewhere, who had been a physics professor. But that was it. My own father didn't even finish high school. So, I was completely clueless about how college worked and just followed my friends on their own adventures, the first stop being Richland Junior College in Dallas, which was only about ten-minute's drive from home. That really worked well for me, affording a chance to get a clue while still living at home.

My dad had always viewed my potential college experience with some trepidation, for college was where many persons have their Christian faith challenged, with all the freethinking and pot and pussy and whatnot. And, frankly, he was right. At least about the freethinking and the pot; I was never much of a player.

But yes, my very first semester, in the wake of the Voltaire experience in high school, I took an introductory philosophy course at Richland that smote me about as thoroughly as the French man's little book. I'll never forget that class or the instructor; if I had been a girl or gay, he would have been my first professorial crush.

We learned about Plato's forms, Kant's categorical imperative, and Berkeley's idealism. But perhaps most compelling was Descartes's proclamation, *"Cogito ergo sum"* (I think therefore I am). Do you know where the statement came from? Descartes had been on a bit of a mission to distill undeniable truths, facts that simply could not be doubted. And that's the only one that endured. "I think, therefore I am." I am having thoughts, therefore I must be existing, in some capacity. I might be asleep or dreaming—shit, I might even be dead—but whatever *I* is, *I* exists at this moment. A verb can't exist without a subject!

The accompanying message was that we can't really *know* anything beyond *cogito ergo sum*. Everything else—everyone else—could be figments of my imagination, and may not even exist at all. But I know, at the very least, that I am existing, that I am. This is the only notion of which I cannot be skeptical. Everything else beyond this warrants skepticism.

The idea resonated profoundly with me and would serve as the perfect foundation for my forthcoming college career. Perhaps all undergrads should begin their educations with an *Intro to Philosophy* course as such, the first lesson of all being to doubt everything you've been told to date, and everything you're gonna be taught from here on out—including all this crap about Descartes in this class!

As extreme as it all sounds, it is a guiding principle behind both our legal system and science. If you are going to make a claim that someone has committed a crime against you, society will entertain your claim, but the burden of proof to support it lies on the prosecution. We're not just gonna lock someone up because you or the state says so. Science works similarly. Again, society will entertain your claim, whatever it is, but the burden of proof lies on you to produce the data to support it. Otherwise, it's just a claim.

The implications for religion are so glaring that it's difficult for me to decide how to transition to the next topic. Perhaps I should clarify that despite being so moved I wasn't done with Jesus yet. I had been raised in a home that couldn't care less about skepticism and science, a home that preached "You shall not force a test on the

Lord your God," that the essence of faith is "the conviction of things not seen."[3] And I still had faith while in community college. Good ol' fashioned Christian faith. Descartes made the most tremendous amount of sense to me, but I was able to keep logic and faith separated from one another, at least for the time being.

Only two or three semesters after *Intro to Philosophy* starring Rene Descartes, I took a very general, relatively unstructured psychology course in which we were assigned to read a book called *The 3-Pound Universe*. Not coincidentally, I had already perused it in the library on my own time, but was now thrilled to be obliged to buy it and read some more. It was a great book for me, a smorgasbord of provocative topics in psychology with a fairly strong emphasis on altered states of consciousness, from dreaming to schizophrenia and beyond. It was particularly engaging material for someone who had just completed his own adventures in LSD and was ready to start studying to become a legitimate psychologist.

One passage that caught my attention real good comes from interviews with John Lilly. He's the guy who invented sensory deprivation tanks where you float in body-temperature salt water in total darkness. According to the book, Lilly invented these contraptions in an effort to better understand the experience of dolphins, which he had been studying for his career. Today, people use them to meditate and such. Lilly's adventures apparently inspired two Hollywood movies: his dolphin work, *The Day of the Dolphin* (1973), and his LSD trips in isolation tanks, *Altered States* (1980). Yes, I've seen and recommend the latter, but don't know much about the former.

In any event, part of the interview goes as follows:

---

3 Luke 4:12 and Hebrews 11:1, respectively.

"You know," [Lilly] adds, "[mathematician Kurt] Gödel's theorem, translated, says that a computer of a given size can model only a smaller computer. It cannot model itself. If it modeled a computer of its own size and complexity, it would fill it entirely and it couldn't do anything."
"So the brain can never understand the brain?" we ask.
"That's right."[4]

I honestly don't know if Gödel's (or anyone else's) theorem translates as such, but the proposition that the brain simply does not have the capacity to ultimately understand itself seems plausible, given the circularity. And I actually found the notion reassuring, particularly from a spiritual perspective (at least initially). If consciousness cannot be fully understood, that is, explicitly reduced to biology, chemistry, and physics, the possibility remains that there is something more to it, that perhaps there is a "soul," or something akin to one, that endures when the body dies. Perhaps other non-Lillian scientists scoff at the notion of eternal life simply because it's beyond the domain of human science. But maybe there's nothing mysterious about the human soul at all: It's just as real as the stomach and liver and everything else but simply outside the realm of understanding because it's the thing trying to do the understanding! Perhaps aliens with more complicated brains would laugh at us for being so confused and might see our puzzlement over the soul amusing. Suddenly with this type of thinking, it seems that science and religion are finally standing on some of the same ground. My slippery slope just became a little less slippery and sloped. I could cling a little longer.

This optimism was bolstered in a very well-written chapter later in the book, "Border Stations: The Near-Death Experience." The authors, Judith Hooper and Dick Teresi, do a great job of pre-

---

4 Hooper, J. & Teresi, D. (1986). *The three-pound universe* (p. 277). New York: Dell Publishing.

senting data and arguments both supporting and challenging the near-death experience (NDE), with its "tunnel, brilliant light, out-of-body-travel, [and] panoramic life flashbacks," followed by "unshakeable belief in postmortem survival." Being one who cherished the notion of postmortem survival, it was relatively easy for me to pay attention to the pro-NDE arguments and rush past those from the naysayers. As objective and reassuring as ever, Judith and Dick close with this: "The NDE, if it is genuine, raises questions to which there are no answers . . . Sorry, but we have to leave this chapter without an answer."

Unfortunately, however, I just couldn't let Lilly, Gödel, and the incomprehensible go. These are things that I liked to contemplate, and eventually too much contemplation spoiled the truce I had established between science and religion. That is, for the first time in my life I began to truly appreciate the *convenience* of spirituality.

I had previously learned in my *Intro to Psychology* class that human brains simply do not like ambiguity. Although everyone seems to agree that this is the case, no one seems to know why. With amusing circularity, the explanations that I've heard seem far-fetched, if not downright silly—yes, the explanations themselves are more evidence supporting the notion, in that they all feel like desperate, unsatisfying attempts to answer the question!

It soon became clear that one way to solve many of the restless, nagging paradoxes and incomprehensibilities is to throw God into the mix. Things like the beginning of time, the nature of space before the Big Bang, and the current edge of the universe—all of these mysteries are suddenly tidied up nicely when we clump them into one big mystery, an incomprehensible God who specifically has a commandment that we should not question or test him.

Since it's not necessary to go as far as the edge of the universe to be perplexed, everyone can benefit from the salve of gods. In a passage I like to read over and over, Ernest Becker asserted that the mere act of existing can be intrinsically baffling, if not frightening:

William James and . . . [Rudolf] Otto talked about the terror of the world, the feeling of overwhelming awe, wonder, and fear in the face of creation—the miracle of it, the *mysterium tremendum et fascinosum* of each single thing, of the fact that there are things at all.[5]

I don't know a lick of Latin, but that term resonates well. And so does "overwhelming awe, wonder, and fear . . . of the fact that there are things at all."

God can fix these discomforts of contemplation, and others as well—including the most popular, perplexing, and unacceptable problem of all: *mortality.*

Indeed, perhaps the most inconceivable notion for me to comprehend is that of me no longer existing! I'm not even sure if I can do it, partially because the act of trying to do so involves the very activity that I'm trying to imagine not happening (that is, I'm trying to think of not thinking, analogous to the old "Don't think of a white elephant" imperative). Eternal life, whether in Heaven or Hell, solves this problem as well. (Of course, most of us are biased towards the Heaven alternative.)

In these ways, God serves as bookends for the incomprehensibilities, corks for the holes of perplexity. All we have to do is have faith, and suddenly the paradoxes of our feeble minds are no longer paradoxes. God started time, and God will end it. Trees and dolphins and geodes are here because God put them here. Dying is not really dying; it's more like going to sleep, only much, much better.

Comfort ensues.

Not for me, though. I was officially beginning to doubt my Christian affiliation at this point. Not that I was legitimately considering any other formal religion any more seriously. Maybe Buddhism, but I never saw it as much of a religion anyway.

---

5 Becker, E. (1973). *The denial of death* (p. 49). New York: The Free Press.

Once I got my freshman credits under my belt, stopped using drugs (except for alcohol and pot), and got a clue about how college worked, I followed the exodus of friends who had left Dallas the year before for The University of Texas at Austin. I majored in psychology, of course. That was all I had ever considered for a major, except for a brief stint fantasizing about photography. I guess I entertained philosophy as well, but everyone had been discouraging me with the obvious, that there's not much a job market for philosophers.

Choosing a minor was much more difficult. Professors advised me to toughen up my transcript by taking more biology and math courses and such. However, I was neurotic as hell about putting my coveted GPA at risk. So, still eager for more philosophy, I took a class on ethics, along with an elective from the same department called *Classical Mythology*. The mythology professor was one of the best I had ever had, so I went with Classical Civilization as a minor, partially motivated by the prospect of taking more classes with him. That was smooth sailing. My GPA would thank me.

And I did take another class with Dr. Gonzales: The next in his series was called *From Paganism to Christianity*, which surveyed pre-Christian religions of the European and para-European world, some with which I was quite familiar (like Norse), and others that I had never even heard of (like Mithraism).

Despite being incidental, the assaults against Christianity were many and vicious. I know they weren't intentional because much later, after the course was over, Dr. Gonzales would disclose to me during his office hours that he himself was Christian (Baptist, even?). The realization shocked me because his class was the final nail in the coffin for what was left of *my* Christianity, and for organized religion at large, for that matter.

I hadn't been particularly moved by the delightful stories of

Classical Mythology, as we discussed them somewhat superficially and with frivolity. For example, we had learned that Dionysus was the god of wine and partying, an instant fan favorite among us college undergraduates, we being obsessed with beer and titties and whatnot. However, in *From Paganism to Christianity* we delved deeper, learning that Dionysus was born of a virgin on December 25th. In fact, we learned that other gods were born on the winter solstice as well, like Egyptian Osiris and Persian Mithras, the connection apparently being that this was the most important day of the year to many ancient peoples, as it signaled the coming of longer, warmer days and the growing of crops. As I now hear many a pagan declare these days, it turns out that "the reason for the season" may not be the birth of Jesus *per se*, but the optimism of turning the corner from winter to spring, and hence, more abundant food and better health for all.

We learned about myriad other parallels between the ancient gods and Christianity, each being a backhand slap to the face because I had always assumed that Christianity was unique and original. Naturally, there's controversy and it kinda depends on whom you ask, but yes: The manger, the virgin birth, the disciples, the miracles, the temptation, the last supper, the betrayal, the resurrection, the ascension, *et cetera*—it's arguably all been done before. As we proceeded through *From Paganism to Christianity,* it became increasingly doubtful that Christianity is original at all. Even those non-ridiculous parts of the Bible that I had continued to cherish, like the Golden Rule, are covered elsewhere, including Hinduism, Judaism, Buddhism, and yes, even Islam.

Perhaps a reason Christianity has endured and become so popular is because it is a relatively new version of the same age-old myth, founded in a bit of a chronological sweet spot. The relatively modern minds who wrote it borrowed some things from older religions that had staying power but they were smart enough to whittle away much of the absurdity that had doomed some of those more ancient religions. However, the context in which

Christianity was pitched was not so modern that it could be subjected to uninhibited and widespread criticism (as an even newer religion would be, for example, if it was presented today). Perhaps a perfect storm of time and context allowed it to gain a particular momentum that would take centuries to undo—at least for modern society; it came undone for me personally during the course of that class. Once the seal was broken and I became able to critique Christianity without fearing for my soul, it became glaring that it was expiring as well, with its endorsement of slavery and the oppression of women and homosexuals and so on.

Even before *From Paganism to Christianity*, college had been teaching me something else, that every individual and every culture is *centric*: Everyone believes that he, and his time, are *it*, the one that matters the most. Humans are narcissistic by nature, and so necessarily are, too, the cultures they comprise. Individuals (and societies) feel more in touch with reality than the people who lived before them or who currently live on the other side of the river. But their narcissism doesn't allow them to contemplate how the people on the other side of the river are thinking the same way about them, or how the people of the future will look back at them with pity. They believe, or *know*, that their beliefs are correct.

Ironically, I found that studying the history of religion was one of the best catalysts to help me step outside the centrism and narcissism, to see how childish it is to be so self-assured about something that can't really be defended. It became easy to imagine how that I might have an alter-ego over in Iran, a Muslim college student who is 110% sure that his religion is right and that mine is wrong—just as I have felt up to this point about his. How incredibly self-centered of us. We're both equally wrong, because our respective beliefs are not based on reality; they are based on what we have been told, different myths endorsed by our respective cultures.

As I started to appreciate the fiction of it all, it was hard for me to imagine my classmates—many of whom I assumed were Christian—*not* having similar experiences. I would sometimes look around that gigantic auditorium, looking for a sign on anyone's face, but there was nothing out of the ordinary there. Just some traditional looks of engagement, a few smiles, some sleepy faces, and a lot of pretty girls. No one seemed as aghast as I felt. Me, I was forced to finally admit that I had not only been wrong about the Bible, but was also wrong about God and Jesus, even my very liberal, ill-defined versions of them.

But once again, the realization was not a catastrophe. As the dust settled from this disturbance, I realized I was simply still maturing, that I would have to continue to adjust and adopt the next label, this time *agnostic theist*, one who believes in a god of some sort but is unsure of his nature. I will even continue to pray, but I'll have to address "god" instead of "God" when I do.

Instead of conceptualizing the different religions of the world as mutually exclusive—and therefore all false—we can focus on the other side of the coin, that they are actually all congruent. God is too great to be understood by feeble human minds. Different cultures necessarily have different conceptualizations of him because each has been forced to attempt to describe him through the eyes of his own times and peers. Osiris is actually Mithras is actually Zoroaster is actually Jesus. We've been worshipping the same god all along.

And what a crying shame that so much war and destruction have been born of religious conflict when we haven't even been in disagreement. I guess that's human nature; I have to understand that. Not forgive it, but understand it. Egocentrism, ethnocentrism. But I'm gonna be a bigger and better person and see through all that crap. "Spiritual but not religious," that's what I am.

A few semesters after *From Paganism to Christianity*, in 1993, my paternal grandfather died of natural causes. He was old, like most of the Landers when they succumb. I didn't know him well, and probably hadn't spent more than a hundred hours with him total, if that. But he always seemed like a sweet guy; I have no recollection of him being mean or even abrasive. He was tallish and thin and sometimes smoked a pipe. Like lots of kids, I was captivated by that smell. I kinda revered him, as children often do adults who are calm and not oppressive.

Besides his pipe, I have a couple of fond and poignant memories of "Papaw." Once, during some holiday (I think Christmas), he, my brother, and I had what we would later refer to as a "farting contest." It wasn't planned, but totally spontaneous, one of those moments in which the planets were simply aligned just right, with three boys left alone, each a little gassy. I can still remember laughing uncontrollably, and watching Papaw lose it as well. We connected that day, at least a little.

I also remember when Papaw's memory started to slip. His was the relatively kind type, in that he never seemed distressed about it. I recall another special occasion, definitely Thanksgiving this time, when we were all crowded around the TV watching the Cowboys game with him. Papaw was a little disoriented and would lose sight of which game we were watching: During those moments in which the network would show a highlight from the Lions game earlier, he'd jump up and shout, thinking it was still the Cowboys (hey, our colors are similar!). When we corrected him, gently, he laughed and didn't seem embarrassed.

When he died, I took a little time off from school and drove up to Bronte or Winters or whatever tiny, dilapidated West Texas town that was for the funeral. We call that area "west" despite how central it is on a map. It is quite west-ish, if you consider the population density of the state, which is concentrated towards the east. In any event, I had to borrow my ex-girlfriend's car, because mine was old and feeble and I just didn't want to get stranded out there in that desolation.

The funeral was much more tidy than I felt one should be, but I'm not sure why I anticipated otherwise. There were only like eight of us, my little family of four and my dad's brother's equally small family. I can't recall if it was at a church or a funeral home; the two may have been the same out there. It could've been a school for that matter—the place didn't have any spirituality what-soever. I don't remember seeing a casket. Maybe he was cremated.

Since I had spent so little time with my grandfather we weren't really attached in a meaningful way, beyond his pipe and farting and peaceful senility. So, I just kinda went along for the ride, trying to look sadder than I felt and just watched the others. It was very intimate: The eight of us, plus the minister, were sitting in a circle on some of those cheap folding chairs you might find at a small-town convention center. My dad and uncle were having uncannily similar experiences to one another, which were quite intense and therefore antithetical to mine. It was a little unsettling, bordering on frightening, one of those moments when you're really alive—there's no bullshit; real, profound stuff is going down. As the min-ister was talking—and it was a very Bible-laden service—my dad and uncle both had their eyes closed and appeared to be in deep, passionate thought. Every time the minister would say something about Papaw not being gone but instead being with the Lord, and all of us being reunited with him later, they would say, "Amen! Praise his name! Yes, Lord!" and stuff like that. But neither of them looked happy; this shit wasn't Sunday school. They both looked so incredibly serious when they spoke, yet oddly comfortable at the same time, as if they had done this many times before. I'll never forget that scene, how they were both doing the same incredible thing, whatever it was.

About three quarters of the way through the minister's spiel, my feelings of awkwardness suddenly transformed to clarity. I was hit so hard by the freight train of epiphany that I was seriously concerned that the others *must* be able to tell by the look on my face: This ceremony is not for Papaw.

This ceremony is for my dad and his brother, the two who have been hurt the most by this inconceivable event, that is, the loss of their father. Sitting there in that little room with my little family, it suddenly became so perfectly clear why we even believe in Heaven and have ceremonies like this to assert its existence. It's not that different religions are different cultural mechanisms to access the same universal truth; it's that they're all different cultural fantasies to soothe the same universal fear.

It's literally *unbearable* when our loved ones die.

But somehow we keep existing. We miss our loved one, but we're probably—on some level—at least equally concerned about our own impending demise. Typically, we can't even really *conceive* of our own demise, but it becomes as tangible as ever, sitting in the room with the corpse (or ashes) of what used to be the Most Powerful Being in our lives. That god who used to feed us, keep us warm, and save us from every conceivable disaster, is gone. We're as close as ever to death, but we still can't fathom the notion completely.

So we don't. We refuse to even try. Instead, we choose to believe it's not happening at all, and that it's not going to happen to us, either.

Sitting there, among all the "Amens" and angels, it all came together—*Candide*, Descartes, the *mysterium tremendum et fascinosum*, Dionysus, and now my dead grandfather—and pushed me over a line so that I snapped and became an *atheist*. It was all so sudden and striking that I didn't even have a chance to indulge *agnosticism*, that is, the position that one is simply unsure whether there is a god. No, I was too compelled for that. All religions, all bibles, all gods, all religious ceremonies, all conceptions of heaven —and any hopes about any of these being valid or real—have simply been hoaxes, ways to turn *this* particular unbearable situation into a bearable one.

Driving back home to Austin afterwards, I reminisced about the first funeral I had ever attended, that for my mother's father (the fireman) back in 1989, when I was still enthusiastically regarding myself as Christian. That man had always been an atheist, something that we never really talked about openly, as if he had been a child molester or something. But when he died there was chatter that he must have "found the Lord" right towards the end. People were citing things he had said or done over the last months or years of his life to support their optimism. I remembered having embraced those comforting thoughts myself back then as well. But now, driving home as a born-again atheist, I could only feel cynical. I mocked the notion that had comforted me before, asking myself, sarcastically, "Did *anyone* ever go to hell?" Not in my family, apparently. I kinda felt like a fool for ever buying into any of this religion crap, and so now it was time to be a dick about it.

Well, just as the dust had settled after realizing Christianity couldn't possibly be the only spiritual truth, the dust would settle after converting to atheism. I *still* hadn't given up on transcendence entirely! I just had to loosen up even a little more. Now I would appeal to the most ambiguous conception of immortality possible, not of a soul *per se* wandering around in heaven but that of my "consciousness"—somehow involving a god-free Energy that Binds Us and quantum physics and other things that will never be fully understood. Since education and rationality had made it impossible to have faith in anything describable, I would just have to subscribe to something that couldn't be put into words. As ambiguous as the notion was, it helped make sense of some loose ends, like that tidbit from the near-death-experience chapter of *The Three-Pound Universe*, the tidbit that I'd been trying to ignore up to that point:

> Even more remarkably, dyed-in-the-wool atheists were just as likely to have NDEs as born-again Christians—although the pious more often communed with a biblical God, the nonbelievers with a "warm presence" or a holy light.[6]

Of course: If we atheists can have near-death experiences then eternal life must have *nothing* to do with any god or religion. It ob-

---

6 *The Three-Pound Universe*, p. 306.

viously has more to do with science—wonderfully non-exclusive, all-forgiving science. I'll continue to call myself "spiritual but not religious," only now the "spiritual" will refer to the belief that quantum physics (or something) is in charge of it all.

All of these developments were validated by *Omni* magazine articles and well-made documentaries featuring celebrity intellectuals like Deepak Chopra. They spoke with authority, charisma, and a glow that made it clear that we new-age spiritualists finally had it all figured out, that science and spirituality are the same, and no one will be left out. Now *that's* really beautiful: a universe where everyone is granted eternal life. And again, what a shame that the rest of humanity can't see these truths, but instead continue to kill each other because they're too immersed in their respective myths.

Why is religion so ubiquitous? Granted, I'm not a real religious scholar, but I'm personally unaware of any significant society throughout history that has been primarily atheistic. The ubiquity (or near ubiquity; I hate to say "never") of religion suggests it must have a role in satisfying fundamental human needs.

Over two millennia ago, the amazingly open-minded-before-his-time Lucretius identified one of the most likely reasons religion has always had such appeal:

> *For, in good sooth* [truth]*, it is thus that fear restraineth all mortals,*
> *Since both in earth and sky they see that many things happen*
> *Whereof they cannot by any known law determine the causes;*
> *So their occurrence they ascribe to supernatural power.*[7]

---

7 Lucretius. (2007). Lucretius, from de rerum natura (On the nature of things). (W. H. Brown, Trans.). In C. Hitchens (Ed.), *The portable atheist: Essential readings for the nonbeliever* (p. 3). US: Da Capo Press.

Today, I still find myself truly in awe—even a little scared some-times—when I'm beholding a Texas summer thunderhead ap-proaching. And I've got the luxury of weather.com to find out how dangerous it actually is (or not), including a "map in motion" to see exactly where it is and when it will arrive, if at all. Nevertheless, I'm still a little scared, and very much in awe.

Imagine how a dark, gigantic cumulonimbus cloud with light-ning and thunder must have appeared to the people of Lucretius's time—how could they not posit an angry god behind it! They weren't stupid; it's actually fairly rational, given what they did know at the time. Again, they had to have an explanation—not ex-plaining it was not an option. Kudos, Lucretius, for already doubt-ing it all, decades before Christ was even born.

In a book that is as engaging as its title, *Existential Psychother-apy*, the venerable psychiatrist Irvin Yalom elaborates:

> Human beings have always abhorred uncertainty and have sought through the ages to order the universe by providing explanations, primarily religious or scientific. The explana-tion of a phenomenon is the first step toward control of that phenomenon.[8]

He provides a coherent example, of

> natives [who] live in terror of the unpredictable eruptions of a nearby volcano . . . their first step toward mastery of their situation is explanation. They may, for example, explain the volcano's eruption as the behavior of a displeased volcano god . . . [as a result,] a course of action is available that aug-ments their sense of mastery: if the volcano explodes because the god is displeased, then there must be methods of placat-ing and eventually controlling the god.

---

8 Yalom, I. D. (1980). *Existential psychotherapy* (p. 342). New York: Basic Books.

Absolutely. One way to treat fear of the unknown is to know it—even if you have to trick yourself into thinking you know it!

Again, one doesn't need a volcano nearby to benefit from the salve afforded by gods and creators. Even the Garden of Eden or modern Toronto will conjure the uneasy feelings Ernest Becker discussed, "the *mysterium tremendum et fascinosum* of each single thing, of the fact that there are things at all." And for those throughout history who have not been so inquisitive to be haunted by the *mysterium*, other phenomena of the average person's life would have demanded contemplation otherwise. British biologist Lewis Wolpert, from his *Six Impossible Things before Breakfast*:

> Edward Tylor was an early thinker on the reasons why belief in the paranormal was near universal across history and different cultures. He argued that people were from the earliest times deeply puzzled by two phenomena: the difference between a living and a dead body, and the nature of the people in dreams. This led to the belief that life could leave a body and go wandering, as it does in dreams . . . [raising the] possibility of ultimate immortality [which] was, and still can be, very comforting . . . Sleep is itself a sort of paranormal experience, and dreaming of a dead person would make it more so. And illness, in early times, must also have been almost a paranormal experience, as would be childbirth, the causes being mysterious.[9]

What fascinating propositions! We think childbirth is a miracle today: Imagine how miraculous it was ten thousand, a hundred thousand, or a million years ago!

Letting go of my centrism, I can see that Volcano People were not really doing anything different from what Old Testament People were doing: placating a god. And maybe New Testament Peo-

---

9 Wolpert, L. (2007). *Six impossible things before breakfast* (p. 144). New York: W.W. Norton.

ple are no different from Old Testament People. Sure, sacrifice has become less vogue over the years, but I'm not sure that, for example, sacrificing a beautiful Sunday to go to church is qualitatively different. We're still trying to placate (that is, influence, or even control) God so he doesn't abandon us. By influencing our gods through appeasement, we feel safer.

And even when we're not sacrificing, we pray. Prayer also offers a sense of control. When I pray, I'm communicating with *God*. The more I believe he hears me, the more in control I must feel, whether it be over a volcanic eruption or my presentation to the shareholders at work next week. Faith, then, does not offer only hope: It affords a sense of control, or agency. "Potency," Yalom calls it.

Through all of my adventures as a psychologist—student, patient, licensed practitioner—I've become convinced that a sense of control is one of the most fundamental human needs, perhaps on par with eating, socializing, and mating. Ronnie Janoff-Bulman taught me about one of the more compelling and poignant manifestations of the need for control, that is, by explaining the mysterious but surprisingly common response to rape: self-blame.[10] In a nutshell, many victims would rather blame themselves than admit that the world is a chaotic, unjust place where horrible things happen to innocent people. By taking the blame, she preserves her belief that the world is meaningful and fair, but also attempts to convince herself that she is actually in control so she'll be able to avoid another catastrophe in the future. In fact, Ronnie argues that the rest of us blame victims for the same reason: *We* don't want to consider that innocent people are victimized randomly, which makes *us* feel safe and in control. Furthermore, when we blame victims—whether of rape or poverty or whatever—it helps us minimize our obligation to help them.

---

10 Janoff-Bulman, R. (1992). *Shattered assumptions: Towards a new psychology of trauma* (pp. 123-132). New York: The Free Press.

On the other side of the violence coin, it seems that many perpetrators commit violence to assert their control over the world. So many people who are violent as adults were themselves beaten down as children. They had no control, which can be excruciating, humiliating, and devastating. When they begin to find themselves in a position where they can dominate someone else, whether those opportunities begin to appear during their own childhoods or later, some of them take advantage of the situation, and it's reinforcing to them to exercise some control when they couldn't before. It's like payback, in a way, only displacing it from his perpetrator to another innocent victim, someone who was innocent just like he was way back when.

If studying classical civilization had not ruined my faith, studying psychology probably would have anyway. People who spend their lives studying the brain are no longer intimidated by it—nor by consciousness, personality, or its other products. Yes, even the human brain starts to make sense so that one no longer has to throw up his hands and chalk up human nature and experience to souls and spirits or ill-defined cosmic energy fields or whatever. Now, I'm not going to suggest that we will necessarily understand the mind perfectly someday (recall the John Lilly/Gödel paradox discussed above, the proposition that something can't completely understand itself). However, heading in the direction of understanding may be sufficient to convince one that even the human mind is a product of nature and doesn't require a God to have created it. Something profound definitely happened to me when I eventually began to appreciate that the human mind is *understandable*, even if not by me specifically.

We know that the human nervous system is comprised of billions of neurons that transmit electrical signals along their lengths.

Most of these lengths are very short, fractions of a millimeter, while some—for example, the ones that transmit sensations from your big toe to your lower spine—might be a meter long. They really are like biological wires, the long ones even have biological insulation called *myelin*.

At the end of the neuron, the electrical signal that travels across the cell causes a chemical to be released into the extra-cellular space so that neighboring neurons can receive it. If those neighboring cells receive enough such *neurotransmitter*, they will initiate their own electrical signals which they can then send elsewhere. And these processes—the electrical transmission, its transformation into a chemical signal, and back into an electrical signal—are understood quite well. Not perfectly, but there's not an alarming amount of mystery about them anymore.

Those wires running from our toes and other appendages are organized neatly as they enter and ascend the spinal cord up into the brain. There are actually two separate systems working in parallel: one for touch sensations, and one for pain. The touch fibers cross over as they enter the spine and ascend the opposite side (so, your left toe touch fibers ascend the right side of your spinal column). However, the separate *pain* fibers for that same toe don't cross over until later (so, your left toe pain fibers ascend the left side of the spinal cord). Turns out this separation of church and state may serve a functional purpose, and hence may have been naturally selected: If we suffer an injury to one side of the spinal cord, we only lose touch *or* pain to that side, not both. Apparently, if you lose the touch on one side, it helps you function if you can still feel pain, as there is some degree of overlap between the sensations.

Ascending the spinal cord to the brain, the fibers remain neatly organized so that those innervating one body part tend to stay close to those innervating nearby body parts (so, the fibers for the index finger ascend the spinal cord next to those for the middle finger). The organization continues as you ascend the cord and as additional fibers from more elevated parts of the body are added. At some point, if you were to view a horizontal slice through the cord, parallel to the ground, you would have a rough *somatosensory map* of your body. You could stimulate this thing with an electrical probe and create feelings of touch (or pain) throughout your body in a quite predictable manner.

And the orderliness continues as the fibers arrive at the brain, spreading out over the wrinkly cortex so that those brain parts that process touch in the foot (the right foot in the left hemisphere—don't forget the crossing-over!) are next to those areas that process touch in the calf of the same leg . . . and so on.

Of course, those parts of the body where touch is more important (for example, the hands) will involve more brain tissue than those where touch is less important (for example, the abdomen). Fingers can peel fruit, husk seeds and nuts, and manipulate sticks and stones; abdomens just don't need that kind of precision. Our lips also use more brain than one might suspect. Using them for articulating speech sounds and eating and such demands a lot of brain area, too. Some of the side effects of this are good (for example, it makes kissing such a rich experience), but others are bad (a sore or zit around the lips hurts like hell). By the way, all of this organization is not unique to humans: It works the same way in other mammals but varies accordingly so that, for example, rats have a large area of sensory cortex devoted to their whiskers.

Many students are surprised to learn that the genitals have relatively little brain devoted to them, genitals being the centers of our universes. However, despite how good orgasms end up feeling, genitals themselves don't actually have good spatial resolution—they're more like abdomens than fingers. Sure, they love to be touched, but they're not so picky about exactly where. Diffuse pressure works just fine, as long as it keeps moving.

And it's not just touch; the other senses and such are processed in orderly fashions as well. Right next to the somatosensory cortex processing touch, there is an analogous *motor cortex* that is devoted to producing motion. As with the somatosensory map, the amount of brain tissue devoted to each body part is in proportion to how important motion is for each respective body part (again, fingers being big, abdomen being small, and in this case, genitals get virtually nothing).

Sounds are processed in a different part of the brain than touch, and that area is also neatly organized, so that sounds at 1,000 Hz are processed near those that process sounds at 1,500 hertz, and relatively far from those that process 10,000 hertz, and so on.

The organization is most remarkable in terms of the visual system. As your imagination may be suggesting, yes, images of the environment are indeed projected onto the back of your eye via a system of lenses not unlike a camera. When photons of light strike light-sensitive cells in the retina, they initiate a surprisingly not-as-complex-as-you-might-expect process in which the electromagnetic energy of photons is transformed into a biological, neural signal, similar to how neurotransmitters relay messages from neuron to neuron throughout the rest of the nervous system.

Some of the neurons from the eye are only indirectly involved in seeing, as they detour to the primitive "reptilian" midbrain where things like eye movements and pupil dilation are controlled (this is why a "vegetative" patient like Terri Schiavo with profound loss of cortical, "mammalian" brain tissue can still appear to be looking around but she's not really "seeing" in the traditional sense). Those fibers that do the actual seeing travel to the thalamus, which fine-tunes and filters the information, contributing to the smooth and steady perception that we'll eventually see. (Interesting to note: Last I heard, the thalamus is one place where LSD has its effects, essentially reducing the brain's ability to make vision smooth and steady.) From the thalamus, visual stimulation goes to the visual cortex at the back of the brain, where it is further processed and ultimately brought into consciousness.

Magnificently, the seeing fibers arrive at the visual cortex in an orderly fashion analogous to the other senses, so that portions of our visual field that are near one another are processed near one another in the cortex. Does this mean if we could look directly at a brain, itself in the process of seeing, that we could see a picture of our visual field on the brain's cortex?

Not exactly—but almost! In the early 1980s, Roger Tootell and his colleagues injected a monkey with radioactive glucose, which is absorbed into neural cells as they become increasingly active (that is, stimulated). He directed the monkey's gaze towards a screen upon which a stimulus was displayed, something akin to a wagon wheel (the monkey, of course, is under general anesthesia; it doesn't know what is happening, just like when you had your wisdom teeth or gall bladder removed or whatever).

The monkey is later sacrificed for science, and its brain is studied.[11] Unfathomably, the section of brain that is devoted to processing the area of real-world space occupied by the light-wheel literally *has a freaking "picture" of the freaking wheel on it!* No, you wouldn't actually be able to see the wheel on the brain if observing the brain directly while all of this was happening, but the radioactive glucose allows us to see which cells were most active, in retrospect.

The very sobering point: Brains are surprisingly orderly, sensible, and predictable, just as you would imagine an evolved machine to be. The more you learn about brains, the less amazing—no, let me take that back—the less *mysterious* they are. And as the brain becomes increasingly demystified, the less we have to assume something spiritual or transcendent behind it all. And the less we have to assume spirits behind the brain, the less we have to assume spirits behind anything else.

---

11 Regarding animal research, I wouldn't do it, either. However, it's important to realize that literally millions more animals are euthanized at animal shelters than in scientific laboratories every year. If you want to save animals—which I agree is a noble cause—you'll get much more bang for your buck by focusing on the neutering and spaying movement or by volunteering at your local animal shelter as opposed to, say, protesting at universities that conduct animal research.

Now, I readily admit that somatosensory, motor, tonotopic, and re-tinotopic maps do little to account for the more complex human experiences, such as memory, abstraction, and self-awareness. However, the unfortunate but fascinating phenomenon of epileptic seizures does.

Recall that a seizure is the problem in which neurons in the brain become hyperactive, firing spontaneously and excessively, whether due to genetically inherited anomalies or to environmentally acquired injuries. In some seizures, consciousness is maintained but one can lose control of her motor functions. A shaking might start in her fingers because the first cells to run amok are in the finger part of her motor cortex discussed above. But as the hyperactivity spreads over the surface of that strip of brain, it takes over her hand next, then arm, then shoulder, then head—a devilish puppeteer who will even go as far as to make her crap her pants. Some patients may engage in more complex behaviors, like she might eat or brush her teeth while in an epileptic trance—or even go to a party and have a great time, believing afterwards that she had been at home sleeping.[12] Spastic cells in other areas will affect the senses so that one might feel a wind that isn't there or smell oranges or feces for no legitimate reason.

The most interesting experiences occur when the temporal lobes are affected, those parts of the brain that seem particularly important in emotions and memories. A temporal lobe seizure may overwhelm the patient with joy, fear, sadness, rage, nostalgia, or even orgasm. *Déjà vu* is common in this condition because it, too, is nothing mystical but just another short circuit of sorts. Memories might be superimposed on reality, like for Oliver Sacks' patient Mrs. O. C.: "I know you're there, Dr. Sacks. I know I'm an old

---

12 *The Three-Pound Universe*, p. 211-212.

woman with a stroke in an old people's home, but I feel I'm a child in Ireland again—I feel my mother's arms, I see her, I hear her voice singing."[13] It seems, then, that even our emotions and memories—those parts of us which we cherish and pride for making us particularly human—are mechanized in the brain, at least to some degree.

When that most highly esteemed profession of brain surgery came about, doctors began to treat seizures by destroying (or sequestering) those brain cells that continue to misfire despite gallons of medication. Amazingly, these surgeries are done while the patients are awake so that the surgeon can poke the brain and consult with the patient in order to make sure she's in the right spot.[14] And sure enough, by applying electrical current to different parts of the brain via a tiny electrode, the surgeon can control the patient a bit like a puppet, eliciting experiences akin to those described during spontaneous seizures.

One of the prolific pioneers in the field, Wilder Penfield, specialized in evoking sights, sounds, and other subjective experiences that were often difficult for patients to describe. Some of these appeared to be hallucinations, such as when patient #36 reported, "Yes, I hear . . . a woman calling . . . It seemed to be at the lumber yard . . . [but] I have never been around any lumber yard."[15] Other hallucinations were more like memories, as they were verified to have been based in actual experiences, such as that for patient #38: "Yes, Doctor, yes, Doctor! Now I hear people laughing—my friends

13 Sacks, O. (1985). Reminiscence. In *The man who mistook his wife for a hat and other clinical tales* (p. 130). New York: Summit Books. See also: Sacks, O. (1995). The landscape of his dreams. In *An anthropologist on Mars: Seven paradoxical tales* (pp. 153-187). New York: Alfred A. Knopf.

14 It's a bit ironic: Brain tissue itself doesn't actually have pain receptors in it, so this doesn't hurt. This is also why a brain tumor can get as big as a baseball before the patient notices.

15 Penfield, W. & Perot, P. (1963). The brain's record of auditory and visual experience: A final summary and discussion. *Brain, 86*, 596-696.

in South Africa . . . two cousins, Bessie and Ann Wheliaw." Penfield could also cause emotional experiences with his electrode: One patient laughed, another cried—but fear was most accessible. Patient #30 reported, "Yes, I felt just terrified for an instant." Number 15, a 14-year-old girl exclaimed, "Oh, everybody is shouting at me again, make them stop! . . . Something dreadful is going to happen . . . I saw someone coming toward me as though he were going to hit me." Other patients had more spiritual-like experiences, like #14 who apparently felt some sort of transcendent connection to Penfield's anesthesiologist: "I almost spiritually spoke to that woman" (the anesthesiologist was actually male). Number #23 reported, "I am going to die . . . God said I am going to die."

That we can conjure God's voice with an electrode is actually not as surprising as it is interesting. Popular neuroscientist V. S. Ramachandran explains that "Every medical student" is taught that spontaneous seizures can cause patients to have "deeply moving spiritual experiences, including a feeling of divine presence and the sense that they are in direct communication with God."[16] Whether due to more subtle, enduring brain dysfunction or simply because such patients are so moved by the spiritual seizure experience, some "become preoccupied with religious and moral issues even during the seizure-free . . . periods." Many experts now wonder whether some historical religious figures from Joan of Arc to the Apostle Paul may have had temporal lobe epilepsy themselves, as some of their experiences were apparently consistent with the diagnosis.[17] The more you read about all this stuff, the more you begin to entertain the demoralizing, frustrating accusation: "It's all in your head." Not just our fears and insecurities, but also our religion.

---

16   Ramachandran, V. S. (1999). God and the limbic system. In *Phantoms in the brain* (pp. 175 & 179). New York: Quill.

17   For example, *The Three-Pound Universe*, pp. 1-3; 329-330; 352.

Yes, for whatever reason evolution deemed fit, there clearly are brain areas or mechanisms that mediate spiritual experiences. Seizures can stimulate these pathologically, or we can stimulate them deliberately by taking LSD or ecstasy and such. As Lewis Wolpert says, "A simple drug like LSD could only have such effects if the circuits for these experiences were already in the brain."[18] I don't think we know why they are there, but they apparently are.

And maybe we don't even need seizures or LSD to stimulate them! Lewis goes on to discuss the provocative hypothesis that *hypnosis* has a role in—if it cannot explain entirely—elements of religious ritual. Hypnosis is one of the more mysterious phenomena in all of psychology, on par with dreaming, if not more interesting in ways. Now, we know that hypnosis cannot force people to do things they wouldn't otherwise, so don't get any crazy ideas about using it to get laid or having people rob banks for you. However, Lewis cites mind-boggling research showing that hypnosis can, for example, induce anesthesia or hallucinations or—get this— cause one's *physical* reaction to a skin-prick tuberculosis test administered to one arm to manifest on the other (non-pricked) arm! Given that, it's a little anticlimactic when Lewis cites other research showing that people can be hypnotically induced to recount events that haven't even happened, such as having heard gunshots in the night or, of course, being abducted by aliens.

Hypnotized people are apparently not lying about their hypnotized experiences; those experiences are kinda transpiring, at least on some neurological level. For example, Lewis also describes brain imaging research showing that persons perceiving black-and-white images but *told to perceive color* under hypnotic suggestion show activation in the color-perceiving parts of their brains! No, this doesn't mean that one can affect the environment with her mind (like bending spoons or whatever), but it does mean that she can

---

18 *Six Impossible Things before Breakfast*, p. 109; his discussion of hypnosis that follows is on p. 110-115.

affect her own body with her brain (a finding that must have some relevance for the well-documented placebo effect).

If hypnosis can make the visual areas of our brains see color when color isn't really there, then hypnosis can make our temporal lobes have spiritual experiences when spirits aren't really there. While reading Lewis's discussion, all I could think of was my own father speaking in tongues at our church when I was a little kid, vis-à-vis aboriginal ladies I've seen more recently on some anthropology documentary, becoming "possessed" by spirits while dancing around a fire. Given what I know now, it seems more than plausible that my dad and those ladies have been doing the same thing: hypnotizing themselves through the rituals endorsed by their respective cultures, thereby stimulating those spiritual centers in their temporal lobes and having profound experiences of altered states.

I lost the last bit of my own spirituality one day while perusing books about death and dying on the fourth floor of the colossal Perry-Casteñeda Library on the University of Texas campus. It wasn't long after my Papaw's funeral in the mid-1990s, the ink not yet totally dry on my new Proud Atheist card. Although I was no longer able to entertain the notion that God or any other god was real, I was still clinging to notions of immortality through some ill-defined mechanism, something that must involve quantum physics and energy fields and other stuff that I would never fully understand. The near-death experience (NDE) gave me hope—particularly that part about atheists having NDEs as often as anybody else, which I naturally interpreted to mean that life after death is for everyone. But even that all fell apart when I came across *G-LOC*. Whatever breeze had been left in my Sails of Belief in Immortality before that moment finally stopped blowing. I felt it quit, no kidding, standing there; I remember the exact spot.

G-LOC stands for "gravity (or g-force)-induced loss of consciousness." The basic idea is that if one is suddenly subjected to increased gravitational forces, such as during extreme maneuvers in a jet fighter, she can go unconscious. Medically, the phenomenon is understood well: The force of gravity simply forces blood from the brain so that it pools in the lower extremities and such. Losing consciousness via G-LOC is essentially the same as natural fainting or excessive bleeding, the only difference being that blood leaves the brain for different reasons. Regardless of why blood flow is compromised—whether it be to low blood pressure or extreme gravity—the brain is one of the first organs to succumb, largely because it has the highest elevation and because it demands so much blood way up there. Indeed, this is a function of fainting: to lower the head so that a relatively meager heartbeat can feed the brain adequately, which helps facilitate recovery and prevent brain damage.

While flying a jet, you can't afford to faint or to put your head between your legs to prevent fainting. So, pilots are trained in those carnival ride-looking human centrifuges to test their limits and so they can learn to identify and cope with G-LOC before it overwhelms them (for example, by slowing down).

Thousands of pilots have been run through these things in laboratories, allowing researchers to study and quantify the G-LOC experience with significant precision. And the punchline: Many pilots, at some point during G-LOC, experience *dramatic altered states*, eerily—or I guess I should say not so eerily—similar to NDEs. Yes, healthy pilots in G-LOC can experience

> tunnel vision and bright lights, floating sensations, automatic movement, autoscopy [sensation of seeing one's own body from an external perspective], out-of-body experiences, not wanting to be disturbed, paralysis, vivid dreamlets of beautiful places, pleasurable sensations, . . . euphoria and dissociation, inclusion of friends and family, inclusion of prior

memories and thoughts, the experience being very memorable . . . , confabulation, and a strong urge to understand the experience.[19]

No wonder atheists have NDEs as often as Christians: It's because the NDE is a medical phenomenon, not a spiritual one. And no wonder dying people in India tend to see Hindu deities, those in New Guinea see sorcerers, and Native Americans see "Native American objects such as a 'war eagle,' deer, moose, bow and arrow, and moccasins."[20] It's not because life after death is for everybody—it's because life after death is for *nobody*. Even the mighty NDE is just another fucking neurological malfunction.

Now I understand why NDEs seem to be associated with some kinds of dying and not others. Your brain has to be deprived of oxygen to have the pleasant dying experience, like through cardiac arrest, bloodletting, or choking. I've never heard of an NDE associated with blunt force trauma to the head, even though people almost die from it all the time. Surely, deities and angels would not have some sort of preference for certain types of dying, showing up and offering comfort during a drowning but turning a cold shoulder to a hammer to the head. That obviously would not make sense. But G-LOC makes sense.

Now I understand why all the "research" supporting NDEs is merely anecdotal, that no legitimate controlled experiments have ever validated the phenomenon. The clever experiment would involve putting distinct objects or signs in particular places throughout emergency rooms so that they could only be seen by a hovering out-of-the-body spirit. According to physicist Victor Stenger, "This experiment has been tried several times without a single subject

---

19 Whinnery, J. E. (1997). Psychophysiologic correlates of unconsciousness and near-death experiences. *Journal of Near-Death Studies, 15*, 231-258.

20 Groth-Marnat, G. (1994). Cross-cultural perspectives on the near-death experience. *Australian Parapsychological Review, 19*, 7-11.

succeeding in reading the message under controlled conditions."[21] In other words, autoscopy is not real, either. It's just another hallucination. Of course it is, given it's part of G-LOC. Sure enough, turns out autoscopy can also be elicited during brain surgery.[22] I suspect before too long the whole "near-death" experience is going to be something we can purchase for recreation, just like a massage or tour of the Louvre.

At least for me, spirituality can no longer be defended in the face of these medical explanations. I'm afraid that the most sensible assessment is that we really are just biology and chemistry, held together according to the laws of Newtonian physics. Indeed, quantum physics no longer offers an out, as *real* scientists, such as astrophysicist Dave Goldberg, are now taking the floor to inform us that the new-age spiritualists have misunderstood quantum physics and falsely advertised it through, for instance, the "abomination" of a film *What the #$*! Do We Know?* Dave specifies that "It is remarkable (and frankly, alarming) the degree to which quantum uncertainty and quantum weirdness get inextricably bound up in certain circles with the idea of a soul, or humans controlling the universe, or some other pseudoscience."[23]

---

21   Stenger, V. (2012, April 16). Life after death: Evaluating the evidence. *Huffington Post*. Retrieved from http://www.huffingtonpost.com/victor-stenger /life-after-death-examinin_b_1428710.html

22   For example, Blanke, O., Ortigue, S., Landis, T., & Seeck, M. (2002). Stimulating illusory own-body perceptions. *Nature, 419*, 269-270. Actually, many of Wilder Penfield's patients had described autoscopic-like sensations decades ago.

23   Newitz, A. (2014, June 16). 10 scientific ideas that scientists wish you would stop misusing [Web blog post for io9]. Retrieved from http://io9.com/10-scientific-ideas-that-scientists-wish-you-would-stop-1591309822

I suspect that the faithful would retort by arguing that none of these biological explanations for experience and behavior mean anything, that God simply allows his spiritual centers of our brains to be fooled by LSD and seizures just to provide more temptations for us to rise above. You've got to have faith. This is what faith is all about: ignoring demoralizing logic and reason and embracing hope unconditionally.

But I can't do it anymore. I'm tired of trying to make all of this work. It's too much, a cruel and unusual challenge to my faith. I'm perfectly convinced now that spirituality is all in our heads, our so incredible—but so incredibly fallible—brains, with all their glutamate, glycoproteins, and other goo. Of course there's no ghost in the machine. It's just a machine.

And my machine hurts! I don't want to die. Mark Twain was wrong when he argued that annihilation will be okay because we've already experienced it before we were born. He's wrong because there's a critical asymmetry that he's overlooking: When we didn't exist the first time, we hadn't had the experience of being alive yet. Now that we have existed, our second episode of annihilation will necessarily have a different quality, as it will rob us of the life that we cherish so desperately, and there will be no other episode of existence in which to look forward.

No, I see our situation more like Blaise Pascal, and "marvel that people are not seized with despair at such a miserable condition."

CHAPTER 6

The Doomsday Defense

*I ain't happy about it, but I'd rather feel like shit than be full
of shit.*

— Suicidal Tendencies, "You Can't Bring Me Down"

BESIDES HELPING ME COME TO TERMS with my spirituality (lack
thereof, that is), college transformed my attitudes about other matters, and in similarly dramatic fashion. The other ground-shaking
life-changer was learning about *defense mechanisms*, acknowledging
their reality and how they affect our lives, if not run them sometimes.

Indeed, as a young undergraduate student, I had been defensive about defense mechanisms! I used to scoff when an instructor
introduced the notion, almost always in the context of Sigmund
Freud and some nonsense about penis envy or something. Hell, I
had done LSD and had myriad other "mind-expanding" experiences—there was no way some silver-spoon, douchebag professor
from New England was gonna teach me and my tattoos about consciousness and reality! But I can see now that *I* was wrong, simply
not willing to admit that my contact with reality was somehow
compromised. I'm telling you now, it was (and it still is).

When teaching my own college courses these days, I don't talk
about the transformation of my spirituality directly, given that it's a

little personal and doesn't flow well with many curricula. How-ever, I do like to disclose to my students how I was wrong about defense mechanisms, which often arises naturally in psychology courses. At the very least, I'm hoping that students will be encour-aged to examine themselves and entertain the prospect that they, too, might be mistaken about the notion as well, just as I was sitting in the same seat twenty-something years ago. I want to demon-strate firsthand that it doesn't have to be humiliating to admit when you've been wrong. In fact, as I argue to the class, such be-havior can be *liberating*, if you allow it to be. It's hard to say it without sounding cliché, but there really is something empowering about being able to appreciate and embrace our mistakes—includ-ing our misperceptions of reality, and those of ourselves. You really can't grow without it. It's excruciating at first but gets much easier with practice.

So yes, after years of both receiving and administering psycho-therapy and evaluating thousands of patients—from disgruntled cheerleaders to psychotic murderers—I have ultimately come to believe that defense mechanisms are as real as biological organs, like hearts, lungs, and kidneys. No, I'm not talking about all the details of wanting to kill your dad so you can screw your mom, but the general notion of emotional repression is, undoubtedly, a pro-found and pervasive part of our lives.

It's fascinating to listen to neo-Freudian psychologist Phebe Cramer speculate how the repression or denial of aversive stimula-tion begins as early as any other human behavior. She cites her late colleague René Spitz who argued that even the most fundamental act of *sleeping* may be "the prototype of all defense."[1] Certainly, sleep is more about rest, recovery, and growth than anything else, but I'm intrigued when I remind myself that excessive sleeping is a textbook symptom of depression. I think about how much I crave sleep when I'm down myself. Why? Because I want to avoid reality,

---

1 Cramer, P. (2006). *Protecting the self* (p. 52). New York: Guilford Press.

plain and simple. Sometimes when I wake up on a depressed day, I don't want to *think* or *perceive* or even *be* for a while—so I don't: I go back to sleep. If we appreciate sleep as a potential mechanism of denying reality, we might conceptualize suicide as the epitome of it.

Phebe points out that infant life is strewn with frustration and excessive stimulation. We're failing at everything we attempt, whether sitting up, crawling, or communicating with others. I've learned elsewhere that some developmental neuroscientists suspect that simply being conscious as a baby may be overwhelming at times, as one is still trying to learn the basics of the most fundamental experiences, such as depth perception and how to predict how something must feel in the hand depending on how it looks to the eye. Perhaps some of the inexplicable crying we see so often is due to confusion as much as anything else. Those toys we give our kids where they put blocks of different shapes through holes is a lot more educational than some people reckon; kids really are in the process of figuring all that stuff out. Given that these issues had to be dilemmas at some point during our neural development, imagine the perplexity that must be aroused when Daddy comes home from work and slams the door on his way in and ignores me! All of this has to be too much to handle at times, perhaps making sleep even more precious during infancy than it is during adulthood.

As kids mature they acquire more options to avoid noxious stimulation through more advanced motor movements and cognitive operations. Phebe provides an elegant example of research in which a preverbal baby is left with a stranger. When mom leaves the room, the baby cries. When the stranger picks the baby up but positions her so that she can't see who is holding her, she relaxes a bit. However, when turned to face the caretaking stranger, she turns her head to avoid looking at him (that is, she denies him, or represses his presence—perhaps pretending, on some level, that it's mom holding her instead?). Sure enough, when the baby is not allowed to exclude the stranger from her field of vision, she resumes crying. The whole scene reminds me of similar behavior as an adult, when we reflexively cover our eyes and ears when we don't want to see or hear something, like during a horror movie.

Repression gets much more interesting and sophisticated as we develop even more control over our mental faculties. At some point, we learn how to control our attention, including by numbing it down so much that it's almost like we're sleeping while awake. *Dissociation* is a phenomenon with which we're all familiar, as it can happen even when we're not being emotionally defensive. When teaching, I like to illustrate via the example in which we drive our cars along familiar routes and end up getting to our destination without having really paid attention to what we were doing along the way. We were on autopilot, our mind elsewhere, so much so that we might even be alarmed that we made it all! Sometimes I cannot, for the life of me, recall having passed through a certain traffic light, but I know that I must have. Such "zoning out" is often used in benign situations to cope with boredom while we sit in class or some other lecture, again almost forgetting where we are at times. Regarding repression, something similar but more profound can happen when we are being traumatized, such as being assaulted by another person. Specifically, some of the most intense instances of dissociation we hear about are actually common reactions to sexual assault. For an example from the grey area between boredom and assault, I used to dissociate often when my dad was yelling at me growing up. I'd be looking at him, nodding, but my mind was elsewhere. I'm serious: I couldn't recall what he said half the time, despite the fact he was yelling quite loudly.

If we're not good at dissociating mentally, we can numb ourselves chemically. For some, taking drugs is the most efficient and certain mechanism to repress discomfort and pain. If you don't like drugs, you can soothe yourself by overindulging non-chemical distractions, such as food, sex, or shopping. Often when we suffer some losses, such as a romantic relationship or a pet, we just shop for a replacement instead of facing the loss head-on.

Of course, we can also repress without numbing ourselves or engaging in distracting activity. Mature, adult brains can do all sorts of cognitive gymnastics, altering our perceptions of reality while fully conscious and sitting perfectly still and drug-free. A classic example to which most of us at least have the capacity to relate is when we have been rejected by a romantic interest and we reflexively discount them as "not my type anyway." The rejection hurts, but we defend against it by telling ourselves that there really is no loss or suffering, that we actually got what *we* wanted. We pretend we're in control, calling the shots, but it's pure ol' fashioned denial. Similarly, I often notice that whenever I proclaim "I don't care!"—regardless of the context (my voice often being snappy and raised)—I often *do* care, but am simply trying to deny my anxiety, sadness, or shame. The most reliable instance is when I'm accused of hurting someone's feelings and I reflexively assert that "I don't care." I do; I'm just trying to trick myself into thinking I don't, because I don't want to admit I fucked up, especially like that.

Phebe tells of a more poignant, clinical example of denial:

An unusually attractive young woman, stylishly dressed in the mode of her peers, entered my office for the first time. Despite her "together" appearance, she was clearly distressed: Her hands shook, her lips quivered, and she was struggling with losing control. Within minutes, she was sobbing uncontrollably, the cause of which upset I had not yet had the opportunity to discover. What was striking (and has remained fixed in my memory) was her reaction to the flow of tears and the heavy sobs. As the tears continued, she said to me, "I'm a very happy person." I looked at her, somewhat questioningly, and she repeated, "But I really am a very happy person."[2]

---

2 Ibid., p. 64.

The vignette captures an important essence of emotional repression: Denial is not simply lying. Part of us is so convinced of the defensive version of reality that we truly believe it is the case. These presentations are a dime a dozen in the realm of substance use. I once evaluated an alcoholic woman in jail who had to be treated at a hospital emergency room for alcohol poisoning just days before I met her, and she looked at me straight in the eye and told me enthusiastically that she did not have a drinking problem, like I was a crappy psychologist for even suspecting she did. I'm telling you, this stuff's not just in movies. It's very real. That was a real human being, with a normal IQ; I know, I measured it myself. We deny other addictions similarly, whether sex, gambling, shopping; you name it. Victims in abusive relationships can deny like this as well, almost as if they are addicted to the toxic relationships they are in.

There are many names for different maneuvers of repression, but the goal is the same each time: to reduce emotional discomfort. Most people are at least vaguely familiar with *rationalization*, in which we are almost always engaging when we defend our questionable behavior by stating "Everyone else does it!" The emotional discomfort that we're trying to reduce in these situations is often *guilt* or *shame*, which we try to deflect by noting that our behavior is not so unusual. We're in turmoil, however, because we want something but part of us knows we're violating one of our principles in order to have it. Pay attention to how it feels the next time you say "everyone else does it," or when you feel tempted to say it. For me, there really is a characteristic feeling, something I might call a numb irritability. I can literally feel myself being stupid, and a little grumpy. I have to numb myself out in order to buy into the deception, and I'm irritable because I know others don't believe me and are quietly challenging me.

There's *displacement*, when we redirect feelings, often anger, from a forbidden target to one over which we have more control. I watched the movie *21 Grams* while working on this chapter, and I think some displacement may have been at play in that scene where hyper-religious Jack Jordan, played by Benicio del Toro, was so hostile (abusive, in my opinion) to his kids at the dinner table. Jack had been fired from his crappy job as a golf caddy earlier that day, but he had to stifle his anger because his immediate supervisor who had to do the actual firing was a good man who was otherwise good to him, and the superiors who ordered the firing were simply inaccessible. That evening, Jack's kids are scuffling over a dinner roll until the little boy hits the little girl on the arm. Instead of scolding the boy, he forces the girl to present her other arm to the boy so he can hit that one, too (à la "turn the other cheek"; so, not only is he *displacing* his anger to his innocent girl, he's *rationalizing* it via the popular Bible verse). After that cruelty, he then ends up smacking the boy, too, anyway. The scene is a bit creepy and disturbing: Jack's behavior is clearly not about redirecting his children; it's about venting his anger towards an exempt stimulus to vulnerable ones.

Splitting is a particularly interesting defense mechanism because the uncomfortable feeling being repressed is a very specific one: *ambiguity*. As discussed in various places throughout this book, human minds generally don't like uncertainty. For some, uncertainty is almost intolerable, so they repress it by taking an extreme, polar position. Listen to Joseph Burgo, author of *Why do I do that? Psychological Defense Mechanisms and the Hidden Ways They Shape Our Lives*:

> When we feel unable to tolerate the tension and confusion aroused by complexity, we "resolve" that complexity by *splitting* it into two simplified and opposing parts, usually aligning ourselves with one of them and rejecting the other. As a result, we may feel a sort of comfort in believing we know something with absolute certainty; at the same time, we've over-simplified a complex issue, robbing it of its richness and vitality . . . Feelings of anger and self-righteousness often

accompany this process, bolstering our conviction that we are in the right and the other side in the wrong. Ambiguity and compromise are out of the question because they plunge us back into the painful realm of ambivalence.[3]

Joseph adds that splitting seems to be a fundamental part of politics; it's what polarizes many "polarizing issues." Sometimes I wonder if much of the enthusiasm of pro-choice activists also stems from splitting. Sure, many women want to reserve the right to have an abortion, but I can't help but wonder if some of the fervor is defending against the pain of what having an abortion really means. On the other side of the political coin, I wonder how many conservative pro-death penalty and anti-gun control folk are actually more on the fence than they are able to admit. For a more clinical example, consider people you know whose feelings towards you seem to vacillate from affection to hostility, especially during conflict. They're splitting, unable to conceptualize you as both good and flawed at the same time, so you can only be one or the other at any given moment.

Projection is when you attribute to others your own unappealing traits, such as anger. Others would describe you as an angry person, but you would argue that you're merely reacting to the hostilities of the rest of the world.

Reaction formation is when we behave in a way that diametrically misrepresents how we really feel. Textbooks might illustrate via a person with puritanical attitudes towards sex who is in reality a raging, horny sex machine underneath. I know this sounds a little too Freudian, so I thought I should include a citation: Professor Roy Baumeister reviews a study showing that, as a group, women who report low levels of arousal to sexually provocative stimuli exhibit

---

3 Burgo, J. (2012). *Why do I do that? Psychological defense mechanisms and the hidden ways they shape our lives* (pp. 83-84). Chapel Hill, NC: New Rise Press.

more sexual arousal than others when measured experimentally.[4] Similarly, in some of the most hilarious scientific research ever, he summarizes another study showing that homophobic men—wait for it—are more aroused by male homosexual pornography than non-homophobic men. Now, don't panic if you're a homophobe; this doesn't necessarily mean that you want to have gay sex. It just suggests that some part of you, deep down, is not as averse to it as you want to be.

I like to conceptualize narcissism as reaction formation. Contrary to some popular notions, narcissists are actually insecure underneath. The arrogance and entitlement are often defensive maneuvers to hide intense, deeply entrenched feelings of inadequacy and shame. I often teach my students (somewhat jokingly, but not entirely) that a simple rule-of-thumb test to distinguish narcissism from more healthy pride is to *insult the person in question*. A person with healthy pride will not mind so much, but the narcissist will become angry. (And maybe even lash out, so proceed with caution!)

Intellectualization is when we distance ourselves from our suffering by appealing to technical knowledge or abstract generalizations. Returning again to the ubiquitous romantic breakup, we overanalyze the dynamics of our failed chemistry, making assertions like "Better to have loved and lost, than never to have loved at all!" It kinda helps, for moments, but some part of us knows it's total bullshit, that the loss hurts bad and doesn't feel better than anything. If we could see ourselves in the mirror, we might notice something creepy about the smile that we're forcing at the moment when we assert the platitude. I'm serious: You can learn to see through it, and it's unsettling when you do. He's saying one thing and acting like he thinks it's the truth, but you can kinda see the

---

4 Baumeister, R. F., Dale, K., & Sommer, K. L. (1998). Freudian defense mechanisms and empirical findings in modern social psychology: Reaction formation, projection, displacement, undoing, isolation, sublimation, and denial. *Journal of Personality, 66*, 1085-1086.

self-deception, this spacey look of disconnection between what he's saying and what he believes. People don't seem entirely human when this is going on, but almost robotic.

Some people live much of their lives in a spacey state as such, what Phebe refers to as "Pollyannish denial," citing none other than Voltaire's *Candide*. It starts as daydreaming as children, but some of us are so good at it that

> the fantasies, unaffected by external events, acquire a salience that rivals external reality . . . Real events are then only recognized insofar as they conform to the fantasy . . . it occurs among adults who are overly optimistic, overly positive . . . The denial occurs not in terms of a failure to perceive what is there, but rather in an imposition of a highly personalized interpretation of what the perceived events mean. The meaning is distorted to make it more pleasant and more self-enhancing.[5]

So, when I explained in my chapter 1 that the experience of my college roommate having accidentally killed our cat eventually brought us together, some readers might be tempted to respond by asserting, "See—everything happens for a reason!" But Phebe might suggest that you're being defensive, trying to deflect the full horror of what transpired by twisting it into some "highly personalized" event that was orchestrated for us.

No, it didn't happen for a reason. It just happened, and Roman and I dealt with it the best we could. Despite eventually coming together, I suspect that both of us would have preferred that it didn't happen at all, and we could have just become closer over something else less traumatic later.

---

5 *Protecting the Self*, p. 45 & 60.

As you read through these examples, from Phebe's sobbing happy lady to Benicio del Toro, you may be noticing a very important aspect of emotional defensiveness: It's so much easier to identify it transpiring in someone else versus in ourselves. Phebe explains that this is largely due to the fundamental nature of defense mechanisms: By definition, since they do lessen pain, it hurts for the suffering person to see through them and to work through them! To seek progress, then, necessarily means feeling the pain we're trying to avoid. In contrast, when observing someone else being defensive, we're not being thwarted by the pain that the defensive person is trying to avoid.

Furthermore, there's likely a more general resistance to the notion that we would ever be emotionally defensive. We are defensive about defensiveness, even when we're not in the immediate act of being defensive! To ever be defensive would suggest that we are weak and can't handle reality, and therefore somewhat out of control of the situation at hand. Recall my assertion earlier that a sense of control is one of the most fundamental human needs, right up there with eating, mating, and socialization. Although when employing defense mechanisms we are exercising some control, in a sense, by tricking ourselves into a preferred version of reality, we necessarily do this at the expense of admitting that we can't handle the real version. Otherwise, we simply don't like the reflexive, unconscious nature of defense mechanisms. To admit that we do such a thing makes us feel mechanical, like automatons, simpletons of sorts. Less human, even.

But I don't think there's anything to be ashamed about. Being defensive is actually a very human trait, because humans don't like pain. On the other hand, we shouldn't resign ourselves to a defensive lifestyle, because *courage* is another human trait, as is the aspiration to grow.

Why are some people more defensive than others? As with any other aspect of personality, nature (that is, genes) certainly plays a role. Some of us simply have a sensitive temperament predisposing us to hurt more, and therefore we simply have more pain to deflect. Phebe adds that defensiveness is also nurtured into us depending on the amount of stress we experience during early development. Recall the image above of dad barging into the house after a long day at work, slamming the door, and running right past his baby on his way to the shower. A single such event is unlikely to affect the baby significantly, but if this type of interaction is habitual he's likely to feel rejected and unloved. A kid can't just leave and find a new family, so he's forced to soothe himself using defense mechanisms. By the time he's ready to move out of the home he's an expert.

Although repression will always have a place in our lives, there are many reasons to aspire for a relatively defensive-free lifestyle. First, it should be noted that repression doesn't really fix anything; it's just a band-aid that helps us get by for the moment. Roy Baumeister cites other research showing that "forcibly ejecting unwanted thoughts from the conscious mind" can result in what Freud called "the return of the repressed," that is, a rebound effect in which the unwanted thoughts return with even greater intensity than before.[6] When we're being defensive, we're just postponing pain, not curing it.

Otherwise, being defensive all the time prevents us from maturing and realizing our fuller potentialities. As Phebe explains, defensiveness only affects internal states, not the external reality. Abiding by the mantras such as "Everything happens for a reason" may help diminish the pain associated with irretrievable losses or mistakes, but it can also encourage passivity and prevent us from seeing our own roles in our dysfunctions. I find in my personal life and professional life as a psychologist that people who appeal to "Everything happens for a reason" are often doing so to avoid taking responsibility for the disasters they create themselves by making poor decisions or by keeping toxic company. By attributing the

---

6 Baumeister & Sommer (1998), p. 1085.

ill effects of our own mistakes to something orchestrated by God or the cosmos, we are less likely to see our own role and therefore change our behavior for the better.

Finally, defensiveness tarnishes our contact with others, including our loved ones. People who are good will respect us, feel closer to us, and like us more when we can be vulnerable and sincerely say "I'm sorry" and when we can openly discuss our fears and weaknesses. And they should like us and feel closer to us, because we are closer when we interact with others in an authentic manner like this. It shows that we trust them. And such behavior is disarming—it gives the person we are talking to the opportunity to open up as well. Most people do want to share their fears and other intimacies, deep down. The irony is that as we work through our defensiveness, we actually become stronger. We feel more alive, not less. Embracing our vulnerability, and that of others, really deepens our interactions and allows wonderful stuff to transpire.

Yes, it's much easier said than done, but it's doable with practice and counseling. Don't assume that just because I'm writing a chapter on defensiveness that I don't do it, either. I'm still learning, too, and always will be. I'd like to share one of my biggest breakthroughs, which occurred just a few years ago, I think it was 2005 or 2006; I'm sure I was still in graduate school, but winding it down.

I had been reading psychiatrist Mark Epstein's *Going to Pieces without Falling Apart.*[7] As the title of his book implies, Mark teaches us to just let ourselves hurt and to be mindful of our emotional pain as it unfolds. Pay attention to it, but don't make any value judgements—in particular, don't criticize yourself for hurting. It was reminiscent of the advice my one good therapist, Jessica, had given me over a decade before which was still in the process of sinking in: When having a panic attack, just let go and float down that river, let it take you away, and don't clutch at the reeds, lest

---

7 Epstein, M. (1998). *Going to pieces without falling apart: A Buddhist perspective on wholeness.* New York: Broadway Books.

you create rapids that pummel your face. Stop fighting; just let yourself die. Enlightened existential psychiatrist Victor Frankl called it *paradoxical intent*: Wish that your greatest fears be realized, embrace your greatest pain and just see what happens. When not resisting, you might see that the threat is not as bad as anticipated.

It was Christmas break, and I had driven down to Dallas from Lawrence to trudge through another holiday. After a long day of Christmas-ing I retired to the guest room, with its nicotine-stained walls, prehistoric blue shag carpet, and crappy TV. And gross: that decades-old reject mattress that must have housed an inconceivable number of dust mites.

To wind down, vent about the depressing holiday, and post-pone what was sure to be a horrific bout of insomnia, I called my ex-girlfriend, Victoria, who was now my regular friend. She had been the longest romantic relationship I ever had, at a not-very re-spectable two years. As I tried to engage Vickie on the phone, she seemed uncomfortable, eventually disclosing that she was now in a committed romantic relationship with some other guy, her first se-rious gig since we parted ways not that long ago.

I felt a grotesquely uncomfortable tension, a feeling I now rec-ognize as being emotionally crushed, but I was unwilling to admit it; I was defending against it. Of course, I didn't let her know I was even feeling uncomfortable. When we got off the phone, there was a sense of finality, and it was so fucking quiet. I could hear the goddamned dust mites crawling around in that godforsaken mat-tress.

Then, Mark's advice kinda snuck into my thoughts. Striking while the iron was very hot and not feeling that I had anything to lose, I decided to do what he had been suggesting: Just relax and pay attention to whatever I was feeling, without expectation or judgement. Let go of the reeds and just let the River of Distress take you wherever it would.

Somehow, I was able to let go. I laid down, lights and crappy TV off, just me and that comically lumpy bed and the nicotine stains hiding in the dark.

It hurt so bad, but I just sat there and let it flow over me, like the Holy Spirit did when Patsy touched me at camp decades prior. I didn't cry this time, but it hurt as bad as that had felt good. I felt like a needy person, a needy person who now felt lonely and help-less because my girl was finally gone—for real this time—and I don't like to be rejected, because I do the rejecting in my relation-ships.

And then, the damnedest fucking thing happened. After about—I don't know, not too long, ten or fifteen minutes . . . half an hour?—it started to hurt less. And then, guess what: The next thing I knew, I was waking up from what appeared to be a full night's sleep! Unfathomably, I felt rested. It was one of those awakenings like on a sleeping pill commercial, with the stretch and the sun on my face, hair looking just fine, beautiful, fluffy white sheets, not a dust mite around, and a big, fat smile on my face.

But no, I wasn't cured. It did hurt some more over time, waxing and waning, but I'm sure it didn't hurt as much as it would have otherwise. If nothing else, I felt less tense about being hurt. I *just hurt*, without the American side effects of being upset about my hurt. I would be okay, and keep on truckin'. The pain that re-mained did not have me. I now had it . . . or at least we both had each other.

Keeping the aforementioned defense mechanisms in mind, one that has particular relevance for my book is *sublimation*: when we cope with our pain by compensating or distracting ourselves through productive or prosocial behavior. Dramatic examples come from psychology textbooks that often cite, for example, a physically abused child who grows up to become a professional boxer. An-other example might be a mother who has lost her child to bullying who then becomes an anti-bullying advocate. More relevant for the masses, one might cope with chronic loneliness or the loss of a loved one by taking on extra duties at work or by filling his spare time volunteering.

It sounds fine; however, even productive, prosocial behavior can be unhealthy if it has control of us, develops into an obsession, or otherwise blinds us. Just as projection or intellectualization or other defenses can be a way of life for some people, so can sublimation. Here, Irvin Yalom summarizes the thoughts of his colleague, Salvador Maddi:

> *Crusadism* . . . is characterized by a powerful inclination to seek out and to dedicate oneself to dramatic and important causes. These individuals are demonstrators looking for an issue; they embrace a cause almost regardless of its content. As soon as one cause is finished, these hard-core activists must rapidly find another in order to stay one step ahead of the meaninglessness that pursues them.[8]

Staying ahead of the meaninglessness that pursues us. That's a very provocative thought, that sometimes our ambitions are motivated by fears of meaninglessness.

One important difference between crusadism and healthy sublimation is that the person engaged in the latter is more in touch with why she is doing what she is doing. She would be willing to acknowledge that she is an activist for anti-bullying legislation because she lost her own child, and she would be consciously aware that this simply makes it hurt less and benefits society, and that although her child would appreciate it, it does not bring her child back. Alternatively, the crusader would more likely deny unconscious motivations, and become uncomfortable and even irritable when accused of them—similar to how the person with unhealthy, narcissistic pride becomes angry when you insult him.

---

8 *Existential Psychotherapy*, p. 450.

If you think I'm a downer for questioning sublimation, you should hear Ernest Becker. His scathing assessment, *The Denial of Death*, earned a Pulitzer Prize in 1974. I find Becker's book one of the most intelligent and provocative works I've ever read, and definitely the most courageous, at least among legitimate literature. Like *Candide*, *The Denial of Death* should be required reading in typical curricula; both should be as popular as *Romeo and Juliet.*[9]

Becker, like countless *Introduction to Psychology* professors throughout history, noted how we humans are different from other animals because we are endowed with the most miraculous abilities that neurons can possibly muster: *self-consciousness* and *abstraction*, particularly, *foresight*.

However, unlike the vast majority of those psychology professors who relentlessly applaud our self-awareness and abstract thinking—as if these traits necessarily warrant celebration and pride because they distinguish us from the lower animals—Becker courageously acknowledges that there is a cruel, horrible side effect of putting the two together: *terror*.

> What does it mean to be a *self-conscious animal*? The idea is ludicrous, if it is not monstrous. It means to know that one is food for worms. This is the terror: to have emerged from nothing, to have a name, consciousness of self, deep inner feelings, an excruciating yearning for life and self-expression—and with all this yet to die.[10]

Becker's book is way too intricate for a summary to do it justice, but the essence of his point is this: We all know that we're gonna die, but the notion is so unsettling that we devote most of our lives trying to ignore or deny the fact. In one of the greatest ironies in the

9 Despite all the worthy praise, some of Becker's discussion is dated, such as the suggestion that homosexuality is necessarily a symptom of pathology (e.g., p. 118).

10 *The Denial of Death*, p. 87.

history of existence, we can become so obsessed with denying our fate that we often compromise the quality of the limited time we do have!

One might assume that ignoring something as profound, ubiquitous, and glaring as mortality would be much more difficult than denying, say, one's alcohol addiction. However, the denial of death comes with surprising ease. First, of course, the notion is inherently distressing so we actively avoid contemplating it deliberately. Otherwise, there are some more interesting psychological dynamics that help us to keep those terrifying thoughts at bay.

Healthy humans, regardless of how rational and intelligent they may be, simply have difficulty appreciating their mortality. Part of our brains knows that we're mortal, but our guts just don't buy it. Ronnie Janoff-Bulman coherently summarizes the post-Freudian (that is, object relations) notion that healthy parenting during infancy instills in us a sense of invulnerability that ironically can prevent us from fully contacting reality as adults.[11] A sensitive parent listens to her baby's cries and responds appropriately, whether covering him with a blanket if it seems that he's cold or offering her luscious teat if he's hungry. Alternatively, maybe the kid is just feeling alone and having some sort of disorientation freak-out and just needs to be held and soothed. The baby's mind is too simple to comprehend the complexity of the world around him and simply learns that every time he feels a need or urge it is somehow magically resolved. He develops a grandiosity, essentially concluding that he is the center of the universe, that it's all about him, a perspective called *infantile omnipotence* or *infantile narcissism*. Despite its "infantile" origins and nature, as Ronnie explains, the "illusion of invulnerability" endures into adulthood, in some form, so that even the most intelligent of adults cannot readily appreciate her mortality deeply. Studying Ronnie's book, I suspect that it's no coincidence that someone like me, who has virtu-

---

11 *Shattered Assumptions*, p. 13-14, etc.

ally no memories of being comforted during childhood, grew up feeling the opposite of invulnerable, that is, particularly vulnerable—and would eventually be writing a book about getting in touch with our vulnerability.

Colluding with the omnipotence with which many are blessed (or cursed) are more fundamental cognitive obstacles to contemplating our mortality, even when we are willing to try. As we discussed earlier when considering the conveniences of believing in God, a consciousness cannot really contemplate itself no longer contemplating. Trying to imagine no longer imagining is a paradoxical task, like trying to force two powerful magnets together at their positive poles. Mundane thoughts are much more accessible, so this is where we spend most of our time by default.

Perhaps an amalgamation of the two aforementioned issues, our experience of *self* is simply too compelling to equate with the "selves" of other creatures that we know are mortal, such as people who live on the other side of the world or even our beloved pets. Now, I've been doing this psychology thing for a while, but I'm not going to pretend that I understand self-consciousness or that I can explain what the self is. But what I do know is that mine—my *self*— is the most salient experience I have—to say the least! I'm the most *real* thing there is to me. In fact, I'm the only thing that I really know is real, à la Descartes's *cogito ergo sum*. How could the universe possibly continue to exist without *me*—I am reality! My *self-consciousness* (whatever it is) is so conspicuous and distracting that it overwhelms my ability to appreciate my true essence, that I'm really just biology, chemistry, and physics.

But sometimes when I'm looking at and contemplating my cat while she's engaged in her feline business, I have these brief Beckerarian moments of clarity in which I can't help but see that we're really not that different. We're both just biological tubes. On one end of our tubes, we each have this mechanical device with exceptionally strong and hard parts fit to consume nourishment. Also on that side of our tubes are the perceiving parts: the eyes, ears, and nose that direct the rest of our tubes towards things that they need and want, like food and sex, and away from things they don't, like big scary dogs. Farther down the line, our tubes digest the food that we've crunched and—with a peculiar circularity—nurture all the parts necessary to sustain our tubes and ambulate them around the world in search of more food. And, of course, we both have backsides, where all of our nonfood matter is purged from our systems.

It seems that the only real, qualitative difference between me and my cat is that the frontal lobes of my brain are more developed, having apparently exceeded some sort of critical mass that has afforded awareness, both of my "self" and of the future. And sure enough, here I am, terrified, while my cat doesn't give a shit. She's over there taking a nap right now, and I haven't had a great night of sleep in months. Ultimately, all because she doesn't realize that we're both food for worms, but I do.

And of course this is the primary reason we defend against our true fate. If we ever are able to appreciate our mortality, we simply can't tolerate it. The notion that we are merely animals, that our existence is finite just like our pets, that our inconceivably magnificent selves will someday no longer be evokes *terror* in us. In fact, it's wholly unacceptable.

So, we don't accept it. We defend against that terror, using the same defense mechanisms we use to fend off any other pain and discomfort, like when we get fired from our jobs, when our ex-girlfriends start dating someone else, or when our parents didn't pay us attention growing up.

We suppress the terror consciously. We repress it unconsciously. We distract ourselves from it. We intellectualize it, we rationalize it, we even try to laugh about it, but deep down we know it's not really funny and all we want is to be young again, or at least to not age anymore. The irony of all of this is so profound: We've developed frontal lobes to our brains that allow us to think abstractly, to marvel at existence, but this very gift scares us so much that we have to dumb it down in order to function! "The irony of man's condition is that the deepest need is to be free of the anxiety of death and annihilation; but it is life itself which awakens it, and so we must shrink from being fully alive."[12]

Back to sublimation, in some ways it seems to be the perfect defense mechanism against existential terror. Becker felt that the fear of death is "a mainspring of human activity."[13] Beyond the traditional, obvious rewards of staying busy (such as making money and gaining notoriety from our peers), rat-racing keeps us *distracted* and therefore shields us from contemplation and the discomfort that it brings.

If we're lucky, we may even create something that will endure beyond us. Now that's good treatment for one's terror: Sure, worms may eat me, but I've left my mark. A part of me will still exist, even when my body is gone. I will not be completely forgotten. Any time even a single person, some other existing entity, is interfacing with my mark, it's almost like I'm still existing.

Personally, I'm ready to admit that a large motivation for writing the book that you're reading—with all of its narcissistic autobiography and egocentric grandstanding—is to cope with my own anxiety about not existing anymore. The thought can horrify me, but there's something about putting my life story and thoughts into a book that makes it hurt less. At times while writing I've felt almost frantic, wanting to finish this thing before something happens to me, like a car accident or stroke or something. I don't have a problem admitting all this; it's all so simple and obvious. And again, being honest with myself and embracing my insecurity makes me feel more *real* and *alive* than when I try to deny it.

Such acts of creating are also great for a society en masse, so no one else is complaining. Indeed, Becker asserted that rat-racing as

---

12 *The Denial of Death*, p. 66.

13 Ibid., p. xvii.

such "is the repression on which culture is built."[14] If I'm following him correctly, he's suggesting that culture (that is, society) is, to some degree, an epiphenomenon, a side effect of the cumulative effects of each individual's fear of death. I'm sure it's more complex than that, but I also think there's more truth to it than it may seem at first glance.

Cultures come in all shapes and sizes: nationalities, ethnicities, political parties, states, cities, football fan bases, criminal gangs, people who are hearing impaired, and those who make movies. Culture offers much more than the societies from which they are born: like-minded camaraderie, *a place to belong.*

And with belonging, we begin to experience something transcendent: that sense of security, maybe even some semblance of immortality. Our cultures are bigger than us and will continue to exist after we're gone, just like some other guy's book will for him. *Belonging* to something that is relatively eternal is at least as good as *producing* something that is relatively eternal. It's more accessible by the masses, that's for sure.

No wonder we are so proud and defensive of our cultures and even aggressive when they are offended. However, the prospect that cultures acquire some of their appeal because of our fear of death should cause us to question whether our radical devotions to them are healthy. Jiddu Krishnamurti had the courage to acknowledge the danger of so strongly identifying with culture. It's a radical stance, if not hyperbole, but bear with us:

When you call yourself an Indian or a Muslim or a Christian or a European, or anything else, you are being violent. Do you see why it is violent? Because you are separating yourself from the rest of mankind. When you separate yourself by belief, by nationality, by tradition, it breeds violence. So a man who is seeking to understand violence does not belong

---

14 Ibid., p. 96.

to any country, to any religion, to any political party or par-
tial system; he is concerned with the total understanding of
mankind.[15]

If you don't want to hear it from a hippie Indian, here a blue-collar
Caucasian conveys the point just as well:

> Culture and tradition is always used as a positive thing, but I
> think there's many negatives to it, because it drives a wedge
> between people, because *one of the things about culture is that
> my culture is better than yours.* Who cares? . . . That's why I'm
> not patriotic. I'm not a flag-waver, I couldn't care less. Be-
> cause to me, the most important thing in this life is being a
> human being . . . I have no shame, you know, in saying that
> I'm not patriotic, or anything, because it's irrelevant to me.

That's Mark "Barney" Greenway, the lead singer for iconic death-
metal band Napalm Death.[16] I know: I don't have any quotes from
mainstream, popular sources—which is a point I'm trying to make.
Mainstream society doesn't make such comments because it's blasphemous to criticize culture, just like it is to criticize optimism.
Such thoughts are demoralizing and unacceptable, at least partially
because culture is so deeply associated with *belonging* and all the
good stuff that it brings, perhaps even the denial of death.

Is all culture and tradition bad? No, of course not. As with anything else, we need to practice rational, educated moderation. But
culture and tradition do become toxic when they begin to impose
on the more important rights of individuals. Iraqi founder of the
Global Secular Humanist Movement, Faisal Saeed Al-Mutar, asserts
most succinctly: "Society, Culture, [and] Tradition don't have

---

15 Krishnamurti, J. (1969). *Freedom from the known* (p. 51). New York: HarperOne.

16 Greenway, M. B. (2012, September 6). Interview by MK Ondergrond. [Audio
recording, with video animation]. Retrieved from http://www.facebook.com
/MKOndergrond (Italics added, I think.)

rights. Individuals have rights."[17] When I preach similarly and people try to argue with me on this point, I cite how, for example, that physically beating one's wife, female circumcision, and even "honor killings" are practiced and accepted in some cultures. Obviously, that shit's not okay, regardless of how long the respective culture has been doing it. Amazingly, some people will still look at me puzzled, at least in response to some examples. And it's not just right-wing, patriarchal traditionalists; some ultra-liberal folk will as well, because they've become *overly* respective of culture. These are people who are so obsessed with being liberal that they've actually become *closed*-minded. "Crusaders," according to Salvador Maddi.

As reassuring as a culture can be, it's often not enough. We need more. Becker again: "Mankind has reacted by trying to secure human meanings from beyond. Man's best efforts seem utterly fallible without appeal to something higher for justification, some conceptual support for the meaning of one's life from a transcendental dimension of some kind."[18] Of course: *God.*

Quite clearly, the most enticing method to manage one's terror is religion. In addition to providing a soothing culture in which to belong, religion makes everything we do much more meaningful than it seems. Our behavior is no longer human (that is, animal) activity but now spiritual, glorifying the Creator or otherwise becoming part of His Plan.

Most importantly, however,

> religion solves the problem of death, which no living individuals can solve, no matter how they would support us . . .

---

17 Al-Mutar, F. S. (2012, November 30). [Facebook post].

18 *The Denial of Death*, p. 120.

religion alone gives hope, because it holds open the dimension of the unknown and the unknowable, the fantastic mystery of creation that the human mind cannot even begin to approach, the possibility of a multidimensionality of spheres of existence, of heavens and possible embodiments that make a mockery of earthly logic—and in doing so, it relieves the absurdity of earthly life, all the impossible limitations and frustrations of living matter.[19]

Yes, religion does solve all the problems of "living matter." Death? Not a problem, because it's not really the end. In fact, something that is so much greater than life that it's inconceivable awaits me. Life until death? Well, it's not the drudgery it seems, because no matter what I do, I "do all to the glory of God."[20] And when it all becomes too much to handle, I just put everything in his hands. That may sound like a cop-out to some, but it's not. Oh no, to the contrary: The more I'm able to trust God and surrender to his will, the greater being I am!

Indeed, one still gets to be a hero by pleasing his gods and deferring to them even if he never does anything productive in his life otherwise. He can even be *destructive*, having more incarcerations to his name than dollars, but still be heroic by practicing, in some ill-defined capacity, religiosity. A mantra of some of the forensic patients I meet at work these days, often expressed in the medium of tattoo, is that "Only God Can Judge Me." The perspective would be comical, if some of the perpetrators weren't using it to justify acts of violence and even murder. And of course it's not just gangsters; many law-abiding, white-collar folk employ a similar maneuver to validate the less productive things they do, too.

Otherwise, insofar as adulthood has deprived us of that "illusion of invulnerability" that we experienced during infancy and

---

19 Ibid., p. 203.

20 1 Corinthians 10:31.

childhood, God can bring it back. Becker paraphrases psychoanalyst Otto Fenichel: "people have a 'longing for being hypnotized' precisely because they want to get back to the magical protection, the participation in omnipotence, the 'oceanic feeling' that they enjoyed when they were loved and protected by their parents."[21]

And religion does even more: It puts reason in its place. Religion is the one forum where we are not only allowed to ignore logic, but we are commended for admonishing it. In religion, faith is king. And the more faithful you are (that is, the less logical you are), the more heroic you get to be.

Religion is truly brilliant. No wonder it's so popular. It really can cure everything.

Coming down the home stretch of *The Denial of Death,* I felt disappointed as I began to realize that Becker had no solution for us atheists. He never gets to the part about the joys of being liberated from repression. On the contrary, he teaches that "Full humanness means full fear and trembling, at least some of the waking day . . . It can't be overstressed, one final time, that to see the world as it really is is devastating and terrifying."[22] Dang, man; I was afraid of that.

So, apparently Becker was not suggesting that we abandon all of our defensive quests for immortality, despite their ultimate futility. There is a place for some repression. He asserts that

> when we talk about the need for illusion we are not being cynical. True, there is a great deal of falseness and self-deception in the cultural *causa sui* [that is, meaning-of-life] project, there is also the necessity of this project. Man needs a

21 *The Denial of Death,* p. 132.

22 Ibid., p. 59 & 60.

"second" world, a world of humanly created meaning, a new reality that he can live, dramatize, nourish himself in.[23]

But we have to be careful. Repression becomes neurosis when "the techniques that they have developed for holding [the terror of mortality] at bay and cutting it down to size finally begin to choke the person himself."[24] Recall Yalom's *crusadism* from earlier. Even ambition and productivity can be destructive and unhealthy if they have us instead of us having them.

Worth acknowledging, being choked as such is just fine for some folks—it can even be addictive. We really can get caught up in our neuroses, perhaps because they are preferable to the alternative, that is, fully engaging reality. Becker: "Not everyone is as honest as Freud was when he said that he cured the miseries of the neurotic only to open him up to the normal misery of life."[25] People like Freud and Becker seem to be suggesting that even our neuroses can have an ulterior function, as they can distract us from the *real* anxiety that we should be having.

Sure enough, one of the first things they prepare us for while studying to become psychologists is that some patients will quit just as they start to get better. I now appreciate why, because even pain can be paradoxically soothing, if it's *familiar* and *predictable*. Sure, it hurts, but at least I know what to expect from day to day. Plus, if I change—even for the best—it necessarily means that I've been wrong about reality until this point. Never mind; I'll just stay put, as I prefer *predictable* and *right*. Finally, another fear with which improving patients must cope is *responsibility*, as they lose their entitlement to be cared for, to be swaddled.

So, then, what is mental health? Becker suggested there really is a middle ground, an amount of repression that allows us to navi-

---

23 Ibid., p. 189.

24 Ibid., p. 178.

25 Ibid., p. 271.

gate life but without camouflaging reality so much that it cripples us or even makes us dangerous: "A lived, compelling illusion that does not lie about life, death, and reality . . ."[26] It's okay to use whatever you need to get by, but if you're so invested in the mechanisms that give your life meaning and a sense of immortality that you're being selfish, antagonistic, or destructive, then you're being counterproductive, in the grand scheme of things.

I've encountered criticisms of Becker's perspective that are pitched something to the effect of the following: "Why would evolution, if it's so sensible, equip us with such a debilitating fear of death in the first place?"

Well, it didn't. Most of us, even us existentialists, don't routinely kill ourselves. Sure, there has always been suicide, but not many people resort to it, proportionally. In fact, even today—a time in history in which I suspect suicide is relatively common, if not peaking—it remains unusual, something on the order of 0.01% of the world population a year.[27] As long as large portions of the population are not suiciding, the gene pool doesn't mind too much. So, existence and the fear of death may be overwhelming for some individuals, but it's not, on average, for whatever reasons.

Otherwise, genes couldn't care less if the organisms who carry them are merely depressed or anxious, as long as those organisms continue to procreate. In fact, we all know that feeling bad doesn't necessarily deter humans from wanting to have sex—indeed, it may encourage them! For many, nothing treats a case of the blues

---

26 Ibid., p. 204.

27 According to the WHO, there are about 800,000 suicides a year (out of about 7 billion people). World Health Organization. (2014, September). Media centre - suicide fact sheet. Retrieved from http://www.who.int/mediacentre/factsheets/fs398/en/

like a good ol' roll in the hay. And for more chronic existential anxiety, what better way to cope with one's mortality than by mating and making a baby, a fresh new person that is half of you, literally.

Although still not debilitating for most, the fear of annihilation must be as rampant as ever in modern times, as technology keeps us overly informed regarding the mayhem throughout the world. Mass media has not been available for most of human history, so we have only recently become confronted with the actual extent of human suffering, destruction, and hatred. Typically, for the average person throughout history, facing death has probably been a relatively infrequent event. And when it did happen, it was typically a more intimate experience, followed by legitimate interpersonal mourning with others—instead of simply putting the paper down and having to go to the office.

Today, it's a challenge to avoid being bombarded with news stories and images that affirm our mortality, in Technicolor and very large numbers. So, of course we're freaked out. And of course we cope by distracting ourselves through rat-racing, shopping, and trying to leave our marks through accomplishments, including children and books like this one. And of course society isn't complaining, because our productive distraction is the machine that makes society function. And of course religion has irresistible appeal, because it readily accounts for all the chaos without demanding much introspection, contemplation, or analysis, instead appealing to faith. Perhaps religion itself is just another mindless distraction.

CHAPTER 7

The Lord Works in Mysterious Ways ... but Evolution Just Works!

What are we to make of a creation in which the routine activity is for organisms to be tearing others apart with teeth of all types—biting, grinding flesh, plant stalks, bones between molars, pushing the pulp greedily down the gullet with delight, incorporating its essence into one's own organization, and then excreting with foul stench and gasses the residue . . . Creation is a nightmare spectacular taking place on a planet that has been soaked for hundreds of millions of years in the blood of all its creatures.

— Ernest Becker, *The Denial of Death*

IN THE SUMMER OF 2005, I and a fellow graduate student at Kansas, Adam, took a road trip to Keystone, Colorado to go mountain biking. I was so excited I could hardly stand it. There was no snow and hardly anyone else around so we essentially had the place to ourselves, free to explore that majesty as much as the sunshine would allow. We had a sweet setup, too, another old friend's time-share condo right at ground zero, so we could just jump on our bikes and be in the mountains in no time.

About two or three hours into the very first ride of the trip, we found ourselves significantly removed from civilization, heading down a gradual slope through an open field, the type that simply demands that you go fast. At thirty-five years old, I didn't care as much about velocity as I might have in my twenties (and even then I was never much of a sensation-seeker), but I got carried away by the scenery and the trail ahead of me, so took the lead and sped ahead with reckless abandon.

After I had gotten some good speed, something on the order of 25 miles per hour (don't laugh—that's fast on a bike, especially in the dirt), the trail suddenly became more of a rut, a tiny canyon about eight or ten inches wide and equally deep. I hit a rock or a hole or something, which forced my front tire into the right wall of the little canyon-rut, and it bit like someone had thrown a crowbar into my spokes. I flew over the handlebars and hit the ground with that violent, vicious feeling so characteristic of a high-impact crash, where you're totally helpless, your existence completely in the hands of physics, but it kinda doesn't matter because everything is such a blur. I hit the ground hard as hell, something serious happened, and I rolled and finally came to a stop in some tall grass, remarkably far from my bike. I was all disoriented, only as you are after such chaos, not even sure if I was conscious or not, for a moment.

As my faculties began to return I reflexively surveyed the damage. Obviously, at the very least, my right shoulder was totally fucked, but I wasn't sure in precisely what manner. I had broken my left collarbone in high school gym class twenty years earlier, and it felt quite reminiscent of that. On the other hand, in addition to that familiar extraordinary pain, the whole shoulder joint just felt all distorted and wrong, giving me the impression that I had dislocated something this time. But after I conjured the nerve to look at it and touch it, it appeared it was indeed broken. Compared to the prior break in high school, this time the respective halves of the collarbone had shifted more dramatically, producing a very distinct lump and neighboring cavity on the other side of the break. Feeling sick and faint now. Head down. Deep, slow breaths.

I lay there for a bit, just to give myself time to calm down, which I eventually did. Once the dust settled, everything began to feel increasingly similar to my previous break and I became pretty confident that nothing novel and catastrophic was happening, like internal bleeding or organ rupturing.

Coincidentally, Adam had gotten flats in both of his tires right about the time I wrecked; I suppose he had run through some thorns or something that I had missed. I didn't feel like waiting for him to fix them because I knew I was gonna be in excruciating pain until I got to the ER, which was very far away, where ever it was. So, I cradled my arm and started walking back up the deceptively tranquil trail from whence we came. Adam would fix his tires, then bring both of the bikes and the rest of our shit back.

While walking through all that gorgeous country, I continued to calm down and even hit a stride of sorts, and ultimately had a very compelling experience, one of the most ever for me.

It was a beautiful day, like 70 degrees, sunny with a few good clouds, and whatever perfect humidity is. And it was also perfectly quiet, and I was perfectly alone, like I often aspire to be while vacationing in the wilderness. Even though it had become pretty clear I wasn't dying, the thought of death was still a little more accessible than usual. But the experience remained oddly peaceful. I remember feeling that I would prefer to die in a place like that, on a day like that. Just sit down and fade away, looking at the mountains and trees and clouds. It was one of those rare moments in which I was kinda willing to die.

Alas, as with every peaceful moment in history, the calm eventually gave way to some anxiety. My mind wandered to the prospect of some wild dogs, a bear, or some kind of large cat finding me in my ridiculously helpless state—which began to make the thought of dying suddenly less appealing. There is no way in hell I could have run, much less climb a tree or rock or something. It would have been an incredible challenge to even get a hold of a stick to try to scare a predator off. Right, good luck actually fighting it or them. With a broken collarbone you might as well be tied up.

And, strangely, broken collarbones are not that rare. I've broken two bones in my life—my respective collarbones. It seems weird that human beings are so vulnerable but we've managed to make it this far. What a pusillanimous little bone, but how incredibly incapacitated you are when it breaks. To make up for it, they tend to heal well on their own; the doctor typically doesn't place it, and there's no cast, just a sling. But you have to have time *to rest.* When undisturbed, the fractured portions bleed marrow or some other goo that dries and binds them back together. Later, that stuff calcifies, and voila, you're good to go. Again, the key is you have to rest and stay pretty still. Not such a big deal in the United States in the 20th and 21st centuries. But what an incredibly big deal back in caveman days!

I hadn't had much formal education on evolution at the time, having only picked up the basics of natural selection from high school biology books, the Discovery Channel, and fleeting regards during my liberal arts college education. But, walking alone through the Rocky Mountains debilitated like that, with relatively realistic thoughts of being consumed by wild cats or bears, some of it started to come together in a very tangible way. Suddenly, I was able to appreciate natural selection more than I ever could before—particularly the part about *social bonds.* I could almost taste it!

Camaraderie was a life-or-death issue during the course of our evolution. Back in caveman days (I'm told that we actually didn't evolve in caves; it was more like savannas), when you broke a bone, solitude could very likely result in your *death,* because, if nothing else, you would be easy pickings for all sorts of hungry critters. However, if similarly broken—but in the company of other people—the situation changes dramatically, as you now have someone to help you more effectively shoo away danger while you recover.

So, Pleistocene men and women *needed* the company of others—there was nothing frivolous about spending time with friends those days. This is not to suggest it wasn't fun at times; indeed, it must have been—it had to be immediately reinforcing one way or another, or it wouldn't have been so popular! Alternatively—more like simultaneously—extended solitude must have felt repulsive.

Evolution must have selected this arrangement. Over time, those people born with mutations rendering them repulsed by company or satisfied with solitude were much more likely to be devoured when they broke their collarbones because they were more likely to be alone when it happened. And once devoured, they could not mate and pass their I'm-fine-with-solitude genes into future generations.

On the contrary, those people carrying genes lending them to prefer the company of others, or to be repelled by solitude, were much more likely to survive, to live through broken bones and infections, and eventually mate with other similarly social humans. Ergo, the I-need-company genes were spread around a lot more effectively than the I'm-fine-with-solitude genes. And, whoomp, here we are today, endowed with a need to connect with others and to belong to cohesive social groups.

Many people are reluctant to even entertain such dry and technical accounts for the human experiences that we hold so dear, such as camaraderie. I recall myself bristling at such notions when I was still clinging to a more spiritual slant to the nature of existence. But now having experienced the transition to godlessness firsthand, I see the resistance like Ernest Becker, that one reason we reject these explanations is because we're afraid to mechanize ourselves and identify too closely with beasts, lest it suggest we are less special than we feel.

However, over here on the other side of the spirituality fence—and about as far from that fence as one can get—I'm thrilled to announce that, paradoxically, I feel *enriched* by the evolutionary perspectives of my behavior and experience. Camaraderie somehow feels more real and legitimate—perhaps even *more meaningful*—when appreciated as a phenomenon that has been honed through millions of years of natural selection, as opposed to having been instantaneously imposed via a magical finger-snap by Zeus or whomever.

I feel even more connected to others, both my friends and even strangers, in a way that is more tangible than ill-defined spiritual forces that are purported to do the same. My drives become part of my essence, a natural essence that I share with virtually every human being ever, Christian or Muslim, alive or dead. No, I'm not suggesting that every time I eat a burger that Joan of Arc or some al Qaeda terrorist in Qatar can somehow taste it, but it does make me feel less different from people in general. We all have similar desires and fears—especially the fear of mortality.

Nor am I saying that teaching evolution is going to bring world peace, but I think it may have more potential than the effort to reconcile the world's religions. The latter simply cannot happen entirely; too many religions are mutually exclusive, and there's too much at stake. That's the problem with immortality: It's too inspirational. What I do notice, however, is that my daily life has more peace when I appreciate the similarity between me and everyone else, that we're all on the same boat to mortality, and on some level, we're all afraid. It helps me, for example, be mindful of my interactions with others, whether it be my girlfriend or the checkout lady at the Quik-E-Mart.

Evolution doesn't just connect me to people: It even connects me to lower animals, who have similar—if not exact—versions of the same drives that I do (even though those animals may not be complicated by the ability *to contemplate* their experiences while having them). But realizing that I'm like the animals hasn't encouraged me to act like one, as I suspect many religious people fear it should. However, it has helped me feel less guilty for *wanting to* act like one, and has helped me to forgive myself when I actually *do* act like one (which isn't very often). For me, this secular, humanistic forgiveness feels more satisfying than the blind, frivolous forgiveness I used to get from Jesus. Ironically, it was spiritual forgiveness that had become routine after a while, insincere, and easy to abuse.

The evolution of socialization had to involve more than simply keeping company with others. Socialization works best when our company likes us, to some degree. They have to feel devoted to us and perceive us as worthwhile, dependable, valuable, attractive in some way. Otherwise, they're less motivated to care for us when we break our collarbones, nor will they be interested in having sex with us once we've healed.

With this in mind, we can now begin to appreciate how negative emotions, such as *guilt* and *shame* could fit in to the picture. (Psychologists do make a distinction: We experience *shame* when someone catches us doing something we feel is wrong, whereas *guilt* is relatively private, in that it doesn't require the publicity.) Pleistocene men and women who carried genes that created ill feelings when they perpetrated behaviors that were not conducive to the camaraderie of the group—such as stealing—would be less likely to commit those antisocial behaviors. As a result, they would be held in higher esteem in the group and treated preferentially, increasing the odds of their survival. Certainly, if I find two of my clan members in a precarious situation and it's up to me to make a sacrifice to help—but I can only tend to one—I'm gonna help the guy who shared his extra carrot with me last summer and let the guy who flirted with my cave-wife burn. And so, something like that, morality was born. It's worth mentioning that we're talking about the *average* cave-person. Sure, shameless/guiltless folk can survive in a group as well (at least in limited numbers) as long as they also have genes endowing them with the gifts of *manipulation* and *secrecy*. Such folks have survived just fine; we call them "sociopaths" or "psychopaths" today.[1]

Perhaps surprisingly, again, this evolutionary perspective orients me and provides direction—ironically, more so than the Bible ever did. Understanding my guilt and shame as products of millions of years of laborious development, a matter of life-or-death for my an-

---

1 Some professionals make a distinction between the two terms, but inconsistently so it depends on whom you ask; many of us consider them synonyms, and prefer *psychopath*. In general, they describe someone who is callous and lacks empathy, negotiating life with manipulation and/or force in order to suit his wants and needs. However, technically speaking, a person never has to break the law to be a psychopath. You have probably encountered many more people with psychopathic tendencies than you are aware.

cestors hunting and gathering on the African savannas millions of years ago, I feel like I have a legitimate reference to guide my behavior. All I have to do is learn to pay attention to my feelings, how to identify when I'm feeling guilty or ashamed. Nowadays, this compels me to examine my behavior and scrutinize it carefully, and I can make a decision based on how my options sway those negative feelings. The trickiest part has been working through the defense mechanisms and actually contacting the guilt and shame—just like physical pain, human minds don't like to feel them, so they reflexively try to push them away. But once you begin to contact them, this system becomes more reliable and less confusing than the Bible, which is ambiguous and will inevitably give you contradictory advice if you read it long enough. Perhaps guilt was a gift from God after all. Administered slowly, over millions of years of evolution on the African savannas.

The overarching mission of the field of Evolutionary Psychology is to better understand modern human behavior by explaining why and how it was naturally selected. A real evolutionary psychologist, Leda Cosmides, along with her anthropologist husband, John Tooby, have formalized a discussion about the role of evolution in modern mental illness.[2] The notion they present, profound for me, begins with the fact that evolution is (typically) an extraordinarily slow process. However, one of the products of evolution, modern humans with their abstracting frontal lobes, has discovered technology. Relative to evolution, technology proceeds very quickly. It's even accelerating, that is, it feeds itself and goes even faster as new advances are realized.

---

2 Cosmides, L. & Tooby, J. (1999). Toward an evolutionary taxonomy of treatable conditions. *Journal of Abnormal Psychology, 108,* 453-464.

So, as the simplest of calculus would predict, technological advances have now greatly outstripped our evolutionary adaptations. Ergo, we now find our current selves housed in bodies and minds that are still optimized for ancient living conditions, that is, hunting and gathering in tribal communities, living outdoors, and being intimately engaged with nature and other humans on tasks directly related to survival. As you can see, there is a glaring mismatch between how we were designed to live and how we are actually living today. Not surprisingly, this can lead to both physical and psychological distress. Surely, people have been discussing the irony of the pitfalls of luxury ever since luxury was invented. Leda and John's notion of "development-environment mismatch" seems to explain a lot of it.

They open the discussion by exploring non-mental health issues, that is, more medical examples, such as the "trivial" instance of overeating (by "trivial" they probably mean that this is a commonly cited example, as opposed to suggesting it doesn't matter). Pleistocene men and women were equipped—that is, naturally selected—to crave fat, salt, and sugar because these are particularly nourishing to human bodies and brains. The craving and appreciation for these foods are strong because such valued foods were relatively scarce back when the craving developed. In other words, there was a match between the supply and demand that functioned well. Today, however, at least for many of us in bountiful America, our supply is effectively endless, but we're still equipped with the same cravings that were suited for a much smaller supply. Ergo, we're obese and ridden with heart disease and tooth decay—which Leda and John describe as "virtually unknown in populations that [still] hunt and gather." It's also no wonder that hunger satiety takes time to set in: Everyone's quite familiar with how much easier it is to overeat than to under-eat. When Pleistocene women and men were fortunate enough to land some deer, they didn't stop after they had enough. They kept eating, and didn't start to feel full until way after they were actually full, because there might not be any more deer for a few days. Stuffing oneself back then could have been a life-or-death issue. Ironically, the tables have turned, huh!

I suspect that experts who really know what they're talking about could go on forever, but I have just a couple more examples of development-environment mismatch you might find engaging. One I enjoy teaching in my college classes whenever the discussion arises goes as follows. We did not evolve on boats, and therefore boating can be a terrible experience for many. This is because the brain on a boat is receiving conflicted messages, to which some people are particularly sensitive. The motor cortex and feedback from the legs are telling the boater that he's standing still but his vestibular system is telling him that he's in motion. For the human Pleistocene brain on land, such confusion was an alarm, the only natural deduction at the time being that the organism had consumed something poisonous. Ergo, the safest thing to do in such a situation would be to vomit. So, here we are today, conquering the planet with our boats—but for many, the earth wins, leaving the vanquished heaving over gunwales, feeding its fish with their vomitus. (By the way, a similar phenomenon happens at some movies—*The Blair Witch Project* in 1999 was notorious for inducing nausea in patrons, with its bouncy camera simulating movement while we were really just sitting in seats—me on the edge of mine, for sure; that movie worked well for me.)

And for those tough guys who make fun of the vomit-prone for being sissies, the joke's on you: Given a mass poisoning of our primitive tribe, our sensitive, barfing comrades are actually most likely to survive—and after all the macho guys with the cast-iron stomachs die, the "sissies" get their women!

While the iron is hot, we might as well venture into defecation. Bear with me; we won't stay long. But yes, I've taken up backcountry hiking over the last few years and have been moved by how much more magnificent a bowel movement is when squatting in nature versus sitting on a toilet. I'm serious: If I ranked all of my best dumps ever, the entire top 10 would consist of natural ones, despite comprising such an infinitesimal portion of total dumps taken. The irony is that by creating a situation that makes us more comfortable overall (that is, the toilet), we're putting our colons in an unnatural position that impedes the crapping process.

Okay, that story was a bit of a set-up (although it is totally true!). I was also interested in arousing icky feelings in you, which I suspect are quite rampant by now. But I'm not trying to be crass—I want to talk about those feelings, and suspect the discussion may proceed best if the feeling in question is fresh on your mind. The point: That feeling of disgust that you are feeling right now is also naturally selected. A genetically endowed repulsion to feces (and rotting food and so on) has self-preservation value—that is, avoidance of infection—while genes endowing any sort of attraction to such infectious things will soon become scarce in a gene pool. That revulsion is strong and deep, not just for hilarious playground jokes, but because it needs to be.

Of course, the repulsion is more complex than this, but that's likely where it starts, evolutionarily. And of course, our culture has also indoctrinated us to steer away from feces and such, to not even discuss such matters, which complements well our innate revulsion. But as many an evolutionist has noted, the rules of our culture are often simply resonating something that natural selection has already established, in this case "Stay away from doo-doo because it is so gross that it can be dangerous. No matter how hungry you are, don't eat *that*, despite the fact it just came out of you. Don't be near it; don't even *talk* about it." Other naturally selected laws of human nature endorsed well by culture include "You must beget children, but not with your own kin" and "Do unto others as you would have them do unto you." Our cultures enforce these rules, but it's an easy job in most instances because the foundation is already there. I'm not even sure if "enforce" is the right word; it may be more like *embrace*.

Back to poo, Ernest Becker takes it all to another level, arguing that our revulsion to feces and such, both personal and cultural, is not only about health but also related to our fears of mortality. He talked about "gods with anuses" to describe the duality of humankind, in respect to our narcissistic claims of having conquered the earth—but while we still have to shit, just like the rest of the animals.[3] Sure, we wipe our dirty butts, but often ineffectively. We even get it on our hand sometimes!

Becker says that the relatively animalistic behaviors like defecating are taboo because they are potent reminders of our mortality. To acknowledge them puts us on the same playing field as animals, and animals are mortal and don't have souls, so shitting and humping like them raises doubts that perhaps we don't have souls either. What kind of god would make us so different from the beasts (that is, immortal), but also so similar (that is, with urine and ejaculate and menses)? In a truly spiritual universe, an immortal being wouldn't even have an asshole, nor would it breast-feed its children like a dog. So the more we can disguise our animal parts and behaviors—with deodorant, clean underwear, scented toilet paper, feminine products, and nursing blankets—we can distance ourselves from the animals and convince ourselves that we're different. So different that we can live forever!

Becker goes on and on, culminating in what I am sure is the greatest line from any literature, ever since the beginning of the written word: "No mistake—the turd is mankind's real threat."[4]

It's true. The rectum and its product really do put us in our place. I've had mild bouts of hemorrhoids in the past, managed adequately with over-the-counter preparations for such. I'm not trying to be gross frivolously! I'm dead serious, just like Ernest Becker was: I've never felt more beastly than when applying ointment to my *sphincter ani externus*. The experience puts me in touch with my animality even more than crapping in the woods.

I like to imagine chatting with Ernest Becker about this stuff, sitting in rocking chairs on the porch, drinking cold beer. I can just hear

---

3 *The Denial of Death*, e.g., p. 51.

4 Ibid., p. 227.

him now: "Yeah, Dave, it's really hard to believe in God with your finger in your butt."

I'd laugh. "Yeah, well, I'll see your anus, Ernest, but I'll raise you a *masturbation*. That's right: gods who *beat-off*." It's easy to understand why masturbation is so shunned by religion, it being arguably more vile than crapping, and hence even more incompatible with immortality. Plus, masturbation has the benefit of being even more private than crapping, which affords people the opportunity to deny that they even do it at all! Privacy is what makes it a sin. Crapping would also be a sin, if we could at least pretend that we don't do it.

We'd go on and on. We'd rant about "gods who kill their babies," that is, abortion. Permitting abortion is about as incompatible with spirituality as any human behavior possibly could be. As long as abortion is legal, we're no better than the lion king when he kills entire litters sired by other lions in order to get their inferior genes out of the pool.

Similarly, we can't permit voluntary euthanasia of dying, consenting adults because to do so would also make us too beastly. I can't speak for Ernest, but I might even argue that in a world without spirituality, even suicide would be respected, at least in some cases. Yes, sometimes I think that when survivors of suiciders call the deceased "selfish," it's actually the survivors who are being self-centered.

In any event, Leda and John skip the evolutionary (and spiritual) discussion on feces and apply their development-environment mismatch notion to mental distress, such as anxiety. When I'm teaching this stuff to my college classes, I often begin with the example of *fear of heights*. A fear-of-heights gene would have been very beneficial from the beginning of human existence, as we don't need to be goofing around up in trees or on rocky precipices. We need to get what food we can and get down, carefully, lest we fall and break our collarbones and—well, you know the rest. A mutated gene that caused one to crave heights and to be frivolous about them would have been less likely to stay in the pool, for reasons that should be obvious. And no, it's not strange that a minority of modern people are thrill-seekers with relatively less fear of heights. They would have served us normal people well at times when the *only* food around was in a tree or up on a precipice. And when they did bust their ass fetching it, we healthy scaredy-cats would tend to them, for reasons that should also be obvious.

So, today, most of us carry the relatively safe fear-of-heights genes. The mismatch problem is manifest in that our technology presents us with many more heights—and much more incredible heights—than our ancestors had been experiencing during evolution. We have buildings, bridges, and airplanes—accessible heights that our ancestors rarely encountered, if ever. When you put those Pleistocene-era fear-of-heights genes into modern people, we're much more likely to be afraid, and even overwhelmed, given all the heights to which we have access.

No wonder I'm so inconceivably afraid of flying! Can you imagine anything less natural? I'm supposed to be walking in a field, looking for berries, roots, and maybe—if I'm lucky—a wounded miniature hippopotamus-horse-pig thing, but instead I find myself in this inconceivably complex tube made from steely rocks that travels hundreds of miles per hour several miles above the earth! That's right: You're the one who's weird, if you're *not* afraid.

And there will always be people afraid of flying, because those fear-of-heights genes will never be weeded out of the gene pool unless, for some reason, the fear of heights somehow causes that majority of the population to mate less. So, for example, if the World passed (and enforced!) a law that we must only fornicate on precariously high watchtowers, then the fear-of-heights genes would finally begin to disappear over time.

The development-environment mismatch logic can be applied to myriad other psychopathologies. One of the first things we learned in panic disorder treatment is that the panic attack is essentially a natural *fight-or-flight response* being initiated out of context. Fight-or-flight evolved to help us survive when confronted with threats to our physical integrity, like saber-toothed cats or even strange people who have a different skin color than us. However, today, the mechanism is triggered in unnatural contexts (such as while sitting in a classroom or at a board meeting) because of the accumulation of modern stressors, such as our grades, romantic failures, our pending presentation, and last week's layoffs. Once the fight-or-flight response kicks in, it only gets worse as you continue to sit in that meeting—you're supposed to be fighting or running by now! So, yes, when you find yourself in situations of escalating stress as such, one possible treatment is to whup someone's ass (I'm kidding; going for a jog will be more effective overall.)

Fear of crowds seems like an easy one to grasp (given we didn't evolve at shopping malls or football stadiums), which may then provide a segue into other experiences, such as suspiciousness or even some paranoia. Evolutionists often identify *male sexual jealousy* as an adaptive phenomenon, as unsightly as it can be. Functionally, however, it would motivate a man to monitor his mate, not just to help care for her but also to help ensure that he's devoting his resources to raising his own genes (including those jealousy genes), not someone else's. It's easy to imagine how a relatively healthy jealousy mechanism as such could run amok in today's world, with so many people to monitor, in a much more mysterious environment. Back in the good ol' days, I knew most of the people around me, or at least knew someone who knew the ones I didn't. Today, my wife is working miles away from home with all sorts of douchebags I've never even met, checking her out at the copier all day, begging her to go to happy hour . . . all while I'm busting my hump for The Man at the cable company so our kids can have as nice of clothes as possible . . . at least I *think* they're "our" kids.

Another instance of development-environment mismatch that seems very relevant these days relates to posttraumatic stress. Psychologists who practice therapy talk about *vicarious traumatization* or *empathy fatigue* in which the therapist himself begins to show symptoms of anxiety that appear to stem not from his own personal experiences but from being bombarded by stories of trauma and suffering at work all day. People in law enforcement and emergency medicine and such must have similar experiences. I strongly suspect that something related is happening to laypeople as well, perhaps not as dramatically but more widespread. For the masses, the stories of trauma and suffering don't come firsthand but through the media, but it's sufficient to unsettle them. Many of us today are probably walking on eggshells more than we're even aware, largely because some part of our unconscious (or even conscious) is terrified about all sorts of calamity that we saw on the news recently.

The mismatch reasoning can also be applied to our camaraderie discussion from before. Over the last few hundred years, technology has suddenly afforded us the "luxury" to live large portions of our lives in relative solitude. Many of us choose to, I suppose because it seems easier, given modern living conditions overall. However, just like *crave-fat* genes and *fear-of-heights* genes, we still carry the *I-need-company* genes. Remember, none of these genes are trivial: They are necessary to survive, or at least were.

Perhaps cabin fever has a lot more to do with not being around people than it has to do with spending time in cabins *per se*. I notice that I get a little kooky when I spend too much time alone. But it's amazing how easily this kookiness, which includes depression but is not limited to it, evaporates when something happens to remind me that I'm connected to others, something as simple as a dinner or a beer with a friend, a casual phone call, email, or text message. When those things aren't accessible, a simple trip to the grocery store can ground me sufficiently, at least for a while. Fellow shoppers are sometimes friendly, and the cashier lady almost always is. After being cooped up too long, I just need to be reminded that other humans are accessible and potentially receptive to my efforts to bond. Interestingly, often I can't convince myself this is the case simply by contemplating it—I have to *demonstrate* it, that is, by physically interacting with others. The reality is more effective than the fantasy.[5]

---

5 This is the foundation of cognitive-behavioral therapy: The *cognitive* aspect means that we do need to work on our thinking, but the critical *behavioral* aspect means that we must also act in order to learn.

And maybe those same better-to-be-around-people genes are why I feel compelled to watch so much TV: Because I live alone and get lonely, and I find the personalities on TV soothing. Television can be more satisfying than reading a book or listening to music because I can see a human face and even get to know the person behind it a bit, so much so that it's like they're talking to me sometimes. Hell yeah, I even talk back on occasion. This assessment helps me feel less ashamed about watching TV, that is, to consider that maybe I'm just feeding a gene that helped my ancestors survive. Sure, it's kinda creepy, but I'm also starting to understand why I get so sad when my favorite celebrities die. I don't really know them, but I am kinda *attached* to some stars—they've kept me company over the years! I suspect this is part of the reason why we can get so choked up during that part of the Oscars when they review the celebrities who have died over the previous year. Like family members, they arouse our feelings of mortality even more than other relatively random deaths we see on the news. We really will miss them; I don't think it's anything to be ashamed about.

And it's also easy to see why we're so addicted to virtual socializing. When I'm lonely, that iPhone tune signaling a text message has been received is so exciting, on an uncannily deep level. It's moving because it's stimulating these ancient social reward centers of my brain, reminding me that I'm connected after all. Sending a text message or getting a "Like" on our Facebook post is a lot easier and more accessible these days than having a face-to-face conversation, so we can readily experience more instances of text messages and likes than we can actual human contact. It's very similar to the salt-fat-sugar craving: We can tickle those reward centers as often as we want, to the point where it utterly devours our attention. But I think in the end it's not quite as satisfying, so we crave it, not unlike a heroin user craves his unnatural fix. Again, it's nothing to be ashamed about; just something to contemplate.

And it's easy to see why I'm so attached to my cat. A relatively sentient animal can commandeer our social drive (the more sentience, the better), even more so than people on TV can. That's why we miss them while on vacation, and why we're destroyed when they die. They're not people, but at least they're real, and we even *touch*. They comfort us physically and emotionally, and us them. We care for them, not wholly unlike we'd care for our own children, if we had them. I'm fairly sure that our pets stimulate the same neural mechanisms that have evolved to compel us to care for our kin and closest friends, although not necessarily as intensely.

Again, I find the evolutionary accounts for all of this suffering—from movie-induced nausea to media-induced trauma to plain ol' loneliness—more validating than spiritual accounts. I admit, sadly, that evolution doesn't offer me eternal life, but it explains my suffering in *this* life, my real life that I *know* will transpire. With evolution, when I'm feeling lonely and depressed, I no longer have to wonder whether there's something wrong with my soul, or if I'm being punished for having been bad. And I'm no longer utterly confused when God doesn't answer my pleas for companionship, leaving me to try to figure out how my solitude fits into some part of some Plan or Test. These days, when I feel lonely and depressed, I can see that it's much more simple: It's just my genes talking to me. They're telling me that being alone is not good for you. It's *dangerous* to be alone. You need to be around others, lest you get hurt or sick and become unable to care for yourself or defend yourself. And you're never gonna mate if you keep it up. Be with others, maybe even mate, and you will feel good again (at least for a while).

The Bible is relatively insensitive to many of these issues, and wholly insensitive to others, such as our love for animals. And the Bible can't even begin to help us understand how a bullied kid might want to shoot someone at school. But evolution does. It helps us understand how social isolation might be one of the most powerful impetuses behind severe depression that we can imagine, because social connection really is as critical to survival as eating and having shelter. When a kid is singled out, ostracized, then humiliated in front of groups of his peers who seem to have everything for which he longs and needs, of course it can conjure the greatest anger on Earth and, accordingly, the most ghastly fantasies of revenge. For those who actually act out as such and kill themselves or others it's likely more complicated, but at least evolution gives us a starting point. All the Bible offers are cryptic suggestions about cosmic plans and tests and about hope that it will all be okay someday if we trust in Him and whatnot. It's getting us nowhere, except to hell in a handbasket, ironically.

Sigh: Even romance is finally beginning to make sense to me now.

I've never read *Men are from Mars, Women are From Venus*. However, when I was a graduate student in Neuroscience at Texas in the late 1990s, I was fortunate to work in a lab right down the hall from Martie Haselton who was a graduate student in Evolutionary Psychology at the time. Martie has achieved much success since, currently a tenured professor at UCLA and having toured her research on various documentaries and talk shows, including *The Science of Sex Appeal* on the Discovery Channel, multiple interviews with Diane Sawyer, and on . . . um . . . *The View*. But yes, my first momentous lessons in natural selection were over lunch and not-as-lame-as-you-might-think graduate student parties.

One of the most interesting notions Martie introduced to me is *parental investment theory*, a grand idea born by Robert Trivers in the early 1970s which ended up inspiring much of Martie's research, and much of that of Evolutionary Psychology as a whole before her. Parental Investment Theory asserts that throughout the animal kingdom natural selection has influenced the gender that invests more in begetting offspring to be more prudent and choosy when selecting mates. In a nutshell, females of many species are limited in how many total children they can have, so in order to maximize their *reproductive fitness* they need to make every opportunity count as much as possible. First, females are limited simply by time: Once pregnant, they can't get pregnant again for a while, and insofar as they are attached to their babies after birth they continue to be obligated to them as they mature. Otherwise, bearing children can be physically taxing on the female, and even dangerous. Her fetuses steal her own nutrition and handicap her mobility. Birth complications can literally kill mom. To cope with these limiting factors, females have evolved to be relatively selective when choosing sexual partners. They seek the healthiest males, that is, the ones most likely to produce the heartiest children, as well as the most devoted and resourceful males, that is, the ones most likely to stick around during and after the pregnancy and help at least a little.

On the other hand, a male can invest relatively less in mating, sometimes as little as a few moments of his time, a handful of calories of energy, and a dollop of his endless supply of sperm. Males are not necessarily obligated, biologically or otherwise, to tend to any offspring that might result from a mating act. So, there's been less *selection pressure* for males to be prudent or choosy when mating. In fact, being aggressive and indiscriminate works just fine from the male gene's perspective. His reproductive fitness, to some degree, will simply depend on how much sex he can have. So, he's adopted more of a shotgun approach, that is, to just spread as much seed as possible, some of which is bound to stick. Whenever he's interacting with females, he tends to *over-interpret* their sexual interest in him, encouraging him to make sexual advances even when they're not welcome. Better safe than sorry, as far as a male's genes are concerned. I'm just gonna open this can of worms but not actually explore it in this book, but some have suggested that what is essentially rape may be a "mating strategy" for the males in some species. The most likely instance I've seen first-hand is ducks. It's kinda disturbing to watch ducks do it.

As you read through this discussion, you can't help but see the beastly influence in modern humans. And there you have it: Men, Mars; Women, Venus. Of course—particularly in humans—the dynamics are much more complicated than this, so variety can still flourish in the system. And in general, human males are relatively civilized, that is, feminine, compared to males of many other animal species. Our promiscuity and competitiveness and such are quite evident but not as glaring as they are elsewhere in the animal kingdom. Many men are as attached to their children as much as their wives are, and in some cases, even more so.

Nevertheless, there's something exceptionally sobering as you begin to compare animal mating behavior to human mating behavior. The similarities become more apparent than the differences.

Martie's Ph.D. supervisor at Texas, David Buss, is especially well known in the field. In his evolutionary psych textbook, he describes the mating ritual of the African village weaverbird:

> When a female weaverbird arrives in the vicinity of a male, he displays his recently built nest by suspending himself upside down from the bottom and vigorously flapping his wings. If the male impresses the female she approaches the nest, enters it, and examines the nest materials, poking and pulling them for as long as ten minutes. During this inspection the male sings to her from nearby. At any point in this sequence she may decide that the nest does not meet her standards and depart to inspect another male's nest. A male whose nest is rejected by several females will often break it down and rebuild another from scratch.[6]

Presumably as Dr. Buss intended, all I can envision when I read that passage is modern man trying to engage the attention of modern woman by exposing his Gold's Gym muscles, Armani suit, shiny red Lexus, and—if he holds her attention long enough—spacious, well-manicured lawn. Once in his home, the female is quietly inspecting everything from dust bunnies to sheet thread counts to prescriptions

---

6 Buss, D. M. (1999). *Evolutionary psychology: The new science of the mind* (p. 99). Boston: Allyn and Bacon.

in the medicine cabinet. Throughout the entire process the male is trying to charm the female, fawning over her, pretending he likes children, and continuing to advertise his value and devotion by showering her with fancy dinners, flowers, and eventually jewelry. If he's ultimately rejected by her and later by others, he'll likely be compelled to adjust his approach.

Now, I'm sure that love *feels* different for people than it does for animals, that is, much more rich, spiritual, and cosmic, but we have to acknowledge that regardless of how magical those feelings seem, they are often misguided, suggesting that the feelings of love are just that: *feelings*. I should clarify that the feelings are often misguided at least in terms of America's notion of love; in terms of evolution, they are guided perfectly.

Richard Dawkins paraphrases anthropologist Helen Fisher, who has "beautifully expressed the insanity of romantic love" (my quotation marks are not to imply sarcastic dissent; I totally agree with both Helen and Richard):

> From the point of view of a man, say, it is unlikely that any one woman of his acquaintance is a hundred times more lovable than her nearest competitor, yet that is how he is likely to describe her when "in love." . . . Evolutionary psychologists agree with [Helen] that the irrational *coup de foudre* could be a mechanism to ensure loyalty to one co-parent, lasting for long enough to rear a child together.[7]

I'm actually not sure who's agreeing with whom, but yes: Just like physical pain, the pleasure of eating animal fat, the fear of heights, camaraderie, and guilt, perhaps *love* is also—to some degree—another naturally selected experience for its functional role in passing our genes into the future.

Now, I don't want to lose half of my readers before I even get to the best part, so I want to be perfectly clear: I'm not arguing that

---

7 Dawkins, R. (2006). *The god delusion* (p. 184). Boston: Houghton Mifflin.

there is no such thing as enduring love. I've encountered many people who seem to have found it; I'm truly happy for them, and I envy them. (That said, I don't believe in the notion of "soul mates"; as difficult as it is to find one, there are countless people out there who could potentially fill the role for each of us.)

But enduring love is clearly not the norm. It seems that most people—assuming they can find a mate at all—have to settle for something less. For many, compatibility is the most reasonable long-term expectation, which may not even include much legitimate affection at all. At worst, I see a lot of toxic incompatibility that has never had any business being a relationship in the first place. In the grandest scheme of things, I feel very confident to speculate that if we consider all of the humans who have ever existed on Earth since the beginning of time, the vast majority have died without having had the opportunity to fully indulge true love. In contrast, the pangs of romantic love are ubiquitous. Certainly, the vast majority of humans who have ever existed have experienced the "irrational *coup de foudre*" of romantic love.

There seems to be some controversy over divorce statistics, but the rate really has been about half in recent decades.[8] And of course, many of those who stay together probably shouldn't, but they're just trapped for various reasons, such as family or cultural pressures (both explicit and implicit), financial security, loneliness, fear, or just plain-old defensiveness (for example, not wanting to admit they've been wrong all along). Now, divorce statistics wouldn't be so interesting if we knew that the divorcing couples didn't really feel in love when they married. But we can't say that's the case. Instead, it's *routine* for couples—even those who we all knew were truly in love—to ultimately divorce. And it doesn't just happen in trailer parks: It happens to the successful, talented, intellectually endowed, Oscar winners, and even royalty.

---

8 Miller, C. C. (2014, December 2). The divorce surge is over, but the myth lives on. *The New York Times.* Retrieved from http://www.nytimes.com/2014/12/02/upshot/the-divorce-surge-is-over-but-the-myth-lives-on.html

We've all been at some magnificent wedding that was like a scene from a Hollywood movie, with beautiful flowers, a string orchestra, and some bridesmaid we didn't know who was practically bawling the whole time. We were dazzled by the way the couple stared at each other and recited their own vows; they were nervous and awkward at times but gave off an undeniable aura that smote everyone in its wake. And the reception was brilliant: We drank expensive champagne in real glasses, shared chummy cigars, and there were adorable children dancing around in little tuxedos. It was one of those rare occasions we actually enjoyed chatting with strangers because magic was in the air. The whole time we were fantasizing that one day we'll be having a wedding like this of our own, because this is the real deal, and that's all that really matters in life. A wedding like this would fix everything.

Shockingly—but uncannily routine—things die down and a few years later that couple divorces, and sometimes quite nastily. Harsh critics will argue that they were never *really* in love—that's why it failed! But I don't buy it, and I suspect that many readers won't buy it, either. I'm not ready to disregard those feelings of passion as fake, partially because I've been victimized, too.

I've met Her and become so overwhelmed that I can't sleep, but that's okay, because I'm giddy and smiling all night long. I can't focus the next day at work because I can't stop thinking about her, but that's okay, too, because the fantasies I'm having are much more engaging than my stupid job. When I start to realize she might be having some of the same experiences, my excitement increases without bound, and I start to have hopes about this being *It* and me becoming *whole*. We make it to bed soon, but not before the tension gets right to where it needs to be. By that time, I'm so consumed with excitement there is no way to stop until every piece of her flesh has been in my mouth, the overall experience being the perfect balance of affectionate and dirty. Later, I write her poetry—lengthy, heartfelt stuff baring my soul—and she *loves* it! It's clear by this time that this is indeed *It*, as we spend an inordinate amount of time staring at each other's faces while holding hands and not talking. At other times, we're loud and reckless and the whole entire universe can fuck off, because we're the only two *really* in it.

Oops! Turns out, I was wrong. We both were. It didn't work. Over time, things happened and our perspectives changed. The fantastic feelings we had were replaced by much less desirable ones, such as regret, embarrassment, humiliation, and even anger. And here's the most hilarious part: I've been through this whole shenanigan more than once! And I know many of you have, too. Praise Jesus for birth control. I'm sure I'd have at least one illegitimate child by now if it weren't for it—and by illegitimate I mean conjured by a devilishly deceptive passion, an almost evil spell that tricked me as badly as I've ever been tricked before.

Of course, if I *had* made a kid, I'm absolutely positive that I would love him or her, well beyond anything else in the world, including myself. I'm proud to argue that I'm very feminine in this regard. All of those annoying assertions you parents make that us childless adults can't understand what it's like to have a child? *I agree.* The parent-child bond *should be* the greatest bond in nature, not because Jesus is real, but because evolution needs us to care for our kids even more than our spouses—perhaps even more than ourselves at times. I don't know what that bond feels like. I can't imagine; you're right.

Again, it's important to be perfectly clear: By no means am I trying to suggest that our feelings towards our romantic partners are *fake*, not *real*. They *are* real, just as real as the physical pain from a broken collarbone. That's the point: If the experience wasn't convincing then it wouldn't work! Broken bone pain has to demand a certain behavior—in that case, utter immobility of the broken part—or you could *die*. Similarly, we need an extraordinarily powerful motivation to drive us to merge with another, to forfeit any sense of privacy we typically have—or our genes could die with us. We have to trust our mate, not feel vulnerable anymore, want them—*need* them—so badly that we must rub our naked bodies against them as hard as we can. We can't be shy about their slobber and other juices—indeed, we're more likely to complete a successful mating act the more we're willing to embrace all that good stuff. Along the way and for some time thereafter, we have to be so moved by the whole experience that we're not interested in anyone else. In fact, we're so devoted to our mate (and our offspring) that risking our lives for them would come naturally, without hesitation.

Love must be more special than physical pain because it faces a greater challenge: *transcendence*. Pain and hunger and such are relatively simple experiences in that the neurons that mediate them connect the stimulus site in question (broken shoulder; empty stomach) directly to the brain parts that are responsible to tend to them. However, love and other interpersonal experiences, such as shame and camaraderie, are more complex, abstract, as they need to promote behavior that transcends the individual, that makes acting on behalf of or in reference to others rewarding (or aversive, in the case of shame). Perhaps those warm feelings of spirituality that we experience when we do a good deed or connect with someone else— especially when we fall in love—is what natural selection has devised to motivate such interpersonal, that is, self-transcendent, behaviors.

Recall our discussions from previous chapters in which scientists have shown there are spiritual mechanisms in our brains that can be stimulated directly by drugs, neurosurgery, seizures, or even g-force. Those brain areas must be there for a reason; they didn't evolve for LSD parties. Perhaps they evolved along with our consciousness to afford a feeling of profundity, *irrationality*, so that we'll do some crazy things we need to in order to promote our genes—crazy things like behaving altruistically, even risking our lives for others at times, or wrapping our legs around someone so they can literally put their disgusting body parts *inside* us.[9]

---

9 Richard Dawkins extends the conversation to speculate whether a transcendent, irrational brain mechanism naturally selected for love may have at some point become co-opted in mediating our transcendent, irrational devotion to religion (*The God Delusion*, p. 185). It's a fascinating, if not creepy, notion . . . and conjures thoughts of the most sensual book of the Bible, Song of Solomon.

Maybe that's the only real difference between us and the weaverbird. We both have the instinct to mate, but we humans have this self-consciousness and rationality that are potential obstacles. Where the weaverbird doesn't contemplate its behavior, we have to transcend ourselves and our fears, one of which is admitting that we are also beasts. We need to feel bigger than our animal natures, à la Ernest Becker, so we glorify our mating behavior as something much more meaningful and dignified than it necessarily is. We buy flowers and diamonds and say beautiful things about how love conquers all, but really its goal is just to make babies. Maybe there's nothing really magical about it. Maybe it is just fucking, clouded by our wild imagination and insatiable need to distance ourselves from our instincts, so that we can continue to feel spiritual—and immortal.

Transcendent when it's working, love is devastating when it's betrayed. News stories (and real statistics) show us that one of the largest groups of murder victims in this country is lovers and ex-lovers. Every time I see one of these accounts, I wonder to what degree that couple also thought they were in love. I think about their wedding and wonder if some of the guests there had been overwhelmed with spiritual feelings, dabbing away tears with fancy little monogrammed napkins. I wonder if the murderer himself had been overwhelmed with romantic feelings at some point. His girl raised his expectations to places where they had never been before. She was going to *save* him, and all of his sufferings in the past would finally be forgotten because the future would obviously be so different. Love is what he had been living for all this time, and he felt so lucky to be one of the few who finally found it. This was the kind of love that proves there's magic in the cosmos, that there is someone (or something) watching over us, and that some things in the universe are truly eternal.

If love was truly a cosmic, spiritual phenomenon, I don't think it would treat us like this. It wouldn't be associated with so much deprivation, deception, and destruction. Of course, not all love ends in murder. But loneliness, infidelity, and temptation are norms. It's all very mysterious, and frustrating, when conceptualized as some kind of magic bestowed upon us by God or the Cosmos or something. But it makes splendid sense when seen as a product of our genes, chosen and honed over millions of years of evolution in an effort to create babies. As far as evolution is concerned, passion works wonderfully, in the vast majority of cases. Again, genes don't care how the individuals who carry them suffer, as long as babies are being made and are at least given a fair chance to live to mating age themselves. Genes actually like our loneliness and the irrationality that overwhelms us when we think we've found a solution, our soul mate. And genes are just fine when lovers go their separate ways, because now they can fall in love again and mate elsewhere and enrich the gene pool more than they would have otherwise. Albert Camus's assertion was hyperbole, but poignant nonetheless: "there is no eternal love but what is thwarted."[10]

As much as I've been studying while writing this book, it has been unusual to come across commentary such as this in which love is reduced to just another product of natural selection. I suspect that many pure evolutionists do believe that it can be, but they feel that the notion's simply taboo. They don't want to be ostracized or to deflate their audience, so they just keep it to themselves.

Others give the impression that they, too, believe that love has some sort of immunity from the denigration of evolutionary accounts because it is indeed different, somehow spiritual. Love, for many of those who have no other spiritual outlet, may be the last bastion against depressive nihilism. Love can provide a purpose or meaning to life for those who have rejected other mechanisms of spirituality. Perhaps love is the one human experience that can re-

10 Camus, A. (1991). *The myth of Sisyphus* (J. O'Brien Trans.; p. 73). New York: Vintage International.

place spirituality and make life worthwhile without it. Because love is the most transcendent of human feelings, it provides some vague sense of immortality when we can't find it elsewhere.

But if we entertain the notion that there's nothing spiritual about love, that it is just a spiritual *feeling* mediated by neurons and hormones—just like every other subjective human experience—we arrive at the beating-a-dead-horse question for this book: Does it belittle the experience?

And the beating-a-dead-horse answer is once again: absolutely not! Paradoxically, it may honor it!

Deferring to the evolutionary account does not prevent one from experiencing love, no more than it prevents one from experiencing hunger, physical pain, fear of heights, or guilt. However, it does put the experience into some perspective, perhaps subduing it just enough so that it can be managed instead of running amok and becoming destructive.

When we overindulge love at first sight, we may actually be behaving less human than when we remain grounded and patient. Getting married within just a few months of meeting is the equivalent of a dog getting a good scent off some other dog's butt, then mounting before introductions are even finished. The more human reaction would be to practice patience. Get in touch with your superego (the frontal lobes of your brain) so that it can prevail over your id (the reptilian brain). The irony is that we *think* we're being more human by indulging the passion and sealing the deal, as if we're fulfilling some transcendental, spiritual prophesy, but we've got it all backwards. We're being deceived by our animal genes that just want us to hurry. But we can beat them, once we understand them.

And apparently we are beginning to: The most recent data I've seen is that we are waiting longer and marrying older, and the divorce rate is declining![11] Let the excitement dwindle a bit—which it will, it has to—then think about these extraordinary life-changing

---

11 "The divorce surge is over, but the myth lives on." (NYT article cited earlier.)

decisions. We need to make sure that we really care about our mate *after* we've been mating for a while and before we enter a legal contract—and, God forbid, before we bring illegitimate children into the world, victims of our own impulsivity and recklessness. This is an exceptionally common but serious problem with families (and our society) today: Couples have children not because they're ready, but because they're *not* ready. That is, they have babies because they think bonding over children will help fix their crappy marriage that they rushed into earlier . . . having rushed into them because they were so sure that Jesus was on board with them the whole time.

I want to assure prudent readers by explicitly asserting that as I began to identify with the animal side of human mating, I haven't had the reaction that spiritual folk likely fear, that is, to discard my morals and devote my life to hedonistic debauchery, full of sex parties with panties and dildos flying around my bedroom in a tornado of sweat and stink. No, the evolutionary perspective has not become an excuse, carte blanche, or any other dysfunction. On the contrary, analogous to my reaction to evolutionary perspectives on mental illness discussed above, I mostly feel validated and soothed. The evolutionary perspective finally helps me wrap my head around my own frustrating experiences, such as my insatiable horniness and fear of long-term commitment. It also helps me feel less guilty—but by no means does my guilt disappear. In fact, my guilt becomes more honed and functional compared to when it was associated with religion. Religious guilt always seemed somewhat ambiguous and disorienting, as it tended to blanket my whole person, making me feel that the issue at hand was not a particular behavior but whether I was a good person.

In contrast, I've since learned that naturally selected guilt—once contacted openly and honestly—is less deprecating, as it helps me focus on my behavior as opposed to my character. The Bible simply ordered me to not lust after someone else's wife, but evolution does much more. First, it acknowledges that the urge to commit adultery as such is actually quite common and may even be "natural," so I shouldn't feel so depraved for feeling lusty and tempted. I know now that the animal side of my genes just wants me to mate, regardless of whom it hurts. However, I also realize that there's a more pro-social, human side to my genes that cherishes other social bonds besides sex, social bonds that are built on trust and the golden rule. When I succeed and forgo the adultery in the world of evolution, I have something to really appreciate: Not that I followed orders like a good boy, but that I weighed the options nature presented and I chose the relatively human path, not the beastly one.

This is the exciting and even fun challenge of being a human living in a world of evolution: engaging in a tug-of-war between the animal and human sides of our nature. For most of us, we *do* have some say in how we behave and we can foster our humanity, again, approximately what the Freudians called the superego, and what neuroscientists now know is mediated by the prominent frontal lobes of our brains.

To close my rambling monologue on evolution, I must cite Stephen J. Gould who warns against over-applying natural selection to try to explain everything.[12] Just because something is the way it is doesn't mean evolution carefully selected it to be that way. Some things just *are*, or have stuck around not because they help but because they haven't been particularly harmful. Stephen illustrates via the "puzzle" of the oddly small arms of tyrannosaurus rex. He suggests these appendages were not honed to be small: They ended up relatively small because they were simply outstripped by the jaws and hind legs, which adapted so well by themselves that the beast just didn't really need arms anymore. In other words, the forelegs just got left behind, and it didn't matter.

---

12 Gould, S. J. (2007). The spandrels of San Marco and the Panglossian paradigm: A critique of the adaptationist program. In P. McGarr & S. Rose (Eds.), *The richness of life: The essential Stephen Jay Gould* (p. 428). New York: W. W. Norton.

It seems reasonable to assume that there are salient features of us humans that were not necessarily naturally selected either, at least directly. For example, I've felt that the evolutionary accounts I've heard so far to explain our affinity for music often feel forced and are not very convincing. Maybe there was no selection pressure to create and enjoy music, but our appreciation of it is instead an epiphenomenon, side effect, or even malfunction of some other adaptation. Maybe brains just like rhythm because it gives them something to focus on besides their own thoughts running wild.

Such notions are intriguing because they suggest that some messiness, and perhaps even mystery, will always be with us. It's interesting to consider which aspects of us humans are not necessarily here for a cosmic or even useful purpose, but instead are fascinating leftovers or random gifts—or even curses—from animals of eons past.

CHAPTER 8

Antitheism and the Disprivileging of Religion

One apprehension assails me here, that haply you reckon
Godless the pathway you tread which leads to the Science of Nature
As to the highroad of sin. But rather how much more often
Has that same vaunted Religion brought forth deeds sinful and godless.

— Lucretius, *De Rerum Natura*

YOU CAN'T WRITE A BOOK ABOUT ATHEISM without addressing the following worthwhile dilemma: "If religion works for people, why not just leave them alone? If it soothes them, gives them hope, and helps them function, why challenge that—why all the hostility?"

Well, I promise my intention is not to make anyone feel bad, not even the most radical, misguided Christians in the country. You could strap hate-mongering, funeral-protesting, fundamentalist pastor Fred Phelps to a chair, hook him up to some sort of brain implant device with "Feel Good" and "Feel Bad" buttons, put me at the controls and force me to impose an experience upon him, and I wouldn't choose the bad option. I just couldn't, regardless of what he represents or what he has done.

No, I'd much rather help people feel good. Specifically, I'm hoping to contact those folks sitting on the spirituality fence for whom religion is *not* working. They are confused and distressed about spiritual and existential issues and in need of some communion about it all. I would have loved to have read this book when I was about twenty. I would have felt much less alone and disoriented, knowing there is someone else out there like me struggling with some of the same problems. So, yes, I'm actually more interested in comforting others and connecting with them than I am in inciting conflict. And if anyone's faith is diminished in the process, I only hope that it's as good for them as it has been for me.

As part of that communion atop the spirituality fence, it's perfectly appropriate and natural to discuss whether religion (or even spirituality without religion) can be toxic, which will inevitably antagonize some readers. Besides the good religion can provide, is there also collateral damage? Now, for a debate to be worthwhile, we have to assume that the reward of an eternal life of bliss through faith is merely a fantasy. A real blissful eternity would unfairly bias most people to defend religion, regardless of how many problems it causes in this life, I have to assume.

If we resort to studying history, even Holy Bible-based religion becomes easy to abhor. Some of the best fodder comes from the Inquisition as, according to celebrity atheist writer Sam Harris, "there is no other instance in which so many ordinary men and women have been so deranged by their beliefs about God."[1] He explains that torture was officially sanctioned by the Catholic Church as a method to interrogate alleged witches and other heretics for several hundred years from 1215 to *1834* (that's not a typo; I double-checked it elsewhere). All it took to initiate an interrogation was an accusation by your peers, of which attempts to recant would only have resulted in them being punished along with you. The accused was allowed to confess but the confession would not be accepted unless she named accomplices, who were then interrogated as well. Despite the inconceivable horror and injustice of this process, Sam suggests confession

---

1 Harris, S. (2004). *The end of faith* (p. 79). New York: W. W. Norton. The rest of Sam's discussion cited here comes from chapter 3 of the same book, titled "In the shadow of God."

was the easy way out, as punishment then might only be as bad as life imprisonment. Apparently, the worst was saved for those who maintained their innocence, as they would be subjected to torture devices such as "a pear-shaped vise . . . inserted into your mouth, vagina, or anus, and forced open until your misery admits of no possible increase." If you were a particularly stubborn victim, you might have your arms dislocated, your feet roasted, or a cauldron of mice placed upside-down on your stomach until the mice would "burrow into your belly in search of an exit."

The men in charge of the Inquisition were not renegades; some were fan favorites, like Saint Augustine. Of course, there was no shortage of justification for their behavior from the Old Testament, but Sam argues that even Jesus could be perceived as on board, as suggested by, for example, John 15:6: "If anyone does not abide in Me, he is thrown away as a branch, and dries up; and they gather them, and cast them into the fire, and they are burned." Such verses are actually not unusual. I'd like to add, for example, Matthew 10:34-35: "Do not think that I came to bring peace on the earth; I did not come to bring peace, but a sword. For I came to set a man against his father, and a daughter against her mother . . ."

Some defenders of religion will reflexively remark, "Well, that was all in the past!" And this is one of the points at which we atheists get angry at faithful people and feel so intolerant of religion in general. We're angry because you've just demonstrated what may very well be our greatest grievance with religion: *insensitivity to suffering*. In order for you to validate your religion and to maintain your faith that God is good and invested in your safety today, you have to somehow account for the Inquisition and other similar catastrophes of religion. No matter which coping strategy you attempt to use, you invariably end up minimizing what happened to those countless victims of Christ's misguided sword.

I know what that denial feels like because I did it, too. I may not have asserted "That was all in the past" out loud, but I definitely recall contemplating something along those lines when I was a kid (or perhaps *struggling with* is a more accurate characterization). Later, when I had matured enough so that I couldn't help but appreciate that the torture and murder were *real*—and that they felt just as bad back then as they would to us today—I had to adopt the more effective "The Lord works in mysterious ways." That is, I was forced to characterize the mayhem as a phenomenon that was simply not for me to understand or even question. Either way, it's all denial. Typing this now, I can readily recall those numb feelings of emotional defensiveness, kinda staring off into space in a daze, knowing on some level that it really happened but just not letting myself embrace it and appreciate the implications.

Once the defenses fall and we let go of faith, we are overcome by a sobering clarity: Of course, a religion that *ever* failed so miserably must be the product of humans, not divinity. There is no way that a god would sit back and watch for 600 years while his highest priests tortured thousands of innocents via the likes of anal vice until they denounced him. Something truly holy would never have been subjected to such gross misunderstanding and atrocious implementation in the past. It would be timeless, not a work in progress; otherwise it reduces the billions of people who have lived before us to some sort of experiments for our own well-being today, us living in much better times. What a horrifically narcissistic and insensitive attitude this would be, to disregard the past in order to soothe our own existential fears about our own deaths, most of which will be quite pampered relative to theirs. Again, I did it, too. And now I'm ashamed. In fact, it makes me wonder if some of the hostility I have towards people who remain faithful is projected, that is, I'm mad at myself for ever having been in so much denial, too.

The truth is that we have come a long way so that religion is more civilized than ever before. But this is not because God cares more about us today than he did those living in the Middle Ages; it's simply because we're smarter than we were back then. And, despite how far we've come, we're far from out of the woods. There's still much more divinely inspired torture and murder in the world today than there ever should have been, and religious-based oppression of a less lethal nature remains quite rampant, even in the progressive and privileged West. Overall, we are still in a state of progress, meaning that we are actually an ongoing experiment for the people of the future who will have even better religious lives than us, one where there is even less murder of heretics and less oppression of slaves, women, and homosexuals. We can all see where this is ultimately headed. Eventually, someone's gonna have to write a Brand New Testament that usurps the New Testament. But it will be even shorter than the New, most of the emphasis being on the Golden Rule—the punchline again being that people have never needed spirituality to live the Golden Rule. They have only needed spirituality to help pretend that they were different from animals, that they have immortal souls.

Even if the terrorism and oppression motivated or enabled by religiosity were to be completely eradicated, we'll always have unjustified suffering and innocent victims in other contexts. Just as we atheists believe that the faithful can't fully acknowledge the victims of religion throughout history, we feel that they disregard the modern victims of relatively secular injustices as well. Religiosity and the authentic appreciation of suffering are mutually exclusive, as religions frame suffering as a necessary element of some kind of plan. The faithless atheist sees it more clearly, raw and cruel, without mitigation or meaning.

In *God's Problem*, professor Bart Ehrman's metaphor is exceptionally provocative:

> What would we think of an earthly father who starved two of his children and fed only the third even though there was enough food to go around? And what would we think of the

fed child expressing her deeply felt gratitude to her father for taking care of her needs, when two of her siblings were dying of malnutrition before her very eyes?[2]

You can't unread that passage.

So, yes, whenever I'm around people who are praying, whether at dinners or any other ceremony, I don't bow my head along with them. Today, I look around—defiantly—because I'm not going to give thanks while my siblings are starving before my eyes. Don't get me wrong: I am thankful—exceedingly thankful—for my food, but not to a God who would design things as such. Indeed, I feel that my contact with reality helps me appreciate my food more than a praying Christian. If the praying Christian truly appreciated how lucky he is to have so much good food, he wouldn't be offering thanks for it! He'd be baffled like Bart Ehrman, and he would even feel guilty and wonder what he has done to deserve such bounty. If he truly appreciated how most of the world is hungry while he's praying, he would begin to see the obscenity of his prayer. He might even lose his appetite for a while, if he really understood the problem, deep down.

By thanking God for our comfortable American lives of air conditioning, grocery stores bursting at the seams with food, functioning automobiles all our own, magical cell phones, gigantic wedding rings, and yes, healthy children, we are—by default—validating God's choice to neglect the majority of the world who are deprived of these luxuries. Most of those people don't deserve their lot. They are victims of circumstance, born there instead of here. Bart is absolutely right: Thankful prayers are offensive, plain and simple.

At about this point, books on atheism often detail stories of horrible crimes in order to jolt readers and to lay the foundation for a discussion on how the magnitude of evil in this world can't be reconciled with the notion of a benevolent God in Charge of It All.

---

2 Ehrman, B. D. (2008). *God's problem* (p. 129). New York: Harper One.

For my example of mayhem, I decided that I'd teach you about one of the most disturbing phenomena in all of psychology, one that is rarely discussed even in professional circles. I had merely speculated about this for most of my own education, and wasn't formally educated myself on the topic until—shit, *after* graduate school, when I finally needed to look it up myself because of my job. No professor during the countless psychology courses I took between 1988 and 2006 ever delved into this. I'm not sure why, but I have several suspicions.

Instead of explaining it myself I'm just gonna quote from a scientific research article. The journal has a dry but descriptive title, as many do; this one is *Child Abuse & Neglect*. Volume 22, number 10, published in 1998 has an article called "Factors Associated with Sexual Behavioral Problems in Young Sexually Abused Children."[3] This is not pornography; the point of the journal, and article, is not for anyone's enjoyment. Its purpose is to educate professionals, like me, about very real phenomena, in this case, to help identify which victims are at highest risk to abuse others, for the sake of imposing treatment interventions and preventing further abusive acts.

In this study, researchers looked at 100 sexually abused children, aged three to seven, in treatment centers. The authors were working in Toronto and Calgary but only needed two centers to get their 100 subjects. In the end, they found that two major risk factors for victims to become perpetrators themselves include: (1) if they had been sexually aroused when they were abused; and (2) if their perpetrators had been "sadistic." And, sure enough, some kids experienced both pain and pleasure when they were victimized.

The authors provide disturbing descriptions of the research that are difficult to read, even for my relatively experienced and hardened self. This is a blurb from what is usually the blandest part of such articles, the Methods section, where the authors have to explain

---

3 Hall, D. K., Mathews, F., & Pearce, J. (1998). Factors associated with sexual behavioral problems in young sexually abused children. *Child Abuse & Neglect, 22,* 1045-1063.

how they determined whether kids had been aroused or treated sa-
distically when they were sexually abused. Put on your serious hat:

> For example, for arousal, the child either needed to disclose
> that physical changes occurred in his/her body which would
> indicate arousal (i.e., "Got tickly feelings in my pee-pee,"
> "My dinky got hard like his") or would actually show signs
> of arousal while disclosing or playing out sexual abuse (e.g.,
> red face and heavy breathing while disclosing sexual mate-
> rial, having an erection, masturbating to flushing while en-
> acting sexual abuse on dolls, etc.). Perpetrator sadism was
> noted if the child disclosed how the perpetrator "enjoyed"
> the child's physical pain or discomfort or enjoyed tricking
> the child into fearfulness or terror (e.g., laughing at the child
> while hurting them, forcing the child to beg for the abuse to
> stop while perpetrator continues laughing, etc.).

That passage is one of the most unsettling texts I have ever read.
And I've read a lot, as police reports are a routine part of my job.

I don't know where to begin. All my life, ever since I was old
enough to realize that some kids are subjected to sex against their
wills, I had never imagined that it could possibly be anything like
that. And apparently, *that* is so common, you can research it—in
peaceful and progressive modern Canada!

I went to Carlsbad Caverns for the first time recently. Way down
in that most incredible place, my atheist friend who was with me,
Wally, overheard some woman say to her husband, "I don't understand how someone could see this and not believe there's a God!" I
like to imagine she was morbidly obese and had her kid on a leash.
Anyway, my reflexive, smart-ass response is that despite how beautiful that cavern is, geologists can explain it perfectly, without magic
or anything else.

My more serious response is that, despite how beautiful that
cavern is, there are also little kids all over the world—right now—being sexually abused in a manner that is simply unthinkable, but

paradoxically manages to turn them on to sex themselves, at the extraordinarily tender age of *three*. They become what we call *hypersexualized*, and often go around abusing other kids themselves, some of whom, of course, will also become hypersexualized, and so on. Sexual abuse is here to stay; no public service announcement is ridding us of *that*.

Carlsbad Lady, that's one reason I can't believe in God, or any other divinity, for that matter. I see your magical caverns, but I raise you "forcing the child to beg for the abuse to stop while perpetrator continues laughing."

And of course it gets so much worse. At least those kids are alive. I can't help but think about the ones who are dead, whose *final* experiences on Earth were being forced to beg for mercy, only evoking laughter from their demonic, psychopathic killers.

Unfathomably, it can be even worse. We can find stories where victim's loved ones, whether during the Holocaust or a modern home invasion, have to watch this truly unimaginable horror unfold before their own eyes before they, too, are tortured and put to death—or perhaps worse, allowed to live. Absolutely, unequivocally inconceivable—but it has happened, and it still happens, and it always will. I've heard other war stories of pregnant, living women having their fetuses cut from their wombs with bayonets, and stories of SS Nazis putting born babies in bags and smashing them against brick walls in front of their parents. I've lost sight of the citations, so I can't include those here, but it doesn't matter. We all know that human hatred is capable of such atrocities; we don't even need the citations.

History is strewn with this sort of behavior, the volume of death in the Holocaust so great only because the technology and context permitted it. Nazi murderers were no more evil than anyone else; they just had the means to exercise their hatred more effectively than anyone had before. Other efforts since—including quite recently, such as in the Sudan, Rwanda, and Bosnia—have rivaled that genocide at least in spirit, and would have gladly matched the death

count if the logistics had permitted them. That said, these more recent endeavors have been allowed to spill much more blood than
they ever should have because the rest of the world hasn't felt that
the return on investment has justified adequate intervention. We're
disconnected, whether because those people are poor, black, or so far
away. Whatever the reasons, it must make it impossible for us to
even fully appreciate that they are people, because if we did we
wouldn't tolerate what happens to them.

Those victims may be foreign but the hatred, evil, and insanity
are not. Back home, the same awesome forces motivate murder all
day, every day, on our streets and in our homes, schools, and movie
theaters. Our church—God's house—is not even safe, despite His
assurance that "For where two or three have gathered together in My
name, there I am in their midst."[4] Christians will continue to defend
Him, however. I can readily envision some creepy painting, a deranged artist's conception, of Dylan Roof shooting up the Emanuel
African Methodist Episcopal Church in Charleston, with Jesus sitting
in the corner crying or perhaps escorting the deceased up some
cloudy stairway to heaven. And the vision makes me angry.

I've read the various defenses that Christians provide for why
God permits such suffering in the world, and none of them are re-
motely satisfying. No matter how you cut it, He is either *cruel, apathetic,* or *incompetent.*[5] That is, he's either (a) choosing to impose incomprehensible suffering; (b) not imposing it but allowing it to happen; or (c) wants to intervene but is unable.

Most Christians will quickly disregard option (c), which is fair, as
the notion of an incompetent god is somewhat paradoxical and de-
feats the purpose of having gods at all; surely, the proposition has
only been included sarcastically. Based on my personal religious experience and training throughout the first third of my life, my sense

---

4   Matthew 18:20.

5   Different versions of the sentiment have been expressed by many, from
Epicurus to Woody Allen.

is that most believers subscribe to a hybrid of schemes (b) and (a). That is, God generally employs a laissez-faire approach to running the world, allowing Satan to tempt us and provoke evil but intervening at select other times, whether in response to prayer or unilaterally. In this system, God is not so cruel or apathetic. When a sinner suffers, it's punishment. If a believer is subjected to the exact same suffering and survives, then it's a test. If a believer does not survive the exact same situation, then God actually favors her and is gathering her to His Glory. The Power of Prayer works in a similar foolproof fashion. When our prayers are followed by good things and we get what we want, God answers prayer. When our prayers are followed by bad things, then our wishes were not in His plan and we are being tested; perhaps we were even being greedy for having asked in the first place and are now being bestowed wisdom and strength.

Of course, some suffering and unanswered prayers will fall through the cracks and seem to defy even this invincible scheme, such as those endured by any given 100 Canadian child sexual abuse victims, at which point we are forced to give up and assert that God works in mysterious ways that we are too simple to comprehend—which is itself another test of our faith, perhaps the ultimate test even. Indeed, the more incredible the horror is, the better Christians we are for not doubting Him in the face of it. This maneuver is reinforcing on two levels, as it not only helps numb ourselves to the horror, but it also affirms our own immortality. Both aspects are soothing, and they feed one another.

Well, any objective observer can see through the scam, if he only has the courage to critique it. High intelligence is not necessary; absurdity on this scale is glaring with just an open, rational mind.

The universe is not divine. God is not good. Nothing is tending to our prayers. Our beliefs in holiness and magic are merely coping strategies—defense mechanisms—whose obvious and only goals are to help the living feel better in the face of the brutality of reality.

And yes, Carlsbad Lady, your faith makes me angry. If you truly appreciated the magnitude of suffering and evil in the world, you wouldn't believe, either. Your faith exists only because you are able to minimize the evil. In fact, *it is largely the reason that you can* ignore it! Your faith gives you the "strength" to wander the earth, soaking in God's Glory while anesthetizing you to His Negligence. You are *Candide*'s Cunegonde, satisfied "that what was taking place in my father's castle was standard practice."

We need to stop it. As the innocent victims of torture, murder, rape, and starvation endure their suffering, the least we can do is acknowledge the reality of what is happening. These are not punishments or tests; they are the natural acts of the cosmos simply unfolding as it does—heartless, mindless, and cruel.

None of our rationalizations are helpful. It doesn't matter if the perpetrators are caught and executed. Capital punishment isn't justice; it's vengeance, and unsatisfying at that. It's unsatisfying because it doesn't undo the damage that has been inflicted, nor does it bring anyone back. It is yet another coping strategy, of which we should be ashamed when it does seem to work, because insofar as it soothes us we've equated the lives of the psychopaths with those of their victims.

It's commonplace during news interviews for the surviving loved ones of victims of catastrophe to make assertions such as "I know the Lord was with him when he passed." However, because I do forensic psychological evaluations for a living, I am, unfortunately, routinely able to compare the news story with the actual police reports, and I can assure you that I know for a fact that sometimes when we assume God's presence, we're simply wrong. No, there was nothing peaceful about what happened. If there was any deity present, it was the Devil; I'm afraid the Lord was nowhere in sight.

I have a stellar example in mind but am not going to detail it or even provide a disguised version of it, out of respect for both the deceased and the survivors. This is the part where I begin to feel less angry and more sympathetic, as I couldn't possibly blame a surviving parent, spouse, or sibling for resorting to spirituality to comfort themselves in a situation like this. The horror of real life can be truly inconceivable, wholly unacceptable, *forcing* us to be unrealistic. This may be the ultimate reason why we have religion in the first place. For some people sometimes, religion may be the only viable option. I guess I have to respect that, or I'm the one being insensitive.

While we atheists must not ridicule the defensive maneuvering of surviving loved ones of such victims, the problem is that Americans—being obsessed with optimism and meaning—tend to overreact to the lead and go overboard. Our defensiveness has become a national pastime, a mass hysteria. We watch the news and we say, somewhat superficially, "How awful" the refugee crisis is in Syria, but we don't really allow ourselves to care. Before our sympathy even has a chance to gel, we're distracted by a stylish, noisy commercial about the newest smartphone or a news blurb on what the celebrities wore at some posh awards ceremony last night. Come Sunday, our preacher comforts *us* by reminding us once again that "The Lord is close to the brokenhearted," which validates our position to not get too worked up about Syria and whatnot. After the service, we gaze at that painting of Jesus carrying the baby lamb around his neck, and it's intoxicating. We're drugged numb, brainwashed to believe that all of the pain in the world is acceptable, if not meaningful. We are passing the test!

Every catastrophe becomes another opportunity to flaunt our optimism. Like looking for Waldo, we're vigilant for any sort of silver lining in the horror. In 2011, after tornadoes in Joplin, Missouri killed over 150 people, the internet was strewn with pictures of the cross left standing at the otherwise leveled St. Mary's Catholic Church there, as if that was some kind of inspiration for hope. The irrational courage of the religious was described succinctly by Freud, in what may have been one of his wisest sentiments: "the secret of their strength is the strength of these wishes."[6] And so is the secret of their insensitivity.

---

6 Freud, S. (2011). *The future of an illusion* (W. D. Robson-Scott, Trans.; p. 52). Mansfield Centre, CT: Martino. (Original work published 1927).

It's not just the survivors of natural disasters. After every plane crash, mass shooting, refinery explosion, or building collapse, some survivors are literally glowing with thanks to the Lord while discussing the miracle of their survival to a news reporter. Of course, the unspoken but glaring implication is that the Lord chose to annihilate the victims who were right next to them. Again, I can't criticize the survivor. He's delirious with trauma, and of course doesn't mean what he seems to be saying, that God esteems his life more than those of the deceased, that his loved ones' prayers for his safety were more worthy than theirs.

The word "hero" has become meaningless in America, as we spectators throw it around recklessly to describe anyone who was really just in shock and happened to survive a catastrophe, often driven by nothing more than a traumatic daze. Those who were lucid just did what any decent normal, non-heroic human should do. And of course this is how the heroes themselves describe their behavior, as natural and unremarkable. The heroes are not sensationalizing their behavior; it's the rest of us, in an effort to cope with the horror that we've just witnessed, in hopes that some similar hero will save us if we ever end up in a similar situation.

I'm ranting. We atheist writers can't resist it. It's probably not only because we're angry at religion for minimizing the suffering in the world: We also have more selfish concerns—specifically, *we're scared*. We're scared because some of the people most "deranged" by the denial afforded by religion are not merely being passive in the privacy of their homes. As during the Inquisition, others are lawmakers and terrorists, so we feel threatened on multiple levels. Religious people are capable of anything, no matter how outrageous and disastrous. Part of the problem is that dying for one's religious cause lets him reap the benefits of that cause! Worth reiterating, "the secret of their strength is the strength of these wishes."

To calm and wind it down, I should clarify: I'm not questioning whether looking at the world through Everything-Happens-for-a-Reason glasses helps many people feel good. There's an entire branch of psychology called Positive Psychology that has produced volumes of research showing that thinking and behaving positively really can improve our mood and functioning. But, of course, just because something helps us to feel better doesn't necessarily make it *right*. Ask George Bernard Shaw: "The fact that a believer is happier than a skeptic is no more to the point than the fact that a drunken man is happier than a sober one."[7]

And of course, the exceptions don't get much press, but they're out there. While recently perusing old issues of the *Monitor on Psychology* I came across a news blurb, "Cancer survival not linked to a positive attitude, study finds."[8] Reporter E. Packard summarizes a study by James Coyne, Ph.D.: "Coyne and colleagues reported that emotional well-being in no way predicted survival among patients with head and neck cancer." I especially appreciate how the article is closed: "Coyne believes it's important to not blame cancer patients who don't adopt an aggressively positive spirit . . . 'People have to do what's comfortable with them, but they have to do it without the burden of thinking they've got to have the right attitude to survive.'"

What a refreshing dose of poignant and sensitive reporting—and in a publication from the national association that represents my otherwise Pollyannish field! This is a sad topic and this is sad news about it, but thank you for just letting it be sad and not trying to twist the whole story into some histrionic, Panglossian carnival about hope and optimism.

Now, I'm not suggesting that we flaunt pictures of body parts on the news instead of those of the survivors. People really can be traumatized by simply looking at a picture; you don't have to be at the scene of a crime. But we've distanced ourselves too much. We put too much emphasis on feeling good.

---

7 Shaw, B. (1952). Preface on the prospects of Christianity. In *Saint Joan; Major Barbara; Androcles and the lion* (p. 418). New York: Modern Library.

8 Packard, E. (2008, January). Cancer survival not linked to a positive attitude, study finds. *Monitor on Psychology, 39*(1), 14.

Perhaps this is what Ernest Becker meant when he said that only by dropping the defenses can we appreciate our real humanness. Once we shed the comfort of spirituality, we will appreciate our mortality more deeply. As a result, we will appreciate our losses more deeply, for what they really are. Until then, we're just children being sheltered.

Becker studied Freud, who believed we can't grow up until we first acknowledge that childishness:

> True, man will then find himself in a difficult situation. He will have to confess his utter helplessness and his insignificant part in the working of the universe; he will have to confess that he is no longer the centre of creation, no longer the object of the tender care of a benevolent providence. He will be in the same position as the child who has left the home where he was so warm and comfortable. But, after all, is it not the destiny of childishness to be overcome? Man cannot remain a child for ever; he must venture at last into the hostile world.[9]

Religious folks fear that without faith there would be anarchy and chaos. After all, as bad as things are across the world today, faith has gotten us this far!

The problem with this reasoning is that we haven't explored the alternative much—in this hemisphere, anyway. It's well known in atheist circles that the happiest nations on earth are often the least religious, including Denmark, Norway, Sweden, and the Netherlands. The dynamics behind such a correlation are certainly complicated, but evolutionary psychologist Nigel Barber believes that the atheism-happiness effect is mediated by economics. That is, the citizens of these nations are happy primarily due to "a combination of national wealth and redistribution of resources via high taxation and

---

9 *The Future of an Illusion,* p. 85-86.

a well-developed welfare state."[10] In other less alarming words, "European social democracies provide *existential security* . . . a secure standard of living for everyone." Italics added. The suggestion is that once people achieve existential security through financial stability, they're less desperate to look for it in religion.

Meanwhile, back in the relatively religious "Greatest Country in the World," we pretend that we're happy but the existential insecurity of cutthroat capitalism running amok seems to be killing us. Americans are "less healthy and more likely to die from disease or accidents than those in any other affluent country . . . Even the best-off Americans . . . are sicker than their peers in comparable countries."[11] We "have had a shorter life expectancy than people in almost all the comparator countries and for the last three decades the gap has been widening, particularly for women." The United States also leads affluent countries in teen pregnancy and STDs, as well as overall AIDS, obesity, lung disease, alcohol/drug deaths, and homicide.

A country with those distinctions is not blessed or "under God." That's a country with a lot of misguided public policy, and that is living in all sorts of denial about it.

No, the atheistic society is not the dysfunctional one. While Nigel Barber suggests that it's the security of socialist leanings that fosters atheism, I suspect atheism also fosters socialist leanings. None of the atheists I know, if they were in charge, would ever implement or tolerate an economy that sustains a division of wealth like that in America today. Most of us don't even esteem wealth personally. Being realists, we are acutely aware that materialism is more about

---

10 Barber, N. (2011, February 17). Does religion make people happier? Are atheists actually happier? [Web blog post "The human beast" for *Psychology Today*]. Retrieved from https://www.psychologytoday.com/blog/the-human-beast/201102/does-religion-make-people-happier

11 Boseley, S. (2013, January 10). Americans 'are sicker and die younger' than people in other wealthy nations. *The Guardian*. Retrieved from http://www.theguardian.com/world/2013/jan/10/americans-sicker-die-younger

greed and addiction than security. Also as realists, we are no longer able to ignore the suffering of those around us. We won't feel peace and security until our neighbors have them, too. That includes the Mexicans, both those on the other side of town and those on the other side of the border. We embrace immigration because it's easy for us to see that we might be immigrating, too—even illegally—if we had been born under some of their circumstances.

Even one of the most sensationally depressive philosophers of all time, Arthur Schopenhauer, argued that a nihilistic view of nature could have the paradoxical effect of binding us together:

> In fact, the conviction that the world and man is something that had better not have been, is of a kind to fill us with indulgence towards one another. Nay, from this point of view, we might well consider the proper form of address to be, not *Monsieur, Sir, mein Herr,* but *my fellow-sufferer, Soci malorum, compagnon de miseres!* This may perhaps sound strange, but it is in keeping with the facts; it puts others in a right-light; and it reminds us of that which is after all the most necessary thing in life—the tolerance, patience, regard, and love of neighbor, of which everyone stands in need, and which, therefore, every man owes to his fellow.[12]

It's a beautiful sentiment. Even the great Schopenhauer seems to find some meaning in his pessimism.

People on the fence still clinging to religion often argue that there's nothing to lose if they're wrong about it all. However, it seems there

---

12 Schopenhauer, A. (2008). On the sufferings of the world. In E. D. Klemke & S. M. Cahn (Eds.), *The meaning of life: A reader.* (3rd ed., p. 53-54). New York: Oxford University Press.

may not be that much to gain, either—at least emotionally.

I hadn't intended to write a research-laden scholarly book, but we have to at least briefly consider some that addresses the relationship between religiosity and emotional well-being. One of the most efficient ways to do this is via a *meta-analysis,* that is, a super-study that combines as many preexisting research studies on a topic as possible and reanalyzes the data across them as a whole. It didn't take me long to find one relevant for this discussion: Smith and colleagues compiled 147 different studies that had each already assessed the correlation between religiosity and depression, altogether involving almost 99,000 different subjects.[13] They found that when looking at all of these studies together, the correlation between religiosity and depression was -0.096. In the simplest of layman's terms, this means that religious people are less depressed than non-religious people, on average. However, of all the variation we might see in a population's scores on a depression test, religiosity only accounts for about 1% of it. Yes, that means that 99% of the variation in our depression scores is *not* related to religiosity. It's related to other factors, like genetics—which other studies show accounts for about 40% of the variation in depression.[14] Indeed, depression is a splendid example of a condition that results from approximately equal contributions of both nature and nurture. But, as far as nurture goes, religiosity is apparently only a tiny part.

That religion has the capacity to elevate mood is hardly interesting to atheists, as we readily acknowledge that it can soothe people for non-spiritual reasons. We've already explored many of these elsewhere in this book. First and foremost, religion helps people believe in some sort of immortality. Second, closely tied to the first, it provides a purpose when one can otherwise not find one, that is,

---

13   Smith, T. B., McCullough, M. E., & Poll, J. (2003). Religiousness and depression: Evidence for a main effect and the moderating influence of stressful life events. *Psychological Bulletin, 129,* 614-636.

14   American Psychiatric Association. (2013). *Diagnostic and statistical manual of mental disorders* (5th ed., p. 166). Washington DC: Author.

serving a god to earn that aforementioned immortality. Third, religion teaches people that the universe is not as chaotic and apathetic as it appears, but that it is instead under some sort of meaningful control. Fourth, a religion offers its followers a sense of some of that control (that is, via prayer). And even when prayer does not work, at least it lends an ear when no one else will listen or if what we have to say is too private for human consumption. Finally, regardless of whether one attends church, religion provides a social community or culture that shares one's worldview, helping him to feel a part of something bigger than himself.

Contemplating these benefits (I'm sure there are more), it may seem surprising that the research doesn't show *stronger* positive effects for religion—even given the assumption that the spirituality behind it is an illusion!

I suspect that one critical problem can, to some degree, undermine each of the benefits in the list: *doubt.* That is, many people who identify as religious simply are not as convinced as they appear. Part of them knows deep down that there was no meaning behind 9/11, the 2004 Indian Ocean Tsunami, and the Sandy Hook shootings. Their defense mechanisms are not *that* strong, so doubt ensues. Doubting the meaning of suffering on that scale must be insidious, raising doubt about the meaning of less salient but more personal catastrophes, and even the prospect of immortality, and so on. As we explored in chapter 6, defense mechanisms only work so well. When being defensive, we *say* things we want to believe, but our deepest reaches know they're not true, which creates a separate tension all its own. Religiosity is probably less likely to produce its benefits when it's superficial and forced—which it must be at times, when reality overwhelms it. Perhaps there's even something more tormenting about trying to cling than just letting go altogether. There may have been for me. I have to entertain that clinging was at least contributing to the debilitating panic attacks I had for five very long years, given that they went away around the same time I gave up God.

Other large-scale, carefully designed and implemented—but

surprisingly elegant—research has shown that prayer specifically can have a paradoxically toxic effect, at least on those receiving it following major heart surgery.[15] This study was gigantic: Sixteen authors (including MDs, RNs, and PhDs) plus support staff studied 1800 patients at six hospitals across the country, the entire study taking years to complete. Patients were randomly assigned to treatment groups (receiving prayer or not) and their resulting complications were assessed blindly (that is, by professionals unaware of who was assigned to which group). The main result, again, not surprising to us atheists: "Intercessory prayer itself had no effect on complication-free recovery from CABG" (coronary artery bypass graft surgery). However—in an obscenely cruel twist that even I don't think is funny—people who knew they were receiving prayers had more complications than those who were unsure whether they were receiving prayers! In the paper, the authors don't offer a possible explanation for this latter finding, but Richard Dawkins says that one of them has speculated elsewhere that perhaps those who knew they were being prayed for became distressed because they felt some sort of pressure, that is, akin to "performance anxiety."[16] All is not lost, however. Other legitimate research has shown that prayer can help *the person who is praying*, for example, by reducing his anger.[17] Of course, religious affiliation doesn't matter, nor does church attendance; it's simply the act of praying that provides the benefit. Findings such as this suggest that prayer may be nothing more than meditation, which is not a terrible thing, as long as you don't demand too much from it.

15 Benson, H. et al. (2006). Study of the therapeutic effects of intercessory prayer (STEP) in cardiac bypass patients: A multicenter randomized trial of uncertainty and certainty of receiving intercessory prayer. *American Heart Journal, 151*, p. 934-942.

16 *The God Delusion*, p. 63.

17 Bremner, R. H., Koole, S. L., & Bushman, B. J. (2011). "Pray for those who mistreat you": Effects of prayer on anger and aggression. *Personality and Social Psychology Bulletin, 37*, 830-837.

Besides doubt and its potentially deleterious effects, some people argue that religiosity may actively stifle us in ways that could also sabotage some of its potential benefits.

For someone writing a book with *Nihilism* in the title, I've read very little of Nietzsche. However, I have read a book about him, *What Nietzche Really Said*. Scholars Robert Solomon and Kathleen Higgins explain that the philosopher held that

> believers exchange an active stance toward their environment for the reactive stance of a pet or a victim. Instead of actively engaging with their problems, they treat their lived experiences like hieroglyphics whose real significance is decipherable only on a different— supernatural—plane . . . this shift of focus amounts to a complete falsification of our actual circumstances . . . For Nietzsche, this outlook is damaging to one's ability to function and flourish in one's life. It obstructs one's view of the real world, addles one's ability to see the real forces at work in one's life, and destroys one's ability to recognize how best to address them.[18]

In other words, faith—like other defense mechanisms—can rob one of her *agency*. Responding to conflict by asserting "I'm gonna put it in God's hands" is often just an emotionally defensive maneuver to ignore the actual problem. It turns out that the "real forces at work" may not be as mysterious as they seem, but instead stem from the faithful person's own bad choices or personality/emotional dysfunction. These personal problems need to be acknowledged and worked through, but faith provides an excuse to avoid self-exploration and conflict resolution.

In *The Nature of Existence*, American multi-talent Julia Sweeney specifically criticizes prayer in this regard, pointing out that it is not

---

18 Solomon, R. C. & Higgins, K. M. (2000). *What Nietzsche really said* (p. 88). New York: Schocken Books.

just a cop-out, it's a *deceptive* cop-out because it gives the illusion that we're doing something significant. Prayer is necessarily a compelling experience—we believe, on some level, that we are communicating with God and therefore affecting the universe! But if, in reality, prayer doesn't work, we've done nothing, or perhaps even done some damage via our complacency. Our spiritual cultures encourage us to pray and applaud us for doing so, but they may simply be teaching us to shun insight, agency, and growth.

For the moment, let's just consider everyday opportunities to engage the world actively and to mature emotionally (which can turn out to be much more profound than "everyday" would suggest). For example, I recently had an interpersonal conflict with a more seasoned colleague who was effectively my supervisor at the time. Ours felt like nonsensical tension, the type of head-butting that is commonplace in all sorts of workplace environments. We were quietly at each other's throats but the precise source of the problem was not perfectly clear. In general, it just seemed unnecessary and neurotic, on both of our accounts. It does take two to tango.

Now, if I had still been a religious person, I probably would have conceptualized the situation as some sort of Test from Above. I definitely would have prayed, at the very least asking God for the strength to endure my insufferable colleague. And I probably would have found that strength, because I'm good at being "strong" like that, as I've never been a confrontational person, especially towards any semblance of authority. If I had dared to pray for a *specific* solution or plan of action, I probably would have just seen signs instructing me to do what I *wanted* to do, which was *nothing* and I would have indeed just trudged through it. Regardless, because the supervisory relationship was temporary, I ultimately would have survived it and then chalked the "success" up to His Grace and whatnot. In the event the situation had escalated and crashed and burned into a more dramatic falling-out, then I would have seen it as God's method to deliver me from that evil, and I would have just accepted those new developments and moved on, praying all the way. But I would have learned nothing, nor would I have bettered myself.

Instead, as someone who sees no design whatsoever behind interpersonal conflicts such as this, I knew that if I wanted the situation to change I'd have to change it myself. Simply being strong and trudging through it remained an option, but a less desirable one, in a secular life. Somehow, the prospect of taking charge became irresistible, despite how frightening it was for me. Finally, one day as we were winding down a routine consultation, he asked me (a bit stuffily and impatiently, as usual), "Is there anything else we need to cover?"

I was exceedingly nervous but responded, "Yes, actually there's something somewhat unrelated I need to talk about." After breaking the ice, I felt more confident than anticipated, and it all came out with uncanny coherence: "I've been feeling some sort of tension between us, and it's really been getting to me lately. I don't know where it's coming from, but I just want to know what I can do to help make it go away."

He kinda froze for a moment, making it clear that he knew exactly what I was talking about. Then, he snapped out of it and rambled a bit; I honestly don't recall what he said in response, except that it was somewhat vacuous, just a cordial filler for the uncomfortable empty space. But the content didn't matter: The problem was solved simply by putting it on the table in a non-confrontational way ("disarming" was the word one of my therapy supervisors used to use that I have since adopted myself). From that moment onward, our relationship has felt transformed for the best. We even have some sort of bond now, having had that ridiculous, toxic experience together—and having addressed it, just a little bit, but directly.

I'm quite sure that this panned out in a much more productive and substantial manner than if I had taken the prayer route. Without the crutch of prayer, I was forced to examine myself and see how *I* was contributing to the problem (by being passive aggressive). I had to swallow my pride and take a risk that was very outside my normal repertoire of behaviors. I had to utilize an approach that I didn't learn from the Bible, but one that I learned from my secular education. As a result, I ended up connecting with someone in a way that was wholly unexpected. Plus, I *grew* because I learned that *I* have the capacity to make peace, all on my own. I don't have to endure interpersonal conflict; I can work through it. If my attempt fails even if I address it appropriately as such, well, I've still learned a lot and made progress. I've learned that the other person is not emotionally mature enough to truly negotiate, and *now* I realize (no longer *assume!*) that this may be a situation that simply must be endured. But at least I can now do so in relative peace, knowing that I've done what I could and the problem's not about me, it's about the other person. Now I can move on and nurture other relationships with people who can negotiate.

Certainly, there is a time and place for surrender. Sometimes, putting our suffering in God's hands, whether we believe in Him or not, may be the only real choice we have. Sometimes, conflict and suffering are wholly inevitable and the only dignified way to proceed is with acceptance. The tricky part is tapping "the wisdom to know the difference" between suffering that is truly out of our control and suffering that we are indulging—if not fostering.[19] As a psychologist who is finally starting to feel somewhat seasoned, I agree with Nietzche and Julia Sweeney that religion (if not spirituality in general) can have the paradoxical effect of lending us to passivity and, as a result, stagnation and frustration. We'll continue to get by, sure, but we may be more empty and conflicted than we advertise.

When the problem at hand is a childish power struggle with our

---

19   Quote from the "Serenity Prayer," popularly attributed to American theologian Reinhold Niebuhr (b. 1892). However, there's controversy regarding to what degree Niebuhr's version was original, some attributions of authorship apparently going all the way back to Aristotle; see, e.g., Goodstein, L. (2008, July 11). Serenity prayer stirs up doubt: Who wrote it? *The New York Times*. Retrieved from http://www.nytimes.com/2008/07/11/us/11prayer.html

supervisors, we (and our supervisors) may be the only victims of prayer. But sometimes the repercussions are much more significant, such as in Julia's example of praying for the hungry. Here, it's no longer a private problem: Complacency becomes a global issue, with potentially catastrophic effects. Obviously, lots of people have been praying to end hunger in Africa for an ample amount of time, but not enough of those prayers have been answered. The hungry don't need prayer; they need palpable actions, such as donations, volunteers, and global public policy development. Sure, we can still pray, but we need to do more. We need to see God's signs telling us *to act*.

Harvard humanist chaplain Greg Epstein explains that the issue reaches far beyond hungry Africa and even has consequences for obese America. In a call to the non-religious population to step up to the plate and address global concerns (such as natural resources, war, and economy), Greg quotes his former professor, theologian Gordon Kaufman: "This [ecological crisis] is a different kind of issue than Christians (or any other humans) have ever faced, and continuing to worship a God thought of as the omnipotent savior from all the evils of life may even impair our ability to see clearly its depths and significance . . ."[20] I'm hearing the words of Nietzsche, applied not to the individual but to the world at large, and now with cosmic repercussions. To put it simply, if we rely on God to save the earth, the earth is doomed. (I'm gonna leave it at that and not start ranting again.)

In the documentary *The God Who Wasn't There*, author Richard Carrier shares an enlightening insight: He explains that he couldn't indulge the wonders of Heaven if he were to make the cut because it would be unbearable to know that countless others are suffering in

---

20 Epstein, G. M. (2009). *Good without God* (p. 148). New York: William Morrow.

Hell—including people he had known, and maybe even loved.[21] Of course, we couldn't possibly be so childish to assume that *everyone* we have loved could have done everything so right as to get into Heaven. Knowing, sharing your life with—even loving—a Christian is not sufficient. The deceased has to believe.

I, David Landers, am obviously going to Hell, but most of my family and many of my friends, who I'm quite sure love me, will be elsewhere. Oh, man; why couldn't I have stopped asking questions and just let it be? It's actually tragic that I didn't die that night when I overdosed on cocaine, nineteen years old, still believing in God. How will my loved ones feel in the Heavens now, while I'm in hell burning, lamenting, and gnashing my teeth in pain and regret? Will they feel all chummy with God and Jesus, laid back up there, sippin' on gin?

Apparently, yes: "For, behold, I create new heavens and a new earth: and the former shall not be remembered, nor come into mind."[22] Even before the Bible told me so, my mother had. One of my most vivid childhood memories is of asking my mother whether our recently deceased dogs, Tuffy and Caesar, would be in Heaven. The answer was an unambiguous "no." That's right: We never entertained the notion of Doggie Heaven in the Landers home. Instead, I was taught that once in People Heaven, we simply won't be concerned about earthly matters, events and objects from our past lives.

I remember being puzzled by this as a kid. I found it somewhat reassuring, but somewhat unsettling at the same time. I loved my dogs, and the thought of not caring about them anymore because of some ill-defined spiritual transformation was not very palatable. I felt like I was being told, in a backhanded way, that I was overly attached to our pets—and to anything else on Earth that I anticipated missing upon its destruction. Today, I think this is a terrible lesson

---

21 Flemming, B., Jackson, A. (Producers), & Flemming, B. (Director). (2005). *The god who wasn't there* [Documentary film]. US: Beyond Belief Media.

22 Isaiah 65:17.

for children (and adults, too, for that matter). Talk about unpardonable sins: to disregard our existence—the one that we know is real and to which we have access right now—for one that I'm convinced is fantasy.

Freud again:

Of what use to him is the illusion of a kingdom on the moon, whose revenues have never yet been seen by anyone? As an honest crofter on this earth he will know how to cultivate his plot in a way that will support him. Thus by withdrawing his expectations from the other world and concentrating all his liberating energies on this earthly life he will probably attain to a state of things in which life will be tolerable for all and no one will be oppressed by culture any more.[23]

I suspect that most of my Christian friends and family don't *really* believe, deep-down, that I'm gonna be a wailing tooth-gnasher. The Bible affords an easy out, one that I recall resorting to at times when I was Christian, the most famous out of them all, John 3:16. All that other non-John 3:16 crap about coveting, women speaking in church, and camels going through needles doesn't really matter, when push comes to shove, because it says very clearly that we only have to believe in Him to be saved. Besides helping us to not fret over our own sinful behavior, John 3:16 lets us fantasize about how our non-Christian loved ones might have come over to our side at the last moment. I've witnessed this before, in real-life, unfolding in real-time: the Christian survivors of devout atheists fantasizing aloud that so-and-so *must have* seen the light at the very end, the Moment of Truth. It's so easy. Maybe even Christopher Hitchens saw the light at his End—he did make that suggestion about starting to see things differently once he started facing cancer! All one has to do is believe. It doesn't matter for how long, as long as it's sincere. Praise Him.

---

23 *The Future of an Illusion*, pp. 86-87.

Continuing to listen to Richard Carrier, I had a realization, a bit of an epiphany: If I do change my ways and make it to Heaven and somehow become aware that others are dying forever in Hell, *I'd try to be like Jesus*! I would approach God and request a deal: "Father, if I go down to earth and die for them, would you stop being so hard on the unforgiven? Give them even another chance . . . or perhaps let's just make hell a little less hellish. It just seems like too much." Yes, *I* would give my life for the suffering of the sinners, just like Jesus did! And I'm not bragging; wouldn't we all do the same?

Of course, I would need a guarantee that I would be resurrected after a few days; otherwise, the deal's off. And no funny stuff, God—don't you dare leave me dead! That must have been a concern for Jesus, that God might betray him and leave him dead for a lot longer, like millennia instead of three days—or what if he didn't bring him back at all! Can you imagine? Then God could go back to turning people into salt. Now *that* would have been a real sacrifice: giving His life without the prospect of resurrection.

Now, one way in which I wouldn't be like Jesus, though, is to insist that you believe in me—in the absence of any legitimate evidence—to be saved. That would be narcissistic; what kind of deity would glorify one of the most detestable of *human* traits?

No, for me, one's access to eternity would be weighed much more heavily on, for example, how good she was to other people; I'd be relatively forgiving about lapses of faith. To create a mind that's curious, skeptical, and logical—then condemn it for working correctly—would be absurd. No, I wouldn't be like God; I wouldn't be "a terrible character" who is "obsessed" with worship and punishment.[24] I would actually be merciful and loving. I'm not even sure if Hell would be necessary. Limbo would be sufficient, at worst.

This is why my greatest concern about dying is not Hell. I'm too confident there is no such place. If there does turn out to be a tran-

24 Physicist Stephen Weinberg in: Denton, R. (Producer & Director). (2004). *The atheism tapes* (Steven Weinberg episode). [Television documentary miniseries]. UK: British Broadcasting Corporation.

scendental spiritual entity of any sort, of course it wouldn't be so ridiculous. My biggest fear is that there is no transcendence at all. Just carbon, dopamine, physics, and chemistry. Stardust, I'm told.

CHAPTER 9

The Meaning—er, I Mean *Sanctity* of Life

He said it was impossible; all men believed in God, even those who turn their backs on him. That was his belief, and if he were ever to doubt it, his life would become meaningless. "Do you want my life to be meaningless?" he shouted . . . from across the table he had already thrust the crucifix in my face and was screaming irrationally, "I am a Christian. I ask Him to forgive you your sins. How can you not believe that he suffered for you?"

— Albert Camus, *The Stranger*

AGNOSTIC THEISM—the doctrine that there is some sort of god but its nature is unknowable—seems to be replacing more dogmatic theisms these days, presumably due to the natural intellectual maturation of the masses, facilitated by ready access to eye-opening education through cable television and the internet. The proclamations of the agnostic theists are becoming somewhat cliché: "I believe that there is a god, but not the God in the Bible!"; "I'm spiritual but not religious!"; or "I just believe there's a cosmic energy that binds us."

In conversation, we often announce our spiritual-but-not-religious stance with a sense of pride and conviction—almost glee at times—as if we've figured out what the Christians have missed: the supernatural, some sort of eternal existence, and a spiritual life without the irrationality and oppression of the Bible.

But somewhat unsettling to me—and I am speaking from experience, having been very spiritual but not religious myself in the past—that sense of pride and conviction also has a dramatic, defensive feel to it, eerily reminiscent to that of a Christian speaking at a funeral about how the deceased is now with angels and whatnot. Certainly, the defensiveness stems from different versions of the same wishful thinking, that we are more than the Big Bang and evolution—but part of us, somewhere deep down—suspects it's not true. The agnostic theist has the same fears and needs as the Christian, but his intellect and education have whittled away the stupid stuff. But, just like the Christian, he still can't face the prospect of absolute mortality. So, he clings to whatever hope his modern intellect can possibly endure. His intellect has corralled him into a corner, forcing him to make a claim to immortality that is difficult to discount, even by modern standards, because it's not really clear what his claim even says.

"Dr. Landers, why not leave these people alone?"

Because I believe it's critical to acknowledge that trading in God for some more ambiguous Energy that Binds Us doesn't solve many of the fundamental problems of Christianity. Most relevant for my book, it does nothing to address the magnitude of our suffering, the likes of "forcing the child to beg for the abuse to stop while perpetrator continues laughing." Subscribing to the Energy that Binds Us merely shifts responsibility from God/Jesus and places it elsewhere. If Bible God is not real but the Energy is, well, the Energy is now the one who is cruel, apathetic, or incompetent. Whatever's in charge, its approach to running the universe is wholly unacceptable, and our attempts to respect and defend it are insensitive and offensive. As far as I'm concerned, fuck you, too, Energy that Binds Us! Only when we regard *Nothing* as in charge can we truly be in touch with reality, and therefore fully authentic and respectful of existence.

It's been challenging to find people who seriously entertain a universe wholly devoid of transcendence. There seems to be a bit of a belief gradient even among atheists, some engaging in what almost feels like some sort of camouflaged spirituality. And it's not just lay-people. Towards the end of the highly recommended and otherwise sound *The End of Faith*, Sam Harris—one of the "Four Horsemen of the Atheistic Apocalypse"—argues that

> the truth is that we simply do not know what happens after death. While there is much to be said against a naive conception of a soul that is independent of a brain, the place of consciousness in the natural world is very much an open question. The idea that brains *produce* consciousness is little more than an article of faith among scientists at present . . . Consciousness may be a much more rudimentary phenomenon than are living creatures and their brains.[1]

That passage literally startled me; I had to re-read it several times to make sure I was consuming it correctly! But yes, I feel that Sam is committing a leap of faith that is not qualitatively different than that of the agnostic theist, or even Christian: That is, just because I don't have a *soul* doesn't mean that my *consciousness* is necessarily going to die. Such notions are simply the atheist's Heaven, motivated by the exact same Beckerarian fear of mortality that feeds formal religion, different only in that the behavior is more sustainable in a more edu-cated, skeptical mind.

I don't enjoy singling anyone out, especially Sam, whom I regard as an ally. He's obviously intelligent and he seems really friendly, if not sweet, at least for a famous atheist writer. Heck, he's kinda hand-some. But, he goes on to defend his notion of a non-biological con-sciousness by asserting *"And there appears to be no obvious way of rul-ing out such a thesis experimentally."* Italics added.

This is the mantra of the faithful, a violation of the most funda-mental tenet of science and logic—precisely what you had just spent

---

1 Pp. 208-209.

much of the rest of your great book criticizing! The tenet is that we can't make a claim that cannot be tested, then imply that the burden of proof lies on our opponent's side. My point: Until we have good evidence that consciousness continues after death, logically we have to assume, or at least be prepared for the possibility, that it doesn't. And we don't have good evidence that it does. I don't think we have any evidence at all, the closest thing being those ridiculous ghost shows on the otherwise awesome Discovery Channel. So, just like with Jesus, we have to resort to hope and faith.

One more jab and I'll leave Sam alone. Two paragraphs after asserting that there's no way to rule-out a non-biological explanation for consciousness, he discusses the exercise of conducting experiments on meditation and prayer and so on to help better understand consciousness. Sam *then* asserts "Such an enterprise becomes irrational only when people begin making claims about the world that cannot be supported by empirical evidence." Again, I have no desire to embarrass or humiliate anyone, but I was forced to discuss this in detail because it so exquisitely illustrates how even the most intelligent, educated, and open-minded people on Earth can also suspend their reason to defend against the fear of annihilation and nihilism.

Sam's in good company. Even Richard Dawkins confuses me in *The God Delusion* when he argues that his "Darwinism"—which I had assumed was the purist of evolutionary accounts of existence—should not be associated with nihilism.[2] I find the assertion confusing because I don't see how Darwinism can't be associated with nihilism! Mustn't the purist evolutionary account necessarily be nihilistic, at least to a degree?

Granted, the word *nihilism* has myriad connotations; it's not clear how Richard's using the term. (I tried to telephone him for clarification, but his secretary said he was out on some sort of hippie love-in with Sam Harris, sacrificing grain to the moon or something.) He seems to be primarily arguing that a world devoid of spirituality

---

2 *The God Delusion*, p. 213-214.

does not have to be a world devoid of joy—a point with which I wholeheartedly agree. However, at one point he suggests that he, too, believes in some sort of transcendence.

Richard shares a letter of protest sent to him by some doctor who writes with a "tormented" tone (indeed, uncannily similar to the judge I've quoted above from Camus's *The Stranger*). I don't need to reproduce the doctor's letter in its entirety here, as I'm more interested in Richard's response to it. Basically, the doctor had attacked Richard's Darwinistic position as unacceptable because it destroys hope and must therefore lead to distress and destruction. Richard responds, defending himself as not nihilistic, at one point by stating that the doctor is confused when he accuses Darwinism of "teaching that we . . . are annihilated when we die." Richard never elaborates what he himself believes happens when we die, but the clear implication is that it's something distinguished from annihilation. Now, I've seen enough of Richard's work to convince me that he doesn't believe in an afterlife of any sort, so I have to assume that he's referring to how we can survive through our good works and memories of us and such.

When I consider the permanence of my best works and fondest memories, I reflexively feel somewhat assured and warm inside—but only fleetingly. The comfort feels somewhat superficial and dramatic, and ultimately gives way to nagging feelings that I am—once again—being emotionally defensive against a harsher reality. It feels like I'm making a last-ditch effort for some semblance of immortality, all other attempts up to this point having failed: God, god, The Energy that Binds Us, and Sam Harris's disembodied consciousness-thing.

When I scrutinize the situation as openly and as honestly as I can, I end up finding little solace through my legacy. So sadly, even those more meaningful impressions that we do make on others will not survive for very long, in the grand scheme of things. I personally don't feel that I have a rich library of memories of most of my own grandparents, and I have literally no memories whatsoever of their parents. The people of two to three generations prior are well down the road to total annihilation. Critics will cite the gifted and talented people throughout history who have been able to change the world in a measurable way, but of course their numbers are infinitesimal relative to the rest of us, and even they've only changed the world; they haven't saved it, or themselves, for that matter. And of course, we have to acknowledge that there will be no memories of any sort eventually: Even if the human race does not prematurely destroy itself through war, overpopulation, or other ecological catastrophe, the earth will eventually be devoured by the cosmos. It's a matter of time before all evidence that humans ever existed is gone.

These thoughts are sad and quite uncomfortable; I honestly don't enjoy thinking about them myself. Part of me wants to exclude them from my book, but I can't, because this is what my book is about. Indeed, in my book about atheism, I am forced to assert that I actually agree, begrudgingly, that "Darwinism . . . is inherently nihilistic . . . and [it means that we] are annihilated when we die" (or shortly thereafter).

What happens if we take this plunge? It's hard to tell; most of us are so afraid that we'll be overwhelmed with sadness and despair that we avoid even entertaining such views as viable perspectives at all. We fear that we'll either spiral into a deep depression or lose control and run amok in the streets, raping and pillaging to make the best of what time we have left, since nothing really matters.

On the contrary, entertaining the notion can be profoundly edifying and liberating. Sure, it will be dark and depressing at times—as it should be—but the dark parts don't have to consume us. The truth may even enrich our lives in ways that the fantasies cannot.

Just as commonly as *Candide* is cited in books about atheism, Camus's *The Myth of Sisyphus* is often referenced in essays on the meaning of life. As a tribute, I'm going to cite Jeffery Olen's discussion, as he wrote the first philosophy textbook I ever picked up, *Persons and Their World*.[3] Unfortunately, I didn't read the final chapter from whence this came until many years had passed after I first bought the book in community college.

Recall that Sisyphus was the crafty Greek king who tricked the gods into releasing him from Greek hell, for which he was subsequently punished by having to roll a giant stone up a mountain for eternity, as each time he reached the summit, the stone would roll down the other side. Jeffery explains that Camus likened the human condition to the myth because, in the grand scheme of things, "our actions here on earth are as futile and pointless as the eternal task assigned to Sisyphus." He elaborates that Camus believed that "A world without God is a world without hope—for either an afterlife or a life in this world with ultimate meaning." If this most nihilistic assessment of reality is accurate, would life even be worth living?

Jeffery believes that Camus would say that it would:

> Since experiences are all we have, let us have as many as we can. Let us also live them heroically . . . without any hope or regret, without any illusions about their ultimate significance. Let us live them with the sense that we, and not any God, are the masters of our fate, and let us live them in revolt against false answers to the problem of life . . . That Sisyphus is an absurd hero to Camus is not surprising. What is surprising is this. Camus imagines Sisyphus happy as he walks down the mountain to begin pushing the rock back up. Why? Because he has made his own fate. And because he can scorn the gods and his own situation. And because he can continue to experience all that is around him. And because

---

3 Olen, J. (1983). *Persons and their world: An introduction to philosophy*. New York: Random House. The discussion and quotes that follow come from chapter 23 of the text, "The Meaning of Life," pp. 432-441.

he can go on without hope and regret. In short, because he fully understands his situation yet goes on.

So there it is.

For the first time in my life while studying and contemplating purported venues to a meaningful existence—from Christianity's God to our own legacies—I *finally* don't feel the nagging tugs of emotional defensiveness. I finally have something I can sink my teeth into and abide by without doubt, à la *cogito ergo sum*.

Life is not about faith or obsessing about the future, whether with hope or anxiety. It's about simply existing, with *courage, honesty,* and *authenticity.* These philosophers seem to believe that "What is the meaning of life?" is a silly question. There is no objective meaning to, no extrinsic purpose of, and no legitimate transcendence from the human condition. The most meaningful experience starts with facing this meaninglessness courageously!

I may not even need dreams to get by. I may not even have to aspire for a legacy at all. Perhaps if I live moments heroically, in the here and now, the legacy will take care of itself. And if it doesn't, perhaps my life is still valuable enough. I don't even have to be particularly productive, as long as I'm not destructive. Sure, I can still have aspirations if I want, but I shouldn't give them so much credit. My aspirations are not me, and they don't make my life any more worthwhile than my life without them. And they sure as heck aren't going to make me immortal.

Now, as much as I appreciate Camus's Sisyphean metaphor, I must dissent on one point. I'm reluctant to go as far as calling Sisyphus "happy"; I'm leaning more towards *resolved*. Indeed, it was apparently Sisyphus's passion for life on Earth that got him into this predicament in the first place; he must be longing for Earth while trudging up and down his hellish mountain. Sure, defiance (in lieu of hope?) is giving him strength, but I don't think there's any reason for him to feel "happy." I can't help but wonder if Camus himself was being overly optimistic in his assessment of Sisyphus's emotional state, perhaps in an effort to soothe himself! That's right: We should entertain whether Albert Camus was being emotionally defensive when he said, "One must imagine Sisyphus happy."[4]

In any event, Camus's contemporary, Bertrand Russell, seems to reflect his more general sentiment, as do so many atheist writers:

> In action, in desire, we must submit perpetually to the tyranny of outside forces; but in thought . . . we are free, free from our fellow men, free from the petty planet on which our bodies impotently crawl, *free even, while we live,* from the tyranny of death.[5]

Italics added. It's a beautiful perspective, paradoxically contrasted to the spiritual view. Instead of our earthly life being a "necessary evil" to trudge through while we await heaven, the tables are turned. When there is no hereafter, it's our consciousness of this life that is so magnificent and precious. As long as I'm not dead, I'm alive. This is the mantra of the faithless: The miracle is happening right now, and you're gonna miss it if you don't slow down and stop fantasizing about the future.

Russell adds that hostility towards our fate is not an optimal stance, as some have accused Camus of harboring (for example, note Jeffery's use of the words "revolt" and "scorn" above when discussing Sisyphus's motivations):

> But indignation is still a bondage, for it compels our thoughts to be occupied with an evil world . . . [In contrast,] the Stoic freedom in which wisdom consists is found in the submission of our desires but not of our thoughts . . . from the freedom of our thoughts springs the whole world of art and philosophy, and the vision of beauty by which, at last,

---

4 *The Myth of Sisyphus,* p. 123.

5 Russell, B. (2008). A free man's worship. In E. D. Klemke & S. M. Cahn (Eds.), *The meaning of life: A reader* (3rd ed., p. 57). New York: Oxford University Press.

we half reconquer the reluctant world. But the vision of beauty is possible only to unfettered contemplation, to thoughts not weighted by the load of eager wishes; and thus freedom only comes to those who no longer ask of life that it shall yield them any of those personal goods that are subject to the mutations of time.[6]

When Russell talks about subduing our "desires," he clearly is not referring to subduing our *passions*; he's talking about subduing our desperate *wants*, such as the objects of our superficial and unfulfilling materialism.

These attitudes of Camus and Russell illustrate an unexpected outcome of converting to atheism, and even to nihilism. We learn that hope is not necessary to proceed, as long as we have some *courage*. Now that our vision is no longer clouded by defenses, we see the truth more clearly: Hope does often disappoint, regardless of what the Bible says. No, we don't stop experiencing hopes altogether, just the irrational ones. We can embrace harsh assessments of reality and the human condition and keep moving forward nonetheless. Not only that, we learn to appreciate existence in its own right. We find every moment of life more precious than before, because "experiences are all we have" now. We lose our attraction to materialism and rat-racing, because we can now perceive them for what they are, clingy acts of desperation to avoid these thoughts—these nihilistic thoughts that won't kill us after all—and which may actually enrich us, to our amazement.

The simplicity of this approach is wonderful. It's accessible to everyone and takes little effort, just realization. Realization that you are a miracle, a conscious being who is able to witness, experience, and consume the universe, so much of which will never even be perceived by a sentient being. You don't really have to do anything else other than indulge that privilege, and just *be*; the one caveat being that you shouldn't *destroy*. The rat race for meaning ends here.

---

6 Ibid., p. 58.

I remember rationalizing when I was younger, still very immersed in Christianity but starting to doubt, that believing in God and following him was less risky than rejecting Him, regardless of whether he existed or not. If he was real, then of course I'd earn eternal life, which was indeed the plan that I felt was unfolding at the time. If—just for conversation's sake—I had been deceived and he wasn't real, then I'd still have led a wholesome life, and nothing would be lost. But I just don't see it like this anymore, as there is something to lose by believing in God when he isn't real: The deepest appreciation for life and existence that can only come with a nondefensive acknowledgment of its transience.

Besides acknowledging how life becomes more precious in general when it is no longer eternal, various philosophers have noted that the finitude of our lives has no bearing on the value of the specific things we do each day, both big and little. American philosopher Thomas Nagel:

> First, life does not consist of a sequence of activities each of which has as its purpose some later member of the sequence. Chains of justification come repeatedly to an end within life, and whether the process as a whole can be justified has no bearing on the finality of these end-points. No further justification is needed to make it reasonable to take aspirin for a headache, attend an exhibit of the work of a painter one admires, or stop a child from putting his hand on a hot stove. No larger context or further purpose is needed to prevent these acts from being pointless.[7]

---

7 Nagel, T. (2008). The absurd. In E. D. Klemke & S. M. Cahn (Eds.), *The meaning of life: A reader* (3rd ed., p. 144). New York: Oxford University Press.

Similarly, in a provocative blog entitled "Death and the Meaning of Life," a Keith Augustine cites the value of other finite tasks, such as working on political campaigns to having relationships with others to raising a child.[8] I know few parents who seem to believe that their experience of having raised a child is somehow less meaningful for them because the process had to effectively end.

We could go on forever, as virtually everything we do that makes up our human lives is temporary, regardless of whether the lives they constitute are eternal. Some more of my favorites are eating meals, hiking, going to school, working, visiting friends and family, vacationing . . . Transience is the nature of all human experience, and all non-human experience as well. Even the cosmos will die, eventually.

For a brief aside, Keith specifies an interesting incongruity: "If human beings were naturally immortal—that is, if there was no such thing as death—there would still be a question about whether or not lives had meaning." I agree, but I suspect that people would not be so obsessed with the question, and many would not be asking it at all. The question would not be so emotionally charged, that's for sure. We might be much less contemplative overall if there was no more death. It makes us wonder what exactly do people mean when they ask, "What is the meaning of life?" It seems that some may really mean something more like, "Why even continue living, knowing that I can't live forever?" Perhaps we're expressing a fear more than asking a question.

Well, if you subscribe to a religion, you don't have to ask the question, because not only do you believe in immortality but you are prescribed a meaning to your life: serving your god. For the religious, it should be enlightening to consider the scenario in which your religion was real but the immortality was not: Would you still care about serving god? Probably not so much, to put it lightly. It's be-

---

8 Augustine, K. (2000, December 2). Death and the meaning of life [Web blog post for The Secular Web]. Retrieved from http://www.infidels.org/kiosk/article55.html

cause worship and religion are less about serving God and more about earning eternal life. I suspect that very few people really want to serve a god. Most are just after the eternal life part.

I'm closing this section with lovable scholar of religion and myth Joseph Campbell:

> People say that what we're all seeking is a meaning for life. I don't think that's what we're really seeking. I think that what we're seeking is an experience of being alive, so that our life experiences on the purely physical plane will have resonances with our own innermost being and reality, so that we actually feel the rapture of being alive . . . this is it . . . this point now is the heavenly moment. [9]

In *Existential Psychotherapy*, Irvin Yalom outlines various ways in which even us secular folk can experience "meaning" in our lives, or, as I prefer, *value*. The first of two that I'd like to share is the *hedonistic solution*. No, he's not suggesting that we run amok in the streets masturbating, shoveling down pizza, and looting electronics stores. Instead, he quotes a college student who was asked to submit his obituary as an assignment for a philosophy course:

> Here I lie, found no meaning, but life was continuously astonishing. [10]

Very well put, kid! I would have given you an A+. Irvin elaborates:

---

9 Konner, J., Perlmutter, A. H. (Producers). (1988). *Joseph Campbell and the power of myth* (episode 6). [Television documentary miniseries]. US: Public Broadcasting Service.

10 *Existential Psychotherapy*, p. 436.

The purpose of life is, in this view, simply to live fully, to retain one's sense of astonishment at the miracle of life, to plunge oneself into the natural rhythm of life, to search for pleasure in the deepest possible sense . . . On this one point most Western theological and atheistic existential systems agree: *it is good and right to immerse oneself in the stream of life.*[11]

When Irvin Yalom (or anyone else) talks about living "fully" and immersing oneself in "the natural rhythm of life," we smile and nod but I'm not sure that we're always aware to what we're agreeing. Many people overestimate what needs to be done, as they assume that immersion involves frenetic or sensational activity, like traveling the world or skydiving. Sure, these may have their merits, but we don't have to set our sights so high. In fact, we might be missing the point when we do! If we truly appreciated the more fundamental aspects of living, we probably wouldn't be so driven to travel or skydive and such. We wouldn't be so *desperate* to do those things, that's for sure.

Instead, we're talking about appreciating the mere act of existing. Whenever we can do this, boredom becomes obsolete, as the most fundamental activities become worthy of our time and attention. Taking a walk. Marveling at nature: trees, birds, stars, your own consciousness. The simple fact that we are here at all, along with oceans, comets, Facebook, government conspiracies, and gridlock.

Once we learn to appreciate existence in its own right, so much else begins to seem trivial and superfluous, things like shopping, fancy cars, and even fashion and winning arguments. Other things become much more relevant and rewarding, things like bicycling, charity, ecology, and barbecuing with friends for football games. Overall, life simply becomes more precious, even more so than conceptualized in religious schemes. Although there is no objective *meaning* to life, its *value* is immeasurable.

---

11 Ibid., pp. 437 & 431.

Paradoxical to some, evolution may provide some guidance on how to live fully and immerse oneself into the natural rhythm of life. Natural selection has endowed us with fundamental drives and needs necessary for survival. Once we appreciate how non-trivial this process has been, we can find all the "meaning" we need in indulging them.

First, it's telling to consider that our evolutionary ancestors were probably not preoccupied with having a *meaningful, enriching,* or *exciting* life like so many of us are today. They probably didn't have the time to obsess over such matters; instead, their time and mental energies were necessarily focused on activities directly related to survival, such as finding food, caring for children, and ensuring shelter. When they did have downtime, they weren't being barraged with commercials advertising how much better off the rest of the world was, so they were never lured into rat-racing. Our evolutionary ancestors were living on a much more level and symbiotic playing field than we find ourselves today.

But what could be more fulfilling and rewarding than a life devoted to survival? Ironically, it seems that our modern craving to find a meaningful life is a bit of a function of—well, having a life that is *already fulfilled*! Again, I don't mind humbling myself to illustrate: I'm quite sure I wouldn't be so obsessed with writing this book if I was hungry and wondering where I was going to sleep tonight. I'm writing because I *do* have a roof and food in the fridge, and therefore a lot of time on my hands, which makes me restless. In fact, I have so much time on my hands that I spend too much time thinking. And when I think too much, I sometimes feel scared or empty or small. So, I'm writing—and doing so many other things—to feel full and significant.

All is not lost. We don't have to force ourselves into poverty or abandon projects like book writing and such. But the more we can resonate with our evolutionarily endowed needs, the more we can take some of the pressure off and ease the desperation.

Assuming our basic needs for food and shelter are met, we can

reach the next level of fulfillment through social interaction and belonging. Evolution honed humans as social creatures: We were simply more fit to survive together versus alone. Today, however, our
world is so luxurious that we no longer need others to survive so, for
one reason or another, some of us gravitate to solitude—and this is
our undoing; this is why we feel so empty. For many who do engage
the company of others, they just don't appreciate the significance
and magnitude of what is transpiring: that they are in the process of
surviving. The irony is that when we're sitting around with our
friends conversing about the meaning of life, maybe even feeling
frustrated and unsettled because we can't agree upon a satisfying
answer, the meaning of life is unfolding right there at that moment!
If your stomach is full and y'all have a safe place to sleep later, and
this person who you're with cares enough about you to pay attention
to you and help you when you need it, *you have arrived.* It's happening. You are there, living a full life. Demanding much more is being
greedy, and actually spoils the beautiful simplicity that's literally
right in front of our stupid faces. I like to imagine this is what Voltaire meant in the last line of *Candide* by (spoiler alert!): "Now, let's
tend to our gardens." Let's just live, and survive, and do what we
need to do to eat. It will work best if we work together, and depend
on one another, and appreciate each other for it. Let's have communion, and marvel at the indescribable magnificence of nature and the
cosmos (without having to posit gods behind it, now that we know
better).

In light of the sentiment that prosocial interpersonal engagement
is as fundamental to human survival as eating and sexing, it's not
surprising that of all the routes to meaning that Irvin Yalom outlines,
"both religious and secular, none seemed more important than
altruism."[12]

He describes Eva, a woman dying of cancer who "found meaning until the end of her life in the fact that her attitude toward her

---

12 Ibid., pp. 431-433.

death could be of value to many other patients," those "who might be able to use Eva's zest for life and courageous stance toward death as a model for their own living and dying." She volunteered on a hospital ward for terminally ill children, was in a support group for patients with metastatic cancer, and even seemed to administer some informal but productive psychotherapy to her own oncologist, a "cold, steel-spectacled man," softening his defenses and allowing him to experience some previously hidden emotion with her before she left us.

Now, we have to be careful so that if we do find some good in suffering we don't become so overwhelmed with cheer that we forget that the context is suffering. Just because Eva was able to cope with the cruelty of nature doesn't make the cruelty worthwhile. I would be thoroughly offended if someone would suggest—and they certainly would, at least implicitly—that Eva's purpose, the meaning of her life, was to counsel fellow cancer patients. On the contrary, I suspect even Eva might have rather done without the cancer and her associated ministry if she had had a choice. She may have had several more decades in which to do nothing but knit and spend time with her grandkids. Sure, not as sensational of a story, but at least she could have had more life. And being tender with your grandchildren—that's meaningful, too. Eva didn't need cancer to demonstrate her value. I suspect most of us would rather be alive and uninspiring than inspirational and gone.

Another reason we have to be careful not to overemphasize the silver linings of such tragedies is that we don't want to ostracize the countless other victims who are unable to find meaning in theirs, whether it be cancer, natural catastrophe, trauma, mental illness, or poverty. Many victims are unable to make the best of it, and do not die courageously but instead debilitated with fear. While we're happy for Eva for finding strength, we should simultaneously validate the experiences of those who are unable to cope. The weak victim is no less of a person. Indeed, he may warrant our attention more than the Evas of the world.

CHAPTER 10

What Does a Nihilist Look Like?

But there are far better reasons for self-sacrifice than those that religion provides. The fact that faith has motivated many people to do good things does not suggest that faith is itself a necessary (or even a good) motivation for goodness. It can be quite possible, even reasonable, to risk one's life to save others without believing any incredible ideas about the nature of the universe. By contrast, the most monstrous crimes against humanity have invariably been inspired by unjustified belief.

— Sam Harris, *The End of Faith*

IN MY LATE TWENTIES, as I began to accept that I was an atheist—and later, a nihilist—I underwent some interesting changes and began to experiment with some disturbing behavior. I started drinking more and tinkering with relatively hard drugs again. I began to dabble in antisocial behavior, even committing *theft* a few times, most notably that of a watch from a Dillard's tagged at something on the order of $150. One day I viciously keyed a car in the post office parking lot, just because it was there, and nicer than mine. Most embarrassingly, I became preoccupied with masturbation—even more so than I had been during puberty! I'll save the details of the progression for some other book and just cut to the chase: But yes—I still have no satisfactory explanation for this—I became sexually fascinated with the idea of *death* and *corpses*. This culminated to a point where I would go to the city limits and find animal *roadkill*, of all things, and bring it home in a plastic grocery bag. Later, when the urge had gelled—I can't believe I'm publishing this—I would hold the lifeless creature while I—

Oh, stop. I'm kidding. Nothing really changed as I began to identify with nihilism. In fact, I simply continued along the same path of ethical maturation that I had already begun a lifetime before. In general, I'm only an adult version of the ultra-hypersensitive kid I told you about in chapter 3. However, by far, I have actually become more stable, moral, content, and sane than I ever have been before—particularly compared to when I had identified myself as a Christian with a cosmic purpose. Hence, the punchline: If I had died when Christian—which was likely, given my risk-taking behavior at the time—I would have died miserable but gone to Heaven. Now I get to die much more peacefully, but I have to go to Hell.

The truth is, my substance use has slowed to a crawl, limited to sporadic marijuana episodes, which I have regarded as quite an adventure as opposed to the frivolous event it used to be when I was Christian. As an atheist, I've literally gone years at a time without touching it. Whenever I've ended up with a bag to call my own, I've rarely been able to finish it and end up giving it away. No kidding, I had this one hilarious bag for about seven years, making me the object of ridicule for my stoner friends. It was so dry by the time a guest finally finished it off in 2010 that the buds were literally collapsing under their own weight. Time had apparently made it very harsh, as believe you me, that bag did not go gentle into the good night. There was a large amount of violent coughing and retching, the likes of which I hope I never have to hear again; I thought I was gonna have to give her CPR. Despite all that, it still worked . . . according to legend.

I don't get really drunk anymore, either. I mean, I suspect my blood alcohol level is at legally intoxicated levels about once or twice a month, but I don't get trashed these days. And, as with smoking, I don't drive if I go out to drink; I ride my bike. It's so much nicer to be outside on a bike instead of cooped up even more illegally and dangerously in a car. Otherwise, I haven't even touched (or seen) harder drugs in decades.

And about the masturbation, it's nothing to write home about, either. Like my drug use, it had ironically been most problematic when I was relatively spiritual, at one point arguably bordering on addiction. It was easy to become addicted to porn, back in the good ol' days, when all internet websites were free and there was no advertising, so you could just run wild for hours on end, touring the world's naked people and all the incredible things they will do to get off.

For the record, even at my worst, I was only drawn to the really hard, bizarre stuff for academic reasons. A psychologist at heart for most of my life, absolutely, I've been fascinated by coprophagia and bestiality and so forth, but that kind of porn never stimulated me sexually. On the contrary, I've been slightly traumatized by some of that. The problems that I did begin to experience from more traditional porn were two related issues: chronic libidinal agitation and the objectification of women. Now, at least at the time of this writing, I honestly believe that the internet porn phenomenon actually began somewhat healthily. That is, ready access to porn, particularly the amateur stuff, convinced me that many of the women I would have previously disregarded while clothed were actually more attractive than I had been assuming. No kidding, I think amateur pornography helped me lower my unreasonably high standards.

Alas, it kinda got outta control, and I found myself more preoccupied about potential nakedness than I wanted to be. Eventually, the creepiness of compulsively undressing everyone with my eyes began to overwhelm any benefits. Fortunately—after I had become a devout atheist—I became more able to appreciate what "objectifying" women means, because I realized I was doing it, and I was ashamed. Not only does it disregard others and make them uncomfortable—if not scared—it also degrades *me* and the quality of my life. Objectifying women makes me superficial, and keeps me from being present with others and connecting with them in an authentic, healthy manner. Bottom line, I don't look at porn much anymore. When I do, it's just the most basic Playboy-like stuff. And for the record, yes, my libido has been diminishing to more manageable, natural levels. Still a way to go, but it's happening.

A third addiction that has become more manageable as an atheist compared to when I was spiritual is sports. Like drugs and libido, sports fandom is now something I have, whereas it used to have me. I can still remember sitting at a bar somewhere on Sixth Street in downtown Austin, back in 1992 long before it became the Jersey Shore, and watching then-lowly TCU beat Texas for the first time in decades (yes, we're talking football here). I remember being so overwhelmed and pissed-off, and cursing as viciously as I ever had, at least in public.

During a particularly bitter tirade, I spotted this girl sitting with her friends over on the other side of the bar, and I'll never forget the look on her face: It was pity, tinged with a little fear. My hostile dysphoria was disturbing her. Seeing her seeing me felt like a slap in the face and kinda quieted me for the moment, but I'd continue to get pissy like that for quite some time.

However, after I got a few years of atheism under my belt, I really matured in this regard. For instance, I coped so much better years later at "Route 66" when Bob Toledo and his UCLA goons, Cade McNown, Skip Hicks, and Danny Farmer came to Austin in 1997. They pummeled our asses in our worst game since *1904*. The final score was 66-3, having already been a surreal 45-0 at the half. But David Landers—devout atheist by the time—stayed for the duration because he didn't want to be a fair-weather fan. I distinctly remember thinking: If my team can't leave, I'm not going to, either. So, I and my friend Tom stood there among the other tens of fans remaining and sang *The Eyes of Texas* at the end of the game with the humiliated Ricky Williams, Casey Hampton, Leonard Davis, and Shaun Rogers. (That's right, football fans: Those guys were on the same college team. More rumbling beef than the Fort Worth stockyards . . . broken that day, but each would rise again in gridiron glory.)

Ernest Becker might have argued that we can be so emotional about sports because our team is a culture upon which we rely for a sense of belonging and esteem, and maybe even to help us feel bigger and better than we really are. I'm pretty sure I was doing something along those lines back when I was a "spiritual" person (ironically). Now that I see through that need to feel big it has lost its grasp on me. Atheism has helped by grounding me in other ways as well. For example, now that I am more acutely aware of the suffering in the world, it has simply become impossible to get so worked up over something that is intended to be recreation. Don't get me wrong: I still love spectating sports. It's just that they no longer have the capacity to ruin my day (or weekend, or following week).

Today, as a self-described nihilist, I still get all sappy and teary-eyed every year when ESPN plays Jimmy V's speech during their celebratory week named in the coach's honor. And I live for those emotional stories they do on athletes' off-the-field humanitarian accomplishments. While working on this chapter recently, I was watching the 2012 Fiesta Bowl when they did a piece on Justin Blackmon, the receiver for Oklahoma State University at the time. He had formed a relationship with a nine-year-old cancer patient after they met at some charity event. I cried when I saw it . . . and I just cried again when I watched the piece on Youtube to remind myself of how it went down. Oops, I just cried a third time looking at it again while editing. It's the part where the little girl says at the end, "He's awesome, he's an awesome player, and I care about him, too, and I love him."[1]

---

1 Hostile critics will reflexively focus on the substance use problems Justin has had since joining the NFL. If that's your reaction, you should examine yourself: You may be *splitting*, that is, unable to reconcile both the good and the negative traits in a person (as discussed previously in chapter 6).

It's also around Tebow-mania time. There was a similar piece on Tim Tebow recently, and I cried during that one, too. It doesn't bother me that Tim is religious; I appreciate his actions the same. I have no idea whether Justin is religious, but I'm just pretending for a moment that he's not (I think we can assume he's less religious than Tim, at least!). The point that I want to convey is that, as a spectator, I love what each of these guys is doing, regardless. Atheism hasn't diminished my capacity to be touched by selfless human behavior as such. Nihilism hasn't either. No, I don't believe that I or anyone else has been put on Earth for any specific reason, which actually makes what Justin and Tim have done more beautiful than otherwise. I like to think they are two people who feel compelled to do those things just because they see the suffering of others and realize they can alleviate some of it. Not necessarily because God said they should, but because they want to, all on their own.

Now, if I was spiritual, I'd be crying the same way, but there would be an element in which I would be chalking up at least some of my feelings to God's grace or something. Instead, I see something more pure and *real*, a man behaving selflessly when he doesn't have to. Now that's humanity, when there are no spirits involved.

At least on paper, perhaps the most objectively salient improvement in my life that seems to have corresponded with my transition to atheism was the loss of the panic attacks. As I've said before, I can't attribute the healing to my spiritual transition altogether, given that I was in traditional treatment, but the coincidence is difficult to ignore. The bottom line is that I was panicking when I believed in spirituality, and around the time I gave it up the panicking stopped.

But I have to be honest: Although the panic is gone, I'm still quite neurotic. However, it's usually in ways that tend to respect and soothe the cosmos, as opposed to oppress it. It's pretty obvious to me that I'm the greatest victim of my neuroses.

I'm so sensitive toward animals that I have a very hard time even killing bugs and will go way out of my way to avoid it. When I find one in my apartment, I almost always catch it and place it outside, safely. Whenever even a bee or a wasp gets inside (which seems oddly frequent at times), I don't kill it; I catch it with a jar and cardboard and set it free. Recently I accidentally maimed one while attempting this, and it totally made me sad! I placed it carefully on the patio, like a little kid might, hoping it might somehow reattach its thorax if left alone, but it didn't. I also recently killed a fly in my apartment—this time with the full intent of doing so—but reflexively responded by verbalizing aloud, "Awww!" I sounded like a teenage girl confronted with a lion killing a zebra on the Discovery Channel. And no, I don't like watching that stuff, either. It totally freaks me out, and I have to look away.

So yes, this nihilist would kill a fly, but he'd feel bad about it. And it's not about being a hippie or a Hindi or part of any other population that's pro-animal. I simply don't like to destroy anything that's alive. It just feels wrong to frivolously snuff out the miracle of life, regardless of what medium it's in. The Big Bang is behind that fly, and millions of years of evolution and now it has the magic of life. It's wrong for me to crush it. I'm big, it's little, and once it's gone, it's gone forever. I'd rather just let it be and see what the Big Bang has in store for it later.

I have a habit of making U-turns in traffic and stopping at the side of the road to rescue animals who have ventured on or too close. And I'm not just talking about kitties: In recent memory, I saved (at least temporarily) a turtle, a tarantula, and a very large snake, the latter a good five feet or so in length—and it was not co-operating! It hissed at me, struck its best cobra-pose, and rattled its tail on the ground to try to scare me. I know enough about snakes to realize that it wasn't poisonous, that it was putting on a show, but neither was I gonna let its nonpoisonous mouth molest me. So, I grabbed the only elongated object I could find—the Rock-Chalk Jayhawk umbrella from the trunk of my car—and spent about 15 minutes coaxing the dumb fucking thing to retreat to a neighboring field. I honestly remember feeling sad afterwards, realizing that it was going through all that rigmarole because it was scared, and I don't want to be the agent of *anything's* fear, especially something so helpless that I could easily have killed it, if I had wanted. Having the capacity to dominate something feels awful to me; I don't want any part of that experience. To this day I simply cannot give my cat medicine because I can't tolerate forcing myself upon something that is necessarily gonna fight back, and lose. Most of the veterinarians I've met think I'm a total pussy. They don't say it, but I can tell.

I know: It's absurd, and I'm embarrassed . . . but it gets worse. When I jog, I find myself frustrated at the little flocks of birds who fly away because I'm coming through. It's especially frustrating because I don't want them wasting their energy on me, but the little shits will fly off, only to land further down the same trail in the same direction I'm heading, so they have to keep taking off again as I proceed. Dude—just go perpendicular a bit, not parallel, and we'll be done with it!

I don't like to make people uncomfortable, either. It's so bad I can't even watch it. I don't enjoy a lot of sitcoms because the topic is often about someone being embarrassed. Just now, I had *King of Queens* on in the background while working (I'm not a fan! I only caught the end while waiting for the Heat/Knicks to come on), and the episode was about the husband getting coerced into roasting his boss or something and he doesn't want to do it. He gets on the stage, and it's going badly, no one is laughing—and I literally had to change the freaking channel, for that reason. I'm not kidding; embarrassment is not funny to me. It kinda hurts to watch. I've always been this way. I loved *Gilligan's Island* as a kid but often strained over the inevitable. My favorite episodes were the unusual ones in which Gilligan didn't fuck something up.

In public, I walk slowly around old people because I don't want to make them uncomfortable, being some young whipper-snapper bustling about who might bump into them. I hate playing competitive games, video or board, because I don't enjoy winning much more than losing. I still like games like horseshoes, though, probably because the activity itself is more salient than who wins.

Yes, being overly concerned about the welfare of others contributes to loneliness. In addition to the cliché narcissistic fear of rejection, I also have an equally strong, if not stronger, fear of rejecting others. I often don't make a move because I'm afraid I'll be disappointed, and I don't want to expose her to that, especially if I think she likes me. So, like board games, I typically end up not playing at all. Frivolous sex hasn't been very rewarding, either. It's a catch-22 for me: I love the fantasy of a passionate one-night stand, but I don't find myself attracted to most women who would indulge them. I'm not judging people who do; I just feel like I have more traditional feminine ideas about sex, that the best kind is the emotional kind, with some sort of attachment distilled over time.

I can typically find some sympathy for just about anyone, even some people who most Americans find unsightly, including some fairly alarming and violent criminals. Staff down at the county jail recently told me that I've got a bit of a reputation for being able to complete evaluations with relatively hostile psychotic defendants. But I don't have magical powers. I'll tell you my trick: I care about them and their predicaments, and I just let enough of that show so they can tell. Like I teach my students, just because someone is crazy doesn't mean he's stupid. Many crazy people can tell when someone's concern is legitimate, and they often respond accordingly, just like anyone else (not always, so again, tread with caution).

In my psychology practice, I always charge less than my colleagues, sometimes on the order of half. I do this not only because I feel sorry for my examinees, but also because I'm a socialist, and I even kinda like the idea of communism, at least in theory. (Yet I remain mindful of the words of the immortal Yogi Berra: "In theory, there is no difference between theory and practice. But in practice, there is.") In a capitalist society, professionals abuse the public financially, to put it lightly, and I just don't want to be a part of that machine.

At the grocery store, I get my shopping basket from the parking lot, not from inside the store, because I want to do a favor for the pimply teen who has to fetch these things. If I come across a car with its lights left on in the parking lot, I'll turn them off, if it's unlocked (I'm surprised how often they are; what's wrong with you people?). If the door is locked and I can't fix it myself, I write down the license plate and report it to someone in charge. Inside the store, I pick up stuff that other people have dropped in the aisle. When I check out, I always take off my headphones so I can be present during the interaction with the cashier lady.

I'm always picking up trash, not just at the grocery store, but on hiking trails, sidewalks, wherever. If I'm driving past trash in the road that's too big for me to handle, I'm one of those concerned citizens who calls the police. I recycle almost obsessively, often carrying a can around with me for hours until I can find a proper receptacle. I must look hilarious while jogging because I might have a beer bottle in my hand that I picked up earlier down the trail. I know the world is gonna be destroyed eventually no matter what I do, but it's the principle of the matter.

I'm a regular blood donor and am on the national marrow registry. I sponsor a hungry kid in Africa through *Save the Children.* And I don't complain much about my own food. When I'm dining out and find a hair on my plate, I pull it out, show it to whomever I'm with, and keep eating. I think it's mind boggling that we don't find more shit in our food than we do! I despise the mentality of the kind of person who freaks out about such things, as if it's a long-awaited opportunity to raise hell. Like some kind of obnoxious hippie, I don't have a chance to get mad at the hair because my thoughts immediately go to hungry people and I'd feel like an unappreciative asshole for bitching. I've never sent something back because it wasn't what I ordered. And no, I don't think it's the cosmos trying to enrich my life by getting me to try something new. Someone just fucked up, like we all do, and I'm not gonna let the food go to waste. Now, I'm not crazy: If the food is cold, I'll send it back for a warm-up, but insist they don't start over. Nuke it—don't you dare throw that out!

Some Christians and meaning-mongers would be surprised that a foul-mouthed atheist is easily touched by romantic movies, especially the ones with transcendental/spiritual gobbledy-goo. When I was a Christian not long out of high school, of course I cried at the end of *Ghost*. But even in college, as I began dabbling in atheism, I still cried at the end of *Far and Away* (I'm so embarrassed to admit that, but of course this chapter is all about self-disclosure). And very recently, as a full-blown nihilist, I cried the hardest at the end of *Cherry Blossoms*. The latter is probably less well known to the mainstream, being German, but like many American movies, it's about love, death, and transcendence. In any event, this might be one of my favorite movies of all time, and it moves me in a way that is almost unsettling. I ended up buying the DVD, and am currently awaiting, eagerly, until I feel like it's been long enough to watch it again. In the meantime, whenever I want to feel all mushy inside, I watch the trailer on the internet.

It's not just me. In the documentary *The Four Horsemen*, Richard Dawkins expresses a surprising sentiment. He explains that he

once did a British radio program called Desert Island Discs, where you have to go on and choose your six records which you take to a desert island and talk about it. And one of the ones I chose was *Bach Mache dich, mein Herze, rein.* It's wonderful sacred music and the woman questioning me couldn't understand why I would wish to have this piece of music [because it's pious] . . . It's beautiful music and its beauty is indeed enhanced by knowing what it means. But you still don't actually have to believe it. It's like reading fiction. You can lose yourself in fiction, and be totally moved to tears by it, but nobody would ever say you've got to believe that this person existed and that the sadness that you feel really reflected something that actually happened.[2]

I've read two of Richard's books and lightly perused a third, and this is my favorite sentiment of his I've encountered so far. It raises a lot of poignant questions about the distinction between fiction and reality and the capacities for each to affect us in a meaningful way.

I like classical music sometimes, but am far from versed enough to add to Richard's assessment. I have some favorite pieces, but I couldn't name them, and I certainly wouldn't know who composed them without researching it. But I can tell you that I have a very similar experience when I hear—wait for it—Elvis sing *An American Trilogy.* Every time he belts out "Glory, Glory, Hallelujah," I get chills, like clockwork.

One morning after I had been editing this section of my book, I woke up pondering these issues and lay in bed for a while fading in and out of sleep, thinking about which songs I would take to my deserted island. I paged through my favorite genres and when I got to spiritual-songs-that-are-emotionally-provocative, *O, Holy Night* stood out. I got out of bed, poured my coffee, and searched for renditions on Youtube, still in my pajamas, teeth not brushed yet. I

---

2 Upper Branch Productions (Producer) & Timonen, J. (Director). (2009). *The four horsemen.* Richard Dawkins Foundation for Reason & Science. You can watch the two episodes for free at https://richarddawkins.net/

tried Whitney Houston's first, as I've always been drawn to her and her voice, but the video was a little too cheesy and I felt her version apparently wasn't intended to be the passionate type I was looking for. So, I Googled the "most powerful rendition" of the song, and Celine Dion's name seemed to pop up quite a bit. Back on Youtube, I chose her video that includes the lyrics so you can read along. When I played it—no kidding—I cried harder than I had in some time, so much so I had to get a paper towel to blow my blubbering nose!

Something deep is obviously happening here, but I'm quite sure it has nothing to do with God being real, at least for me. In the moment, what did cross my mind—or more like my heart—was more akin to Ernest Becker's discussions about our need, our *longing*, to have hope against annihilation. I was longing for God to be real, to hold me because no one else ever did adequately when I was growing up. Indeed, the whole thing felt a whole lot like when Patsy touched me at camp. Contacting the longing prompts a cathartic release of pent-up pain, and that feels good.

There are all sorts of entire books exploring why gods and bibles are not necessary to lead a moral life, including *Can We be Good without God*; *Ethics without God*; *Good without God*; *Sense and Goodness without God*; and . . . *The Moral Landscape*. Most of the more general books about atheism have at least a chapter on the topic. Despite how much believers may think bibles are necessary for society to function, we atheists find the notion absurd.

I actually haven't read most of the books I've listed above, largely because I don't need any more convincing, having experienced firsthand the transition from Christian to atheist without any apparent deterioration in my morals (which, I suspect, have been average, at worst). Again, if anything, I've become more moral since becoming atheist.

Otherwise, it simply seems self-evident that morality is a *human* trait and not contingent upon religion or its manuscripts.

Morality is necessarily in our genes. Humans are social creatures—we are not parasites, nor are we so-called solitary animals like cougars and bears and skunks. Social species, by definition, cannot exist without morality—they are social! If it had not been for naturally selected altruism and social cohesion the world never would have become so civilized to write the Holy Bible in the first place. As Christopher Hitchens said, "Human decency is not derived from religion. It precedes it."[3] Or, as I like to say, "Morality was the chicken that laid the egg of Christianity."

Some of the most magnificent civilizations in history, like Greek, Egyptian, and Chinese, were erected long before anyone even uttered the name "Jesus Christ," in vain or otherwise. And many others have been erected since, like Mayan and Aztec, but in geographical isolation so that they never heard of the Golden Rule of the Holy Bible, either—but they apparently lived according to some version of it anyway. Of course, none of these societies were perfectly moral, but I don't suspect they were particularly immoral compared to the average Holy Bible-reading society throughout history. For example, I've been taught slavery had a role in building some (if not all) of those ancient societies, but of course it also had a role in building America—and much more recently! And I *don't* recall ever learning that the Bible had a major role in abolition in this country; if anything, as we discussed earlier, the Bible seems to condone slavery. No, I suspect that abolition was driven more by the increasing intellectualization of American society, just like abolition has been driven in other non-Christian nations as well. And I suspect that the world is destined for increasingly moral behavior as time goes on, not because of bibles, but because of advancing intellect, awareness, and the extinction of secrecy.

Careful scrutiny suggests that bibles are not particularly good

---

3 *God is Not Great,* p. 266.

guides for ethical behavior. As we've been discussing, they very often simply assert rules that most of us are already hard-wired to follow. It's not like murder was relatively rampant before the sixth commandment of the Holy Bible was published and then significantly declined afterwards. Again, speaking from experience, I've met quite a few people who have killed before and I can say with confidence that murderers aren't the least bit concerned about laws—whether from penal codes or scriptures—when they commit their crimes. When most killers kill, they're on a different mental plane than the one that considers rules and punishment. I suspect that very, very few people throughout history on the verge of killing someone somehow changed their minds at the last minute because they were reminded of the sixth commandment.

Another reason many commandments don't work in practice is because they are sweeping statements too broad for widespread applicability. Reality is too complicated and nuanced for rules like this; judging others or even killing them has to be justified, under some circumstances. Ergo, some subjectivity in interpreting the rules is not just allowed but becomes imperative. And when subjectivity becomes an imperative part of interpreting a moral code, that moral code loses a lot of its utility. As we've already explored in this book, recall that the Holy Bible in particular demands so much subjectivity that we have to decide which rules have expired and must be disregarded *entirely* (again, I find those condoning slavery and the oppression of women glaring examples).

And the punchline: For those commandments that just don't suit us and our peers, we simply ignore them, unashamedly. Even in this God-fearing country, with some of the most radical Christians on Earth, adultery is rampant—literally a part of our culture, commonplace fodder for television sitcoms, dramas, reality shows, and news stories. Coveting is another American pastime, as our capitalist society continuously indoctrinates us to believe that we need things that we don't. Largely for this reason, keeping the Sabbath day holy is a long-lost tradition, Sunday now being an important day for indulgence—because we have to spend so much of the rest of our time working in order to stay ahead!

No, I don't find the Holy Bible to be a very useful guide at all. I'm not even sure if I did when I was a Christian kid just beginning to explore the world of ethics. What I do recall, in retrospect, is feeling validated whenever I read commandments, rules, or directions that simply resonated with what I already felt was right. Now *that's* what bibles are good for: allowing us to nod and smile and feel assured that we're good (good enough anyway), that we're behaving as our divinities desire (at least much of the time). Overall, it seems that bibles are not as much about directing us to immortality as they are about giving us hope that we're already en route.

To end the suspense, recent research does corroborate the suspicion that ethical behavior is not contingent upon religiosity. Wilhelm Hofmann and colleagues monitored the ethical experiences of over 1200 adults, some who identified themselves as religious, others who did not.[4] Participants were summoned via their smartphones at five random times every day for three days, at which points they documented whether they had committed a moral act within the previous hour. Among many other interesting things that you can read for yourself, the researchers found that "religious and nonreligious people commit comparable moral and immoral deeds and with comparable frequency." I suspect this is surprising to many non-atheists, but perhaps it shouldn't be.

Imagine a catastrophic scene in a city, where, for example, an earthquake or other disaster causes a building to collapse. Of those nearby left unharmed, are the Christians rushing more quickly than the atheists to help? My gut just says no, which the research seems to validate. One difference might be, though, that in the aftermath the Christians would be inclined to attribute their heroic efforts to their spirituality, while the atheists would attribute it to nothing, or perhaps simply to fundamental human duty. The Christian rein-

---

4 Hofmann, W., Wisneski, D. C., Brandt, M. J., & Skitka, L. J. (2014). Morality in everyday life. *Science, 345*, 1340-1343.

forces his spiritual beliefs by assuming a connection between his beliefs and his heroism when there really isn't one, not realizing that nonbelievers were working right there alongside him the whole time.

On that note, Hofmann and colleagues also found that the religious participants in their study, compared to the nonreligious, did indeed have stronger psychological reactions to their behaviors. Specifically, they

> experienced more intense self-conscious emotions such as guilt, embarrassment, and disgust in response to the immoral deeds they had committed, and more pride and gratefulness in response to moral deeds.

The scientists are not saying that the nonreligious were guilt- or pride-free, just that the religious felt these emotions more intensely. Presumably, these superfluous emotions of the religious stem from them attaching greater significance to their moral and immoral behaviors—that is, they believe on some level that their behaviors are relevant for their immortality. One has to wonder if this creates a cycle that feeds itself, so that the strong emotional reaction reinforces the belief that the behaviors have cosmic significance. The punchline is, of course, the dynamic is purely a subjective experience and has no practical utility (for example, it apparently does not increase moral behavior).

British philosopher Colin McGinn might argue that the emotional experiences of the religious can actually be deleterious, somehow distracting them and robbing them of a more authentic experience—if not even making morality more tumultuous than it needs to be overall. In *The Atheism Tapes*, he shares the provocative anecdotal observation that people who have abandoned religion find moral behavior easier to come by than they had anticipated:

> And in fact it was better, because there's a corrupting part to that conception of God, which is the idea that you're doing

something good because God will reward you and think well of you. And that's a corrupting idea. It's much better to do what's good *because it's good*, and only because it's good, and that's your only reason for doing it. But the idea you're going to get the warm fuzzy feeling, "Oh, God's really pleased with me today, you know, I did this," that's not what morality ought to be about.[5]

Absolutely: Commandments are, by definition, superficial. Morality shouldn't be about obligation—that cheapens it, no matter how "good" you are. Following commandments because they're commandments is servile, not moral. Many atheists argue that the moral atheist is more moral than the moral Christian, because she exercises her morality on a deeper level. Christians talk about earning rewards in heaven, but atheists are moral for its own sake, right here on Earth, with no secondary gain.

It's also interesting to note that the schemes of commandments presented in bibles are reminiscent of what psychologists call the *authoritarian* parenting style, the "Do this because I told you so" approach. As any introductory psychology text will explain, this is the unhealthy way to raise children, relative to the *authoritative* parenting style that does not merely direct our behavior but counsels us on the pros and cons of how we behave. Sure enough, as secular households are becoming more popular in this country, scientific data are coming in to show that

secular teenagers are far less likely to care what the "cool kids" think, or express a need to fit in with them, than their religious peers. When these teens mature into "godless" adults, they exhibit less racism than their religious counterparts . . . Many psychological studies show that secular

---

5 Denton, R. (Producer & Director). (2004). *The Atheism Tapes* (Colin McGinn episode). [Television documentary miniseries]. UK: British Broadcasting Corporation.

grownups tend to be less vengeful, less nationalistic, less militaristic, less authoritarian and more tolerant, on average, than religious adults.[6]

Morality should involve contemplation, analysis, and open-minded consultation with others, not reflexive allegiance to a system that has already proven itself unreliable. Besides being outdated, the Bible's contradictory advice inhibits deliberation because it allows us to reflexively appeal to whichever rule we prefer. If we don't want to associate with sinners (such as by serving homosexuals at our restaurant), we cite 1 Corinthians 15:33: "Bad company corrupts good morals." However, if we do want to associate with sinners as such, we focus on how Jesus justified dining with them in Mark 2:17: "It is not those who are healthy who need a physician, but those who are sick; I did not come to call the righteous but sinners." And just as we shouldn't reflexively depend on the Bible, we shouldn't automatically defer to our parents or cultures—whether religious or not—because they've obviously been wrong, too.

Don't be afraid to engage the turmoil of ethical deliberation! When I was Christian, I recall as recently as an undergraduate in college, I had a very adamant anti-abortion stance, bordering on belligerent. (And yes, I'm quite certain that my rigidity was driven more by concerns related to my own immortality than to the life of a fetus.) In any event, once I converted to atheism, I experienced an obnoxious polar shift to the other side and became an outspoken abortion proponent—again bordering on belligerent. I would caustically joke about getting pregnant just so I could exercise my right to abort. I fantasized about making a bumper sticker asserting, "I used to be pro-choice, but now I'm not: ALL babies should be aborted!"

6 Zuckerman, P. (2015, January 14). How secular family values stack up. *Los Angeles Times*. Retrieved from http://www.latimes.com/opinion/op-ed/la-oe-0115-zuckerman-secular-parenting-20150115-story.html

Today, I'm proud to announce that I've stopped the emotionally defensive splitting and instead sit restlessly atop the abortion fence. Of course, I'm not compelled by any sort of spiritual reason whatsoever. But, as with any life, I simply find a human fetus a miracle of nature and I'm uncomfortable with the idea of destroying it. And of course, I find that fetus much more valuable than any other animal that I don't want to kill needlessly, whether a fly or a dolphin or anything else, because I appreciate what it can become, a fully sentient being who may live life to its fullest, loving others and having a generally worthwhile existence.

But on the other hand, I can see the position of the person whose existence is already established on the earth, that is, the mother. If the state of her affairs is such that the baby seriously threatens the quality of her life—which in turn will endanger the quality of the child's life—I can be flexible.

But damn it, then I waffle back to the other side as I consider the more dysfunctional, miserable kids I evaluate for juvenile probation departments. Many of them are precisely the ones whom liberals (like me) are talking about when we argue how life can be so rough for an unwanted baby and her family.

And now I feel *disgusting* for even typing that, having made even the vaguest of suggestions that one of those kids shouldn't exist. That kid's life is just as valuable, in my reflexive opinion, as the perfectly well-adjusted honor-roll cheerleader prom queen.

So, I don't know where I stand on abortion. I hope I never have to face it directly, but if I do, I promise I'll do more soul-searching than I ever have before.

For a tangential but worthwhile aside, Schopenhauer's position on bearing children was comically depressing, but intensely provocative:

> If children were brought into the world by an act of pure reason alone, would the human race continue to exist? Would not a man rather have so much sympathy with the coming

generation as to spare it the burden of existence? or at any rate not take it upon himself to impose that burden upon it in cold blood.[7]

Ironically, the nihilist may be so ridiculously open-minded and respectful of life that he actually has reservations about creating it. He appreciates the responsibility, not being shortsighted by his own selfish needs. Notice how so many people who consider becoming a parent assert "*I want* to have a baby," suggesting that the experience isn't really for the baby, it's for the person having it. When they do have children, they often devote their lives to molding them into their own images, as if they were on a desperate mission to prolong their own lives. On the contrary, we nihilists frame the prospect of procreation into a relatively selfless proposition: "Should I create a life that necessarily has to exist but ultimately face annihilation?"

We talked earlier about how we individuals are reluctant to change, even during those times in which evidence is accumulating to indicate that we've been wrong all along. Societies experience a similar inertia, a commitment to the status quo from which they do not like to veer. Just as with the individual, societal changes are unsettling because in order to change we have to admit that we've been wrong up until the point of change.

Criminal justice examples are readily accessible. For instance, if we were to decisively abolish capital punishment, what would it mean for the thousands of people we've already executed up to this point? That's a tough apology to make, that now we see the light, and we're sorry we didn't just sentence you to life imprisonment

---

7 Schopenhauer, A. (2008). On the sufferings of the world. In E. D. Klemke & S. M. Cahn (Eds.), *The meaning of life: A reader* (3rd ed., p. 47). New York: Oxford University Press.

instead. We're especially sorry because we've been pretty sure all along that capital punishment doesn't even deter crime, and we have known for sure that life imprisonment is cheaper for taxpayers to fund. Yeah, I'm afraid that capital punishment has been more about vengeance than anything else . . . the ultimate irony of it all being that, in practice, we find that vengeance is not as satisfying as we expected, at least in the long run.

Similarly, the American criminal justice system will eventually have to acknowledge that it has unnecessarily damaged, if not ruined, thousands of lives because of its long-standing hysteria about marijuana. We legitimate mental health professionals (and I suspect most police who work the street and are as intimately familiar with the issue as anyone) know that it's alcohol, not marijuana, that destroys families and kills. But even as this truth becomes apparent, our society can't simply adjust. We're a bit addicted to our past, having been so stubbornly blinded by, among other things, Beckerarian assurances of security, such as tradition and culture, as misguided as they can be.

A society, like an individual, is more authentic and healthy when it is less defensive and more comfortable with change. Societies should also engage ethical dilemmas and proceed deliberately, as opposed to reflexively deferring to the status quo.

Imagine if the cigarette had not yet been invented but was now being presented to us in the 21st century, in a nation without any smokers. We're being told that smoking is really enjoyable and will move billions of dollars through the economy, but the catch is that they're highly addictive and even deadly, so much so that they will kill over 480,000 people a year in the U.S. alone—approximately one in five of all our annual deaths.[8] What would we do with such a proposition? We'd laugh our own asses off while kicking the salesman's through the door.

---

8 Centers for Disease Control and Prevention. (2014, November 20). Smoking and tobacco use - Fast facts. Retrieved from http://www.cdc.gov/tobacco/data_statistics/fact_sheets/fast_facts/

Thinking through such examples, we begin to get the sense that this nation under God doesn't care deeply about human life. If we did, cigarettes would have been banished years ago, firmly and sure. Instead, we're willing to forfeit countless lives (and strain our medical care system into stagnation) because we don't want to offend the addicts by removing a liberty that they've already had for so long. And as easy as it is to pick on the United States, the rest of the able world is just as guilty. If the United Nations really cared for its fellows, it would not tolerate, as it has, the myriad ethnic cleansing efforts that have occurred under its watch, which are too numerous to discuss here.

If Americans were truly humanitarian, our national budget would look a lot different than it does today. I never would have imagined throughout most of my life that I would ever disparage NASA, but now, as a nihilistic realist, I can't help but feel frustrated with the institution. Perhaps the best way to put it is like this: If I personally had one trillion dollars to spend, I wouldn't explore space; I would commit that money to ambitious, progressive projects right here on Earth, such as education and criminal justice. I'd fund research that is directly and unambiguously devoted to improving human life, such as harnessing renewable energy resources or perhaps even converting rising sea levels to potable water. Don't get me wrong: I love outer space as much as anyone, but I'd be happy to marvel at it right here from where I'm standing (just as most of the rest of people throughout history have) if, for example, social services for chronically mentally ill homeless people on this planet could be served better. It's gonna sound dramatic no matter how I say this, but here it goes: We shouldn't be exploring other worlds until we can feed this one. Dramatic, but how could we possibly argue otherwise? Just imagine trying to explain to some starving, shoeless kid who lives in a tin shack why the mars rover is worth it. The scene sounds like a bit from a standup comedy routine, and might be comical, if it wasn't such an accurate depiction of how insensitive our society can be.

Australian moral philosopher Peter Singer:

> It is obscene that people are spending thousands of dollars
> on a handbag or a pair of shoes when there are a billion peo-
> ple in the world who are living on less than a [U.S.] dollar a
> day . . . What should I be spending my money on and what
> does that say about me, about my priorities [when I spend it
> on "luxuries and frivolities"] . . . ? The ultimate ethical ques-
> tion is: How are you going to live your life? And the answer
> that Western culture often seems to give is: Consume a lot,
> buy a lot, and seek your own pleasure.[9]

And we shouldn't forget that many of the objects of our gluttony
are bestowed upon us through the suffering of others, like little
girls working in sweatshops in Southeast Asia or wherever.

The punchline is that we all know that consumption is ultimately unfulfilling anyway, and we've known it for eons. Peter
presents the ancient Greek notion of "the paradox of hedonism":
The more we pursue pleasure, the more it seems to retreat. But,

> if instead you do something else that you think is worth-
> while, perhaps something that is ethically important, then
> you find that you get a satisfaction in doing it, and then
> that's not only the more enjoyable thing to do, but of course
> also the more meaningful and fulfilling thing to do.[10]

The sentiment is such a common one that it comes across as trite,
cliché. However—as is often the case with the obvious—we agree
with the sentiment but we don't live it. We smile and say "How
nice" and pretend to appreciate it, but we don't actually allow it to
guide our behavior, at least significantly. It's way too easy to ra-

---

9 Taylor, A. (Ed.). (2009). *Examined life: Excursions with contemporary thinkers* (pp.
63, 62, 85). New York: The New Press.

10 Ibid., p. 85.

tionalize the status quo as acceptable because so many are in on it. Plus, we have this mind-boggling sense of entitlement simply because we were born here instead of there, now instead of then.

We can better appreciate our greed if we consider all of the people who have ever lived on Earth, currently or in the past. Compared to the vast, vast majority of them, we Americans—even many of us who either can't or simply refuse to live gluttonously—still live like *kings*. Speaking for my modest self, I have a climate-controlled, carpeted space whose roof doesn't leak. I have ready access to as much clean water as I could possibly consume. I have more clothes than I can even store properly and I wear all sorts of highly functional shoes. Some of my daily concerns include how to make all of my food fit in the refrigerator, or what I will do today to exercise. That's right: My life is so luxurious that I have to figure out ways not to rest but to burn calories, otherwise I'll gain too much weight, risk diabetes, and go a little stir crazy.

I'm not even sure if it's a choice anymore. I simply can't disregard the suffering of others who don't have my things by chalking it up to some dynamic of a god that I can't comprehend. I do appreciate the suffering of those others, and I hurt for them. Definitely, the very least I'm going to do is not be gluttonous when they can't; it's simply the principle of the matter. You'll never catch me owning a fancy car, living in an extravagant house, or wearing expensive jewelry.

But I'm gonna do more than not be gluttonous. I'm also gonna donate some of my money to charity as well, money that would otherwise be wasted on junk in a futile effort to bring me happiness. And I'm gonna keep thinking about what else I can do. Whatever it is, I'm confident it's going to be more productive than prayer.

CHAPTER 11

Monster-Jam Epiphany, or When Cameras Took Over the World

To a disciple who begged for wisdom the Master said, "Try this out: Close your eyes and see yourself and every living being thrown off the top of a precipice. Each time you cling to something to stop yourself from falling, understand that it is falling, too . . ."

— Anthony de Mello, *One Minute Wisdom*

WHILE ON INTERNSHIP at Arkansas State Hospital, I was able to check an item off my bucket list when my friend Charlee and I went to the Monster Truck rally in Little Rock. I'm not a true Monster Truck fan; we went for the adventure, you know, to experience something far outside our true interests. To be rude, we were looking for a freak show. That said, part of me secretly expected to enjoy the trucks as well. Grave Digger would be there!

As far as the freak show was concerned, I was slightly disappointed. Instead of outrageously wasted, mulletted Free Birds, the arena was mostly filled with fairly average-looking families. The silver lining being that we no longer had to worry about being assaulted, which had been a concern in the back of my mind earlier.

And the only beer poured on us was our own. No kidding, we had to restrain ourselves not to become conspicuous!

Now, the trucks were not so disappointing; neither of us had a chance to hide our excitement once it started. The noise was gloriously loud, even alarming, but just under the threshold of discomfort or pain. And there was this wonderful smell that I had never experienced before. It's hard to describe, but I can smell it right now in retrospect. It was mostly of spent fuel, I presume, but there was also a hint of oil, grease, and some other sort of metal experience that was a little more like a taste than a smell. It must have been the exhaust, because it hit us like a freight train right after the first full-throttle. You know you're really at a show when you can *taste* it. Even GWAR doesn't have a taste.

However, I'm afraid the sound, smell, and taste were more impressive than the visuals. Some of the jumps and car crushings definitely moved me, but our show was mud-free. Apparently, Alltel Arena isn't down with mud. Figures. But ultimately, it would be okay: To fill the void left by the lack of mud, there was funnel cake, cotton candy, and abundant brewskis. We made do.

Indeed, unexpectedly, the most captivating visual had nothing to do with the trucks, nor was it the antics of a fellow patron. As I was trying to watch the scene unfold through my camera viewfinder, Chuck tapped me on the shoulder and had me put my camera down. She had this look of amazement on her face, like she just saw a ghost (a friendly ghost). She's like, "Dude, check it out," and directs my gaze away from the floor and into the crowd beyond, and sure enough it was astonishing, even more so than the awesome truck currently doin' doughnuts.

All of the previously darkened crowd area was now lit up with camera flashbulbs, the density of which I had never seen before or since. It was like getting a free fireworks show, but one where the technician accidentally pushed the wrong button and sent everything up at once. And it lasted for a while. And then kept going. It was really surreal.

The punchlines are several. First, had Chuck not been there to drag my attention from my own viewfinder, I never would have noticed the fascinating scene, which, as awesome as Gravedigger was, was the most memorable moment of the whole night.

Second, as we all should know by now, these pictures suck! Not only was I missing the spectacle of flashbulbs, I was missing them for a picture that was doomed to compromise the reality of the less interesting scene at the time!

Third, all the other photo-addicts were missing the more captivating scene as well—but providing the captivating scene while doing so—and only getting crappy pictures to show for it!

The moral of this story: We've become addicted to picture taking, largely in a desperate attempt to cling to passing moments. The irony being, of course, we're missing out on life, often for pictures that aren't that great anyway. We've become more focused on preserving the moment than we are of experiencing it directly. We assume we can be present later when looking at our pictures, but we never are, really. And now the moment is more gone than ever. Spoiled, even.

Photography should be fun. But it's unhealthy when our motivations stem from desperation and the desperation has us instead of us having it, like when we're preoccupied about showing people how cool we are for what we did, whom we saw, or where we went.

No, I'm not suggesting that we should stop taking pictures altogether. But I am suggesting that we should examine our drives behind taking them, especially when those are bordering on obsessional: Are we content and having fun, or are we clinging?

As you approach the end of my book, you may be asking yourself, "Was this a self-help book? But I feel like *shit!*"

Well, I don't want you to feel bad, but if you do, it's not necessarily *wrong*. If you are feeling bad, it could be that you are beginning to question unrealistic, overly optimistic attitudes about reality. But don't panic: If you are experiencing such a transition, I pray
that it will be like mine, where you ultimately end up in a much
better place. Now, if it's not and you instead find yourself in a place
where you feel overwhelmed, I encourage you to reach out to
friends or family, and perhaps even a professional psychologist. My
goal has never been to overwhelm anyone; I really do just want to
help, or at worst, do nothing.

I'm really not sure if this is a self-help book. I kinda regard it as
more of a story, an autobiography, but one that I hope might affect
people in a positive way. That said, I thought it might be appropriate to at least have a more explicit self-help portion to this book, to
translate some of the ideas we've explored into more specific
guidelines. To get started, we should reiterate Irvin Yalom's "hedonism" and altruism already discussed in the last half of chapter
9. We won't explore those again, but don't forget about them;
they're important.

LOWER YOUR STANDARDS

It's somewhat ironic that the U.S. Declaration of Independence puts
the "pursuit of happiness" on such a pedestal. Many of us psychologists believe that this is a bit of a paradoxical task: Just like
love or sleep, happiness is something that will elude us the more
we crave it. In the words of the very wise existential psychiatrist,
Victor Frankl: "happiness . . . cannot be pursued; it must ensue."[1]

I don't have all the answers myself, but I do feel that one part
of allowing happiness to ensue is to realize that happiness is not a
chronic state: It's a transient one. If we expect it to last, instead of
waxing and waning, we will be doomed to frustration. If we can

---

1 Frankl, V. E. (1985). *Man's search for meaning* (p. 17). New York: Washington
Square Press.

lower our standards to aspire for *contentment* and *peace*—which actually allow for some unhappiness—the most realistic manifestation of "happiness" may then ensue.

In his book *Stumbling on Happiness,* psychologist Dan Gilbert summarizes droves of interesting research studies that, in a nutshell, show that we humans are not good at predicting what will make us happy. In fact, we're so bad at it that we're not even very good at correctly *recalling* what has made us happy *in the past!*[2]

So, besides engaging a paradoxical pursuit in which the target eludes us the more desperate we are for it, we really don't even know what we're chasing! I'm afraid finding happiness is one of those frustrating paradoxes: You have to learn how to quit trying in order to get there. And when you do get there, you're going to learn that it's a different place than what you've been fantasizing about all this time.

SLOW DOWN

Four-hundred years before Ernest Becker was a gleam in his father's eye, Blaise Pascal penned his almost-famous hyperbole:

> I have discovered that all human misfortune comes from one thing, which is not knowing how to remain quietly in one room. A man who has sufficient means to live, if he knew how to stay at home happily, would not go forth to go on the sea or to a siege . . . I have found that there is one very potent reason for it, that is, the unhappiness natural to our weak and mortal condition, a condition so miserable that when we think deeply about it, nothing can console us.[3]

Caught in a bit of a philosophical circularity, Pascal was seemingly obsessed with—if not tormented by—the way we humans are ob-

---

2 Gilbert, D. (2006). *Stumbling on happiness.* New York: Alfred A. Knopf.

3 Rawlings, G. B. (Ed. & Trans.). (2009). *Pascal's pensées; or, thoughts on religion* (p. 65). Charleston, SC: Bibliolife. (Original work published 1670).

sessed with diversion and distraction! When he talks about hunting rabbits in the 17th century, he could just as easily be talking about rat-racing or shopping in the 21st: "we like the chase better than the capture . . . This hare would not secure us against the sight of death and misery (who can save us from these?), but the chase does se-cure us against it." People

> seek only a violent and energetic occupation, which diverts them from thoughts of themselves . . . They imagine that having gained their object they would then take their ease and enjoy it, and are not aware of the insatiable nature of their desire. They sincerely believe they are seeking repose when, in truth, they seek only agitation . . . So life glides on. We seek rest by combating certain difficulties, and when these are conquered, rest becomes intolerable, for we think either of the troubles we have, or of those we might have.[4]

There's something so wrong—but strangely addictive—about the mental state of being in a hurry, to escape the present moment by longing for the next. It's basic behavioral conditioning, negative reinforcement to be exact. A rat that is being shocked will quickly learn to push a lever if that lever relieves that shock. We're the rats, boredom and contemplation are the shock, and hustling and bus-tling are the levers we press to rid ourselves of contempla-tion—particularly those thoughts of our "miserable condition," that is, our mortality. In this peculiar manner, self-imposed acute stress distracts us from our underlying chronic distress.[5]

The more accessible distraction becomes, the more likely we are to indulge it. That's why we spend so much time buried in our

---

4 Ibid., p. 66-67.

5 Quick psychology lesson: *Negative* reinforcement is when a behavior is encour-aged because it is associated with the *removal* of an *aversive* stimulus. *Positive* rein-forcement is when a behavior is also encouraged, but because it is associated with the *addition* of a *desirable* stimulus. Punishment is neither of these: It's when a behavior is discouraged by associating it with the *addition* of an *aversive* stimulus.

phones and other electronic devices today: Because we can! We press the lever impulsively, frenzied, because it's always there.

Even when we're not physically bustling, we are mentally. I often have this experience when I go for a jog down at the "Green-belt," this surprisingly beautiful system of creek and trails that runs right through the middle of the now overly crowded, loud, stylish, and frenzied city of Austin. The transition from urban to rural can be quite dramatic and sudden, but I've learned if I don't stop, take a deep breath, and stop thinking and just perceive, I'll never make the transition completely. It's truly an amazing experience: When I'm lucky enough to remind myself to pause as such, suddenly the sound of birds becomes surprisingly salient—as if I've just re-moved plugs from my ears. Only *then* do I feel the peace I'm look-ing for, the best kind that only comes from being outdoors.

When we first practice pausing and being present like this, it can actually be uncomfortable, if not downright aversive. But, over time, it becomes tolerable, then preferable, at least much of the time. Eventually—as it becomes more natural—all sorts of wonder-ful things begin to happen.[6]

Today, when I drive upon a yellow light, I often slow down and calmly stop instead of stomping the gas to beat it. It's kinda nice to stop, because I can use the down time to just sit and be grateful or contemplate the cosmos or whatever. I remind myself how all this traffic came to be, and how incredibly magnificent it is to be alive and how lucky I am to even have a car in which to be stuck in traf-fic, and a refrigerator full of food waiting for me at home. When I see people ramming the gas to get through the light, I kinda pity them. I don't think I'm *better* than them, but I feel like I'm on to something that they're missing.

The act of rushing creates distress, for both myself and others, that is totally unnecessary. Alternatively, if I leave in plenty of time

---

6 I'm borrowing the term "pausing" from another highly recommended book, Tara Brach's (2003) *Radical acceptance: Embracing your life with the heart of a buddha.* New York: Bantam.

for my appointment, I get to ponder whatever I want instead of being forced to be angry at all the people who seem to be in my way. Regardless of what we're doing, if we're in a hurry, we're wasting time.

Of course, we have to hurry sometimes. But don't let others suck you in needlessly. The world will rush around you if you just let them. Instead of racing your neighbor in traffic, whether driving or walking or pushing a shopping basket, just put on the brakes, let them pass, and move in behind them. It's judo-locomotion, using the momentum of the world against itself to make your passage more pleasant. When you assume your position behind frenzied drivers (or shoppers) and watch them speed off, you'll feel better than when you end up in front of them. People in a hurry are some of the most unappealing people around; I recommend just getting out of their way and feeling sorry for them.

HUNT AND GATHER

Irvin Yalom (and others) has speculated that our evolutionary ancestors were more content than us today, despite lacking technology—indeed, perhaps *because* they lacked technology:

> Furthermore, people of earlier ages were often so preoccupied with the task of meeting other more basic survival needs, such as food and shelter, that they were not afforded the luxury of examining their need for meaning . . . [they] had other meaning-providing activities in their everyday life. They lived close to the earth, felt a part of nature, fulfilled nature's purpose in plowing the ground, sowing, reaping, cooking, and naturally and unself-consciously thrusting themselves into the future by begetting and raising children . . . They had a strong sense of belonging to a larger unit; they were an integral part of a family and community and, in that context, were provided scripts and roles.[7]

---

7 *Existential Psychotherapy*, p. 447.

My dissertation advisor at Kansas, Stephen Ilardi, specifically conceptualizes clinical depression as a "disease of civilization"—along with other ailments such as diabetes and atherosclerosis, which are "largely non-existent" in aboriginal cultures that still hunt and gather, like the Kaluli of Papua New Guinea.[8] On the contrary, depression is running amok in Western culture, significantly increasing with every generation—despite the fact that antidepressants are being prescribed about 300% more often than they were 20 years ago. So, Steve and colleagues researched the Kaluli to identify the factors of their lifestyle that seem to be inoculating them from depression, factors that Westerners are tragically lacking. And they found six: routine physical activity; regular *face-to-face* social interaction; spending time outdoors; sleep hygiene; anti-ruminative activity (that is, doing something besides brooding); and a diet rich in omega-3 fatty acids. Steve's treatment program, Therapeutic Lifestyle Change (TLC) simply prescribes the depressed Westerner these lifestyle habits of the non-depressed Kaluli. Overall, the results have been beyond Steve's "wildest dreams." For example, he reports that mild exercise alone—thirty minutes of brisk walking three times a week—has outperformed the antidepressant Zoloft all by itself in clinical trials.

DON'T MIND THE OTHER SIDE OF THE FENCE SO MUCH
There are probably countless ways in which our modern techno-lifestyle is ironically compromising life for us. We considered in an earlier chapter how that we may be chronically anxious due to overexposure to trauma via the news. Similarly, it's fair to wonder if we are more sexually aroused than evolution ever intended (and therefore frustrated), due to overexposure to sexual stimulation in advertising and such. Otherwise, through the news, advertising, and just daily living, we can't escape reminders that there are so

---

8 TEDxEmory (Producer). (2013). Depression is a disease of civilization by Stephen Ilardi, PhD. [Video lecture]. Retrieved from tedxemory.org ; For more info about the treatment, see http://psych.ku.edu/tlc/

many others out there who have so much more than we do. This is not natural, either, as we evolved in much less stratified societies than those in which we find ourselves today. I suspect that a lot of modern unhappiness is not simply being without: It's being without and knowing that others aren't, as their wealth is constantly paraded in front of us.

Well, it turns out that we tend to give wealth more credit than is due. A quite robust finding in psycho-socio-economic research is that once people have their basic needs met—they can pay the bills and feed the family and have enough left over for a little recreation—they tend to be as happy as anyone else, even the richest of folk. Adding money on top of the basics does not continue to increase happiness, as we poor people tend to fantasize. Dan Gilbert again:

> Economists explain that wealth has "declining marginal utility," which is a fancy way of saying that it hurts to be hungry, cold, sick, tired, and scared, but once you've bought your way out of these burdens, the rest of your money is an increasingly useless pile of paper.[9]

Certainly, we overestimate the quality of others' experience in all sorts of contexts, besides that of their wealth. When you're out on the town and everyone else seems so happy but you're oddly down, realize that many of the people who are out are out *because* they feel good. For every person seeming to have such a better time than you, there are countless others at home in their pajamas channel surfing, feeling angsty and tormented about whether to get up and do anything at all. And of course, if you could read the minds of those other revelers who seem to be having such a great time, you'd see that many are not as happy as they look. Many of them are faking it just like you, wondering if they should be somewhere

---

9 *Stumbling on Happiness*, p. 218.

else. And even for some of those who are actually feeling great, mediocrity (if not worse) is waiting for them at home—that's why they appear so happy at the moment!

Similarly, on social media, everyone seems to have more friends, romance, fun, family, and vacations than we do. But you have to realize you're looking at a non-random sample; the joy that you see is usually more of an exception than a rule. Most people post happy stuff because they are in a good mood at the time. Overall, those people are just like you: They have good times, and then they have bad ones. The average person just doesn't advertise the bad ones as much.

Besides comparing ourselves to others, we also have to be careful about comparing our current selves to those of our narcissistic hopes and dreams. I suspect that most people will never achieve the fantasy version of themselves, and will therefore be disappointed insofar as they are attached to those fantasies.

Is it wrong to have aspirations? Of course not, but aspirations can go bad when they preoccupy us with the future so much that we can't appreciate how well we're doing now, or if they otherwise doom us to failure later. We should have aspirations; we just shouldn't be too unrealistic about them.

CHALLENGE YOUR FALSE SENSE OF ENTITLEMENT

American comedian (and philosopher) Louis C. K. enthusiastically conveys how spoiled and unappreciative we've become in our wealthy, greedy, technologically advanced society:

> People on planes are the worst . . . they complain . . . "That was the worst day of my life! I had to sit on the runway for *forty* minutes!" That's a story in this country. That's a *fucking hardship*, that you had to sit on the runway. People will listen to that story. They'll stop doing the dishes and turn around and go, "Oh, my god, *really*? For 40 minutes? That's awful! You should sue them!"

What happened then? Did you *fly* through the air like a bird, incredibly? Did you *soar* into the clouds, impossibly? Did you partake in the miracle of human flight and then land softly on giant tires that you couldn't even conceive how they fucking put air in them?

How dare you, bitching about flying! "[But] I had to pay for my sandwich . . ." You're *flying*! You're sitting in a chair in the sky! You're like a Greek myth right now. "But it doesn't go back very far, and I was sort of squishing my knees . . ."[10]

Besides not appreciating the miracles with which we engage daily, our unfounded sense of entitlement makes us feel violated when subjected to practical measures intended to protect us. I had to testify in court literally days after Jared Loughner shot U.S. Representative Gabrielle Giffords at her "Congress on Your Corner" meeting near Tucson, along with several others, killing six, including a nine-year-old girl. To get to the actual courtrooms, I have to walk through a security area with a metal detector. There was a UPS guy ahead of me with a dolly of packages, and the guard asked him to unload them so that each could be run through the X-ray machine. There was a lady behind me (presumably a defense attorney), and she was just disgusted with this process, sighing and saying out loud, clearly for everyone to hear, "This is ridiculous!" She looked at me, seeking some validation, but all I could give her was a blank stare, because that's all I could do, being baffled.

I flew for the first time in 1995, at the tender age of 25. I remember being absolutely dumbfounded at how easy it was to get on a plane and potentially bring weapons with you—especially in the wake of the first World Trade Center bombing. My jaw was still dropped when I took my seat. If I had been in charge, 9/11 never

10 Louis C. K. (Writer, producer, & director; also produced by D. Becky, D. Bernath, M. Caputo, S. Hartman, & C. Jenowitz). (2010). *Hilarious*. [TV special]. USA: Epix.

would have happened. The irony is stupefying: Our obsession with liberty has actually cost us much of our freedom!

DON'T LET CONSUMPTION BE AN AMBITION

One of the reasons that surplus wealth beyond what is needed to meet our basic needs does not necessarily make us happier is related to one of the greatest strengths of biological organisms, also one of the most fundamental: We adapt to our circumstances. Observed on the level of the single brain cell, repeated stimulation activates the cell less and less over time, called *adaptation* or *habituation*. The good news is that it produces organisms that are resilient in the face of chronic distress. We can adapt to the bad things in our lives (within reason), such as divorce, physical disability, or even the death of a loved one.

The bad news is that we also adapt to—that is, become bored with—the *good* things in our lives. We always want something else because no matter how satisfied we become we eventually adapt to whatever got us there. The problem is most evident when we rely on accumulating things for satisfaction. Adaptation is why we have pastimes like *shopping* (and, I'm afraid, *adultery*). If owning things truly satisfied us, we wouldn't shop so much; we'd buy a few things and be okay.

When I was a materialist but trying to change, I found it helpful to use the Alcoholics Anonymous mantra, "Fake it till you make it." I would go to the mall or whatever but force myself to leave the debit card at home so that I didn't even have the option to buy anything. It felt uncomfortable at first, excruciating at times, but eventually started to put everything into perspective. Without the option to buy, I simply felt like I didn't want as much as usual; I was no longer *shopping* but more like *hangin' out*, which became a more pleasant experience. When I did come across something I really seemed to want, I promised myself I'd come back the next day (or later in the week even) if I still wanted it. But it was amazing how often I'd lose interest after sleeping on it. Not always, but something about waiting and sleeping on it helped me distinguish between a compulsive want and a relatively legitimate one.

"But what if it's gone when I get back!" Well, the earth will continue to turn, and you will then learn that you really didn't need it after all. It may sting for a moment, even for a while, but you'll eventually forget about it. Off the top of my head, I can only think of one thing ever that I wish I had bought but didn't (it was a neat set of china at an antique store in Leavenworth, Kansas, circa 2003). Oh yeah, and I wish that I would have brought home this dolphin vertebrae I found on the beach at the Gulf one time. I still think about these things on the rarest of occasions, and I still feel a little bit of regret about my decisions to pass them up, but those feelings pass pretty quickly. Oddly, it's almost like I appreciate the lost items *more* because I *don't* have them, reminiscent of that Camus quote about love, that the only enduring love is that which never has the opportunity to be indulged.

Once I practiced deprivation by forcing myself to do without, not only did I realize I didn't need so much, it became clear that being a wanter creates one of those vicious cycles in which the act of trying to fulfill the desire only seems to exacerbate the need! I had an analogous experience recently with beer. I took a month off from beer drinking, largely because I just wanted to make sure I had all my faculties and energy to finish this book. An entirely unexpected benefit was that I found myself more present and comfortable throughout the day because I was no longer looking forward to evening beers! The irony is that anticipating beer with which to wind down later was actually *winding me up* at times, making me think I needed that beer more than I did.

Another favorite passage from Anthony de Mello has been inspirational in my quest against materialism: "Those who sleep on the floor never fall from their beds."[11]

I don't think he's simply saying that if we don't have anything, we don't have anything to lose. I believe the message is deeper: It's about a healthy *mindset,* in that those who do not seek satisfaction

---

11 de Mello, A. (1988). *One minute wisdom* (p. 99). New York: Image Books.

through materialism (and other doomed, superficial quests, like celebrity) are more grounded, content, and more in touch with reality.

As many a bumper sticker has reminded us, Jesus was the quintessential communist. One of the greatest hypocrisies on Earth is that Jesus and so much of the Bible are all about minimizing materialism, rat-racing, and selfishness, but here we are, the most Jesus-y and Bible-est country on Earth, and yet the most materialistic, ambitious, and (in ways) selfish. We should not want! Green pastures and still waters should be plenty.

DON'T LET AMBITION CONSUME YOU

The following anecdote is one of the most compelling I've ever encountered, hands-down. I read it somewhere years ago, but I haven't been able to relocate the source, despite my most valiant Googling efforts. As I recall, the author had described a conversation between a psychologist and a gerontologist (or was it a neurologist and an oncologist?). It went something like this:

Psychologist:	"Gollee, doing the work you do, you must see a lot of people die."
Gerontologist:	"Oh, yeah. Almost every day."
Psychologist:	"Wow. I bet you hear a lot of incredible things. Do people ever share with you their *greatest regrets* in life? If so, is there one particular regret that's most often expressed?"
Gerontologist:	"Oh, sure; that's easy. *Unexpressed affection.* People regret not telling others how much they cared about them."

I don't know where to begin. Of course, the explicit message is a poignant slap in the face, that we are overly shy about telling people that we care about them—and what a horrific tragedy to finally come to terms with this when it's too late. It hurts just to think about it. Re-inspired by the passage while editing my book, I recently told one of my best friends what I'd say at his eulogy if he were to die before me, and it was a wonderful moment indeed, one of the best I've had in a long time and will never forget.

More generally speaking, the story put me in the habit of looking at my life from my fantasized deathbed. Nothing else has helped me more to keep things in perspective. When I contemplate my life from my deathbed, my accomplishments, such as my college degrees and frequent flier miles earned, seem so much less important than they do from where I am now.

What matters more, suddenly, is whether I enjoyed my daily life or worried it away or rushed through it. Was I as *good* to people as I could have been? Was I *present with* and *attentive to* people and places and experiences, or was I always preoccupied about moving onto the next one? And, of course, did I tell my friends, "Hey, I've been thinking about you" or "It's good to hear your voice." Or, God forbid, "I care about you."

Why does this exercise work so well? On our deathbed, we are able to see the world unpolluted by our ambitions and aspirations—we're no longer preoccupied about the future. And we're honest, because the defenses are down. If we can harness our deathbed vision *now*, we can begin benefitting before it's too late. One's deathbed is a bad time to have an epiphany, especially the ones about wasting our lives obsessing about success. You no longer have time to mentally process your newfound realization, much less do anything about it—such as live some of your life according to the epiphany!

We Americans have to be particularly careful, as rat-racing to attain our dreams is a cultural imperative. I worry that Americans experience an inordinate number of deathbed regrets because of this drive. It's so bad over here that sometimes I wonder if it's in our genes. There's a phenomenon in evolution called *speciation* in which the formation of new species is greatly accelerated because some plants and animals are suddenly—at least in cosmic terms—sequestered from the pack. It can occur, for example, when land masses become separated by water, creating different ecosystems and geographies, leaving the respective inhabitants to evolve down independent pathways.

Perhaps the colonization of America was a speciation of sorts. It must have taken a special type of person to get on a boat during the 16th-19th centuries and make his or her way across the Atlantic Ocean to these mysterious lands. Those people were dissatisfied with the status quo in Europe, and ambitious and restless enough to do something incredible about it. And here we are today: a nation of restlessly ambitious people. Americans

> "for ever imagine the Lands further off are still better than those upon which they are already settled"; if they attained Paradise, they would move on if they heard of a better place farther west.[12]

That may sound like a compliment to some, but I think it can be more of a criticism. We've finally run out of frontier but can't seem to relax and enjoy what we have. Sure, restlessness makes for some great conquest and technological advancement, but we've run ourselves ragged in the process. We're going to go to our graves realizing that we rushed our lives away trying to conquer.

It's not just the American Dream of a successful career, loving family, and cozy wine/cheese tasting parties with our successful friends. We run ourselves ragged competing for minutiae, like finding the best parking spot. I'm amazed at the effort people will expend to get a parking spot near the entrance, like it's some sort of life-or-death competition. Personally, I always go straight to the

---

12 Miller, J. C. (1943). *Origins of the American revolution* (p. 77). Boston: Little, Brown, & Company. The portion in quotes is cited by Miller as follows: Lord Dunmore to Lord Dartmouth, December 24, 1774, P.R.O., C.O. 5, 1533, Library of Congress Transcript.

empty part of the lot, in the back, and walk. The walk feels good, and then I chuckle inside when I pass the person that I saw waiting for a spot, still sitting in their car, all pissy.

Even our vacations are rat races, desperate attempts to see as much as possible and to document how much fun we had. Pascal wondered, again with hyperbole, if we'd even vacation at all if it wasn't for the lure of the attention we get upon our return: "one would not make a voyage never to speak of it, and for the mere pleasure of seeing, without the hope of ever talking about it to someone."[13]

Speaking of "wanderlust," in 2008 I had the pleasure to visit Moab, Utah and the surrounding areas, easily one of the most fascinating and beautiful places I've ever been. However, similar to my monster-truck rally experience, an odder memorable moment was of a fellow photographer. I was standing at a lonely fork in the trail one day, debating which way to go, and this man holding a camera literally *runs* up upon me, panting and sweating, and asks me which trail has the best arches so he wouldn't waste any time on the lesser of the two. I have to note, too, that he wasn't American: He was European—and Eastern at that! I was mortified, being a big fan of Hungarian Bela Tarr's movies—beautifully unhurried and existential—now confronted with a man who could have been Hungarian himself, acting an American fool. I always had this fantasy that Eastern Europeans didn't do this sort of thing, but I reckon they do, too. Sigh.

Of course, I'm not disparaging all ambition and recreation. Like everything else, just own it—don't let it own you. That includes everything from your job to your vacation and even your volunteer work.

---

13 *Pascal's Pensées; or, Thoughts on Religion*, p. 43.

I spent Christmas 2011 at Big Bend National Park (just like I did in 2010) to escape Christmas and capitalism and whatnot. I swear to God: Those Lexus commercials where some chump gets his wife a beautiful car with a big red bow around it make me feel ill. All I can think about are the people in my very own town who can't even afford one crappy car for the entire family and so they have to ride the God-danged bus around. And those jewelry commercials that open with some histrionic supermodel contemplating, "How will I know that he loves me?" Darlin', if proof means him wasting thousands of dollars on metal and rocks for you to hang on your face, there's something wrong with your relationship, in my opinion.

In any event, that trip ended up being one of my favorite experiences ever: It snowed when I was there! It was so beautiful and surreal, Big Bend being in the middle of the Chihuahuan Desert, all rocky and cactus-y the vast majority of the time. And the solitude was divine. I went about thirty hours once without seeing another human being, or any evidence of their existence. It was just me, hiking through the mountainous desert, bundled up quite snuggly, trudging through the most perfect amount of snow there could be.

When I arrived in the evening of the fourth day to return my solo-hiker pass to the ranger station at Panther Junction (so they know I made it out alive), it was closed. The sun was setting and it was starting to become dark. Something stirring in the cacti nearby broke the peace and abruptly grabbed my attention. I could see an amorphous blob of animal, but was unable to identify it. For a moment, I thought it might be a bear, and I kinda freaked out. Then I heard another rustling, even closer to me, and could then make out the perps a little better: They were collared peccary, a.k.a. javelina, these adorable little pig-looking fuzzy monsters. (We're not supposed to call them "pigs," however. Rumor has it that they're not as genetically pig as they appear—I read once they're actually closer to hippopotami! I like to hope that's true.)

While I was trying to get a better look, this roundish family of humans pulled in to the parking lot where I was standing, two pre-or-early-teens sisters, their slightly older brother, and mother. I immediately rolled my eyes, figuratively, and wrote the experience off as thereby terminated. But, I was so wonderfully wrong: It got better. Forcing myself to be friendly, I pointed the javelina out to the first sister who was running up, mostly just holding out hope that she'd slow down and not scream and the critter would linger.

I'll be damned: She was captivated as well, as opposed to spastic. Then the rest of the family approached, one-by-one, mom, of course, bringing up the rear, a nice, sincere smile on her face. I was suddenly impressed by how they all behaved; none of them got too close, they just stood there, right there with me, and watched. Amazingly, they didn't scare it away, so the moment continued. In fact, it continued for long enough that *I* eventually walked off, when I was ready to tend to my business.

When I returned from the bathroom, the javelina and the kids had relocated, the former now standing on an asphalt trail, just eying the kids, and them in return, like some sort of Mexican stand-off. The boy was crouched down, literally less than ten feet from it, about to take a picture with his phone. As it became clear that it was too dark, one of the sisters firmly but politely told her brother not to use the flash, to just skip the picture, otherwise he was going to scare it. Inexplicably, he complied. And he didn't even appear the least bit grumpy about it, instead seeming to agree it was a good idea. They kept staring at the animal until finally it snapped, turned, and trotted off, clippity-clop along that little asphalt path. One of the girls, speaking for both of us, said, "Aww!"

I was especially moved by that one girl's awareness and sensitivity, her ability to have the experience and be present in it without disturbing the cosmos by having to take a picture so that she could brag to her friends about it later. And I was moved by her brother's flexibility. I really liked that family; it was a great end to an awesome vacation. My only regret is that I didn't say something to them, especially to mom, to let her know that her kids make a great impression. I suspect she'd appreciate hearing that, but she probably doesn't need to hear it. They're alright, and they must know it, deep down. I bet there's never been a lot of yelling in their home, and there's been little to no inappropriate corporal punishment. I bet those parents have paid attention to each of those kids since each was born. Everyone listens to everyone else in that family, at least much of the time. I know they do; I saw it firsthand.

THE END

How to Ruin Your Kids
without Even Trying

. . . if you think that the greatest ideal in life is to be invulnerable, then you are on your way to becoming geological rather than spiritual.

— Alan Watts, *Still the Mind*

PSYCHOLOGISTS ARE OFTEN STEREOTYPED as crazy themselves, driven to the profession in hopes to one day understand their own pathologies. I'm not thrilled whenever I realize I'm cliché, but I have to be honest and acknowledge that this has definitely been the case for me.

I took my first formal psychology class over twenty-five years ago in high school and, being crazy as shit, have had my nose to the mental health grindstone ever since. Actually, as I explained earlier, I had begun studying psychology informally even during elementary school because I had this peculiar obsession with substance abuse. I had read several books about drugs, grown-up chapter books, before I had even left the sixth grade.

Despite all the psychology I obsessively consumed, it wouldn't be until graduate school at the University of Kansas that I even heard of the notion of *emotional validation*. Remarkable, because of all the psychological phenomena I have learned about to date I feel it has been the most ubiquitous and relevant issue in chronic emotional turmoil. I don't know why, but it's strangely difficult to find it explicitly addressed in textbooks and such. I just checked my bookshelf at home, and of the eighteen books that I thought might discuss it, only three have the term (or some derivative thereof) in their indices or tables of contents. So pay attention! If more people were more acutely aware of how this works, I think the world would be a significantly better place. I promise this is relevant for you, one way or another.

In a nutshell, emotional validation occurs after one person discloses his or her inner experience to another person (typically verbally, but also via body language), and the recipient/audience (validating) person consumes the disclosure attentively. Although the listener may not *agree* with the speaker's experience, he accepts it as *real* (*valid*)—given the speaker's circumstances, including his temperament, if applicable.

For instance, a third-grader, at breakfast, nervously expresses to her dad that she is scared about her spelling test scheduled later that day. Good Dad *validates* her experience by disengaging from his paper—not by merely peeking around the corner, but by putting it down so that his kid knows he's paying attention and isn't taking her fear lightly. There are an infinite number of validating verbalizations, but he could say something along the lines of "Oh, Sweetie; I can see you're worried. I'm sorry you're stressed. I know how important it is for you to do well at school. But don't forget: I'm going to love you no matter what happens!" It really is okay to talk like this; it's never killed anyone.

That's a fantastic parent. First, he simply makes it clear he's paying attention. Then he acknowledges his kid's suffering without belittling it. Next, Dad offers reassurance, the greatest of which being that, ultimately, you don't need to be afraid because your greatest fear that my affection for you may depend on this silly test is only that, a fear that is not well founded. And I love the part where he doesn't make promises about what's gonna happen—he leaves it open that she *may not* do well! But the earth would keep spinning, even in the worst case scenario. Validate, then soothe; don't disregard, and don't make unrealistic promises about things you can't control.

Alternatively, there are also an infinite number of ways to *not* validate his daughter's experience, that is, to *invalidate* it. Unfortunately, this process takes much less energy and effort and is therefore the default response from many preoccupied adults. The easiest way to invalidate is simply to not pay attention, to remain buried in the newspaper, and simply grunt or something. Even worse, dad could react with *frustration* and frown or scowl or say something like, "Oh, honey, you're such a baby. You always get worried over nothing." Of course, the sky's the limit: Dad can be downright mean, or even *abusive*. But we don't need to illustrate the more dramatically invalidating responses at this time; the subtle ones are sufficient. And by "subtle," I mean *not obvious*: Don't underestimate the impact of subtle invalidations. For invalidation to be toxic, it doesn't have to be dramatic—it only has to be habitual. Subtle and habitual can do the trick, at least in susceptible individuals.

One of the diagnosable conditions associated with growing up in a toxically invalidating environment is borderline personality disorder. At least where I was educated, Marsha Linehan was regarded as the guru on the topic, having written a popular treatment manual for professionals.[1] It's also worth noting that in 2011 Marsha

---

1 Linehan, M. M. (1993). *Skills training manual for treating borderline personality disorder*. New York: Guilford. The info I'm discussing comes from the introductory pages 2-4.

came out of the closet to talk about her own personal experience suffering from the condition, complete with suicide attempts, self-mutilation, and necessary but not-so-therapeutic psychiatric hospital admissions.[2] And for those who learned about borderline personality from *Fatal Attraction* or some other Hollywood gig, don't overemphasize the whole self-mutilation thing, nor the psycho-violent aspect. Many very disturbed people don't hurt themselves or anyone else.

Marsha explains in her manual that kids who are born sensitive and temperamental may actually elicit invalidating responses from their caregivers. One possible dynamic is that a sensitive kid may often trip false-alarms, so to speak, teaching the parent that the kid is overreacting (at least from the parent's perspective). So, when the kid experiences distress, the parent is susceptible to respond as above: "Oh, honey, you're such a baby. You always get worried over nothing."

The problem is that regardless how unreasonable it seems to the parent, the child is truly experiencing distress. As Marsha explains, disregarding the kid's subjective experience impairs her ability to learn how to identify her emotions. She feels scared, but you're suggesting to her that what she's feeling is not fear, or at least it shouldn't be. She can become confused about what fear even is, not to mention its nuances.

If one doesn't learn how to assess her emotions, she sure as heck isn't going to learn how to cope with them on her own. What you end up with is a kid (and later, an adult) who has two primary options when stressed: (a) emotional retreat/isolation; and (b) tantrum/overreacting. Option (a) is often realized when the person does not feel that the world will understand (because it hasn't so far!). Option (b) may be realized when the stress builds to unmanageable levels—the threshold for which will be relatively low in

---

2 Carey, B. (2011, June 23). Expert on mental illness reveals her own fight. *New York Times*. Retrieved from http://www.nytimes.com/2011/06/23/health/23lives.html

such persons. The kid (or later, adult) is going to be heard one way or another.

If these emotional examples feel a bit ambiguous, Marsha also provides an example of one of my favorite types of invalidation that may be more apparent:

Kid:	"I'm thirsty!"
Dad:	"No you're not; you just had a drink."

There really is a time in every kid's life when he's not perfectly sure what to make of fundamental subjective experiences, even thirst or hunger. Omnipotent Dad telling him that he's not thirsty or hungry really can be disorienting if he is indeed having such an experience. And if we can be confused about thirst or hunger, imagine how easily we can be become confused about something that is inherently more ambiguous, such as *scared, dizzy,* or *humiliated*.

If you're still skeptical, realize that kids aren't even sure sometimes whether they have been *physically harmed*. I don't spend that much time around children, but I've observed many times where one is running and falls, pauses, and looks up at the nearest parent to get his/her reaction before crying or not. Human behavior is usually more complicated to sum up in a phrase, but I believe that one facet to this behavior is that the kid is honestly not sure how to assess the severity of his situation. "Am I hurt? Should I be freaking out here?" And we all know that (within reason) the crying *is* determined as much by the adult's reaction as it is by the kid's physical trauma. A cheerful "Oopsie daisy! Look who busted his ass!" is much less likely to elicit crying than an hysterical "OH MY GAWWWWD!!! MY BAY-BEEEEEE!!!" Hell yeah, we teach our kids our neuroses.

Another book from my shelf that actually devotes significant time to emotional validation is Michael Hollander's *Helping Teens Who Cut*. It's a great book, but I feel the title is somewhat unfortunate for my selfish purposes here. That is, again, it may give some readers the impression that invalidation and cutting go hand-in-hand. They don't.

In any event, in addition to not learning how to comprehend one's own emotions, Michael adds that another "consequence of an invalidating environment is that kids feel that life's problems should be easy to solve."[3] Most of us know that in reality they are not, although we may see *other people's problems* as relatively frivolous. So, in addition to creating confusion about emotions and feelings (and how to cope with them), the kid feels inept. Inept makes her different, isolated, corroborating her suspicion that "no one understands me." Self-esteem takes a hit, because she's being taught that others must be more capable.

Of course, isolated incidents of invalidation are unlikely to have long-lasting effects. Everyone is insensitive to their child at times, especially during those moments when we're preoccupied with ourselves because *we're* distressed, say, because of the layoffs at work or the engine light having come on in the car today. The problem is that, in many families, these invalidating interactions don't occur in isolation. They are often *habits*, ways of life, indicative of the parent's own pathology that they inherited from *their* parents (via both nature and nurture, but the emphasis is on the nurture here). I should also point out that although I've been focusing on negative inner experiences, validation is just as important in reference to positive inner experiences. It's not qualitatively different and can be just about as toxic when we disregard our kid's excitement, feelings of achievement, crushes on classmates, and the like.

You don't have to spy on a family at home to observe parents taking it up a notch; it happens with alarming frequency in public. For example, at the grocery store, I'll hear a kid expressing what seems to be an innocuous request, but the insensitive, preoccupied parent responds by ordering him to "Shut up! I don't care what you

---

3 Hollander, M. (2008). *Helping teens who cut* (p. 71). New York: Guilford.

want; I told you that blah blah blah . . ." Or, even worse, the parent swats or squeezes the kid, fingernails digging in real good, enough to where pain was clearly inflicted. I saw this just the other day, the most disturbing part being that the kid didn't even really respond. It looked like those nails had to hurt, but he seemed kinda used to it, sitting there in the shopping basket chair. I wondered what it's like at home for that kid, as opposed to being in a crowded public place.

To take it up many more notches, off the charts, some psychologists regard incestuous sexual abuse as the ultimate invalidating experience. This is not a myth or the product of Hollywood dramatics. Often when a dad or stepdad abuses his daughter, he prepares her first by arguing that he needs to do it in order to teach her about sex or that it is otherwise "good for you." Others tell their victims that they really want to have sex, too, but that they just don't understand their desire yet, that sort of thing. I know sexual abuse is one of the least pleasant phenomena on Earth to think about, even academically, but it's revealing to consider how kids of different ages might experience abuse differently. Someone in their mid to late teens is unlikely to fall for that manipulative shit the perp is arguing. Now, her victimization may be the most disturbing thing that has ever happened to her before, but the flavor of the disturbance will be different from that of a younger kid, less complex. With the younger child, the parent still has much more authority, including over the child's own inner experience. By no means am I suggesting that the kid somehow enjoys the experience simply because Dad said she should. I am saying that the younger kid is less able to own her own feelings. Even though dad may not be able to convince her that the abuse is *good*, he can create an incredible amount of emotional confusion about what's going on. An older kid or adult victim *knows* how wrong it is. It's pure violation, without the added *confusion* about the violation—the invalidation about what's happening.

Worth adding, the cliché in psychological treatment circles is true, that emotional pain associated with abuse can hurt worse than the physical pain. Young victims are sometimes able to conjure the courage to break their vow of secrecy with the perpetrator and go to someone else for help, like another family member, often the mother. However, with surprising regularity, the mom or stepmom or aunt or whoever will be overwhelmed with denial (or something) and react by telling the kid she has a wild imagination or even punish the kid for lying. I'm not making this up for dramatic effect: When patients or whoever are telling you these stories, they often don't cry when they disclose the actual abuse, but they lose it when they tell you the part about mom not believing them.

Perhaps you're on board with this business of how emotional invalidation can create an emotionally disturbed adult. Now try bearing with a little psycho-hocus-pocus for a moment: Many psychologists will go as far to argue that chronic invalidation can prevent one from developing a cohesive sense of *self*. Now, I'm not going to pretend I have an adequate synopsis of what the "self" is; there are entire books on the topic, none of which I have read, at least entirely. And certainly, philosophers have as much right to define the self as psychologists. That said, one psychologist, Marsha, believes that

> Emotional consistency and predictability, across time and similar situations, are prerequisites of identity development. Unpredictable emotional lability leads to unpredictable behavior and cognitive inconsistency, and consequently interferes with identity development.

So, early invalidation renders one emotionally volatile because she cannot properly assess her emotions and subsequently cope with the bad ones through self-soothing. Ergo, her emotional behavior has been erratic in the past, and will continue to be so in the future. Insofar as one's "self" is defined by emotional, cognitive, and behavioral coherence across time, identity is indeed disturbed.

David Shapiro, in this old-timey, kinda-but-not-too Freudian book from the 1960s, *Neurotic Styles*, treads these waters as well, and somewhat poetically, to boot. There's a whole chapter on what he calls the *impressionistic* cognitive style. Shapiro doesn't discuss the invalidating environment *per se*, but I don't think anyone was at the time. Nor do we talk so much about the impressionistic style; we call it *borderline* or *histrionic* personality or traits, depending on details.

It's fascinating to hear him discuss how such patients cannot *own* their emotions, identify with them, or otherwise integrate them into their selves. For example, such individuals

> do not quite regard the content of their [anger] outbursts as something they have really felt, but rather as something that has been visited on them or, as it were, something that has passed through them . . . [One patient,] during the period of regret immediately afterwards or later, [referred to it] as a mysterious thing, something akin to a seizure, a strange passion that had got her in its grip; in short, it was not something that she felt.[4]

Paradoxically, impressionistic persons may seem to present with simultaneously *intense* but *superficial* emotions. Exaggerated, but somehow shallow. Another of Shapiro's patients had "periodic stormy, hysterical outbursts of anger," primarily towards her husband:

> On one occasion, she is astonished that he tells her that he cannot put up with it. "He really means it," she says in

---

4 Shapiro, D. (1965). *Neurotic styles* (p. 126-127). New York: Basic Books.

amazement and adds, "But I don't mean the things I say."[5]

Shapiro is clear that impressionistic reasoning has nothing to do with intelligence, or lack thereof; everyone uses it sometimes, as they should. Sometimes, impressions are all we have. But some folks can hardly scrutinize their emotions and be skeptical of them at all, so they are readily carried away, often ruled by fleeting feelings and whim. When particularly pervasive, his or her

> romantic, fantastical, nonfactual, and insubstantial experience of the world also extends to his experience of his own self. He does not feel like a very substantial being with a real and factual history.[6]

It's the damnedest thing: I've met many people from chronically invalidating environments who assert, oddly but frankly, "I don't really remember my childhood," and they truly will have great difficulty telling you anything substantive about the experience. They deny having been overtly traumatized, as one might suspect, but still remain wholly unable to describe what existence was like until some time in their teens or so. These must be examples of what Shapiro was describing. I think he's suggesting that the person has no coherent identity (or didn't for a while) because they have always been unable to experience their emotions *as part of themselves*. I know, it's very psychobabbly, but I think there's something legitimate going on here. One can lack substance because there hasn't been much of a common thread—that is, of emotional coherence and predictability.

It also needs to be clarified that despite using words like "self," we're talking about *brains*. During our formative years, our brains are indeed forming and therefore sensitive to early experiences. Some of the most dramatic instances of so-called *neural plasticity*

---

5 Ibid., p. 123.

6 Ibid., p. 120.

include the brains of those who have, for example, lost their eyes to accidents early in life. In such cases, the parts of the brain that are supposed to process other senses, such as hearing, compensate by using more brain tissue than is typical, literally commandeering those areas that had been destined for sight.

It's fair to speculate that other experiences besides hearing and vision—such as self-esteem and a sense of self—are also mediated by particular brain areas or mechanisms. And just like those brain areas/activities intended for hearing and vision, if they are not stimulated properly during development, including by the seemingly trivial interactions with our parents, they will not form correctly. (And for the record, neuropsychologists and the like now believe that the "formative years" actually extend into early adulthood, that is, the early twenties, at least in some respects.)

Of course, invalidation does not merely occur between parents and growing children, although these are the most formative instances. Adults can invalidate other adults, whether it be boss to employee, friend to friend, stranger to stranger, or husband to wife. Opportunities for invalidation (or, optimistically, validation) are sprinkled throughout our days any time we're interacting with another person. Unfortunately, in America, invalidating the suffering of others is a pastime, right along with apple pie and Chevrolet.

Rumor has it that the town in which I live, Austin, Texas, has some of the most intense cedar pollen levels on Earth, at least during the winter months, December through March-ish. In places where it's particularly bad you can literally see clouds of green dust floating eerily in the air, a ghostly specter, lurking for victims, like something out of a Stephen King book. The "Green Death," I call it. After a major emission, you may find that your car has been painted green by the Death, so that you can write and draw pictures in it with your finger—*if you dare*. Indeed, some people, like me, react quite violently to this horrible tree's discharge, describing it as ever bit as bad as a full-on case of the flu, incapacitating and making one fearful of cracking a window in their home, not to mention the prospect of going outdoors. A drag, because it's not really cold here in winter.

Despite the seriousness of the problem, you will often overhear conversations such as this throughout winter:

Austin:	"Hey, do you want to go out for a couple beers later?"
David:	"Man, I'd love to; thanks for asking, but I'm feeling pretty sick today. I think I'm just gonna stay in and watch the game."
Austin:	"Ahhh, c'mon! It's probably just allergies!"

Instead of offering any validation or sympathy, people try to diagnose the condition, and then behave as if this somehow solves the problem. Apparently, in Austin, Texas calling it "allergies" is somehow supposed to make it hurt less. Indeed, the diagnosis seems to convey, "Well, despite how you feel, you're not actually infected by germs. You need to buckle down and keep on the move. We have shit to do, here in the A.T.X.!"

Of course, it shouldn't matter what it's called—it could be voodoo; identifying it as such doesn't change the subjective experience. How about something like "Oh; I'm sorry you're feeling sick. Yeah, you look kinda beat-up; do you want to just stay in tonight? We could get a movie . . ." Personally, I'm really appreciative of this latter, more sensitive and personable reaction; just typing it like that makes me feel good! But, alas, I find it's a bit of a pipe dream to expect others to respond as such.

Another one of the more common invalidating responses that we use a lot in America is when someone alludes to a significant experience from his past that continues to have relevance in the present:

Jerry: "I still have a hard time being in the same room with Douglas, ever since he hit on Sara at that Christmas party."

Daniel: "Oh, C'mon! That was five years ago!"

I'm not encouraging the habit of holding grudges, but neither should we simply disregard violations simply because a large amount of time has passed. Maybe Jerry doesn't trust Douglas, and maybe he shouldn't. If I was Jerry, I would wonder if Daniel has issues himself, like if he's afraid of conflict.

Another subtle—but significantly invalidating experience—occurs when someone tells us about an exciting experience she's had, such as a vacation in the mountains, and our reflex is to immediately respond by sharing a similar experience of our own. Instead of sharing her story with her, we unconsciously (or even consciously) try to trump it by telling a better story of our own:

Mary: "Hey, I just got back from Colorado; it was so beautiful. The weather was perfect and we got really close to an elk!"

Bob: "Cool! Yeah, I *love* the mountains. I got to go to the *Andes* last year when I was touring South America. A rare spectacled bear got into our tent and ate my toothpaste! I got its picture—didn't you see my profile pic? It looks like it has rabies! Ha ha ha!"

I'm not suggesting that you *shouldn't* tell your bear story; of course you should. But slow down! Consume more about Mary's elk first. Ask if anything else interesting happened, or just how the rest of the trip was. Give her a moment to be excited about her experience—and you be excited about her experience with her—before you trump it with yours. And sure, one might even consider *not trumping it at all*. Bring up your story on some other occasion altogether, or maybe never! I know, that's a pretty lofty suggestion. I bet hardly anyone ever does such a thing, maybe Ghandi or the Dalai Llama or something.

Even less sensitive of us, someone takes a risk and shares a story of acute emotional distress, and we respond similarly:

Mary: "I'm sorry I haven't called in a while. I've been pretty depressed since Rover died. It's weird: I'm lonely, but I don't have the energy to get together with my friends."

Bob: "Yeah, I hear ya' . . . I'm still not over my Fluffy myself. But instead of withdrawing, I find myself going out *too* much! Seems like I've been drinking more than ever, and I'm in some sort of rut."

I used to pretend that maneuvers such as this were somehow empathic, that sharing a similar experience of my own was somehow soothing to the person who started the conversation. But now I believe it's often self-centered. Instead of exploring the other person's distress with her, we use it as an opportunity to vent our own frustrations. And, at the same time, we're backing away from the uncomfortable position in which we find ourselves, that is, someone needing us to tend to them. Sure, some of the content of the conversation suggests it is deep and personable, but it's actually kinda superficial, a ping-pong match of sorts—indeed, there can be something almost competitive about it. I realize now this isn't what Mary needs. She needs Bob to say something more like:

Bob: "I'm so sorry! Rover was wonderful; I know y'all were close. It sounds really disorienting, to know

what you need to do to feel better, but to be unable to do that. Do you want to get together and
mope with me later? I'll drive and buy, if you'll
let me take you out."

This response is more empathic because Bob makes it clear he
heard Mary and he conveys that he's aware she probably has more
to say than her first line. He doesn't use her moment as an invita-
tion to get attention for his own distress. Instead, he returns the
conversation to her, inviting her to say more. He does what he can
to make it as easy as possible for Mary to say "yes" about getting
together, realizing that she probably needs to but doesn't feel like
it. And sure, later, when they mope together over dinner and
brewskis, he can bring up his dead Fluffy.

The more courage it takes Mary to share her inner experience,
the more significant Bob's insensitive reaction becomes. And the
more it hurts Mary when Bob invalidates her, the more it suggests
she was invalidated as a child. If Mary's parents had validated her
well during childhood—producing a healthy validated brain in
adulthood—she is more likely to see that Bob isn't the answer right
now. She'll move on, and maybe share her experience with Dana
instead.

However, if Mary was invalidated often growing up and now
has an adult brain that is wired for insecurity, she is much more
likely to be sensitive to Bob's comments and feel disoriented as a
result of the failed interaction. She may wonder, consciously or
subconsciously: "Am I overreacting? Was it appropriate for me to
even tell Bob about Rover? He's not helping! I just can't be soothed
. . . or maybe I don't deserve to be . . . No one understands me . . .
they never have." I used to scoff at the notion that adult pain often
stems from unresolved childhood pain, but I don't anymore. That
shit's real, man. Stuff hurts not just because it hurts now, but also
because it hurt *back then.* Yes, our adult experiences often tap our
childhood ones, both pleasures and pains.

Frustrated and worse off than when she started, Mary goes to a bar. She gets drunk and laid because she needs to be touched . . . but then wakes up the next morning in some strange apartment, feeling more disoriented than ever. Tugging cigarette butts from her hair and wiping mascara dingleberries from her eyes, she surveys the room, realizing for the first time that her *homme du jour* is a skanky, Jersey Shore-type, way too young for her, even if he had been perfect otherwise. He's currently comatose, face down, a gigantic tribal tattoo between his muscular, sunburned shoulders. Another tattoo—text of some sort—is uncomfortably placed in the lower of his back, just above his silk boxer-briefs. She doesn't dare read it, already resenting his seed inside of her more than she can hardly endure. The sounds of someone else fucking are making it through the wall from the next room. Mary cringes, then spies her own panties hanging off the corner of the aquarium right next to the bed where she's been sleeping all night. There are no fish—only some kind of fucking lizard in there! It's so big! Who has such a thing for a pet?!

You think I'm goofin' around, but I'm serious! If you don't want your daughter to end up as an impulsive one-night stander, you better learn how to pay healthy attention to her when she's little! That's how that ball gets rollin'. Next thing you know, panties danglin' from some douchebag's iguana cage, pullin' cigarette butts and bottle caps from her hair.

Even another way to invalidate another's distress is to reflexively offer advice. Staying with the deceased pet example, we often say something like "Rover died? Oh . . . well, you should get another dog! There are so many to adopt—you can rescue one from a shelter; Rover would be happy."

Getting another pet in the wake of just losing one is not a lot different than going to a bar and getting laid. But this is the American Way. We don't like to suffer, we don't like to *see* suffering, and we don't like to talk about it. We'd rather sweep it under the rug and replace it, sometimes before anyone even notices.

Michael Hollander again:

The real shame here is that [one's] advice might be right on the money. [But,] For whatever the reason—maybe it's a design flaw—people are more willing to accept advice after they feel they've been understood.[7]

Patients often tell Michael in therapy, "the advice was pretty good, but the timing was terrible."[8] I see! We don't know exactly why— perhaps it is indeed a design flaw—but yes, a person in emotional pain *needs that pain to be acknowledged and experienced before they can move on* and benefit from advice, regardless of how valuable that advice is. Pain needs to be felt, to run its course. Only then can one begin to address the more practical issues of coping. Feel first, then cope. Let's just call it a design flaw.

As I hope you suspect, this all takes a lot of practice. Once you begin to train yourself to not respond with advice, for example, you may find yourself instead imposing your own interpretations and hypotheses regarding what others are telling you—while they're in the process of trying to tell you theirs. For example, Jerry up there may have approached Daniel about Douglas more like this:

Jerry:	"Man, I'm not looking forward to running into Douglas. There's something about him that bothers me. It's hard for me to put my finger on—
Daniel:	"Ahhhh, yeah, he talks too much about himself; he doesn't know when to shut-up!"
Jerry:	"Well, yeah, but there's something else—
Daniel:	"Is it that way he always interrupts you when you're trying to talk?"

---

7 *Helping Teens Who Cut*, p. 53.

8 Ibid., p. 54.

In theory, interrupting someone to finish his thought for him might work, if you get his thought right. Sure, he might feel that you have the capacity to see his side of the story, although he may remain annoyed that you interrupted him and didn't let him speak for himself. But, in the also likely event that you don't verbalize his concern accurately while interrupting him, you just create more distance and isolate him.

Instead, postpone the interpretations until the speaker feels heard. Let them tell you; don't think you're a fancy psychologist because you've got it all figured out. The irony is that being a good psychologist is more about listening first and then asking good questions than it is about figuring stuff out for patients and just telling them. If you do figure out an issue, you don't have to specify it yourself: You can ask even more questions to help the speaker come to the realization on his own! In counseling, as with emotional validation proper, we need to "Think 'mirror' and not 'mind reader.'"[9]

Before we switch gears and finish up, we have to acknowledge that there are limits to the validating process—there is such a thing as being reckless about it. To illustrate with an extreme example, we don't validate the paranoid delusions of psychotic patients. Now, we can validate their *feelings of fear associated with the delusion*, but we have to be careful not to validate the delusion *per se*. We can assert that it would indeed be frightening if the FBI was following us, but we simply find it hard to believe that they are. Of course, we encounter similar but less extreme instances outside of the state hospital. Sometimes our friends really are misperceiving reality, and relentlessly validating their experience without challenging their perceptions may not be productive in the long run. But we can challenge them with sensitivity. "Gentle confrontation," I like to call it.

Also, some people really can be too demanding for comfort. My

---

9 Ibid., p. 141.

lecture was not intended to encourage you to advertise every feeling you have in every context. That's called "dramatic," or clinically, *histrionic*. Don't do that, either; it's annoying as crap. As with most things, moderation is key. People who cope with their neediness by excessively demanding attention will only push others away, perpetuating the cycle of neediness.

I gather that the acknowledgment and expression of suffering are more acceptable in some countries outside of the U.S.A. While on internship at a state hospital, I was moved by a story that our Nepalese psychiatrist told one day during our weekly psychopharmacology brown-bag seminar. I apologize, Nepal, if I butcher the story, but I believe I can recount the essence fairly accurately. He explained that following a death in his community, the family of the deceased was essentially locked up together in a single-room dwelling in which they had to remain together for a period of several days. Communication between the grieving and the outside world was not permitted. It was just you and your loved ones, along with the conspicuous absence of the deceased.

The apparent goal of this seemingly peculiar arrangement was to permit—perhaps more like *force*—the grieving parties to indeed grieve, thoroughly and without reservation. Without television, telephones, or tele-anything else, the persons in the dwelling are not distracted and have little choice but to process, privately and together, what has transpired. I'm not sure how these must have unfolded in Nepal, but it's interesting to imagine how they might in America. I wonder if the average American could even endure such a thing! Sure, we have funerals, but I always sense that the energy in American funerals is spent trying to deny that the person is actually gone, as opposed to just soaking it in, like they apparently do in some places in Nepal.

More subtly, following a therapy session with an adolescent recently, I was briefing his mother on her son's progress. She herself was upset about something unrelated, disclosing through tears that her brother was dying from cancer. Mom was from Italy, where much of her family, including the ailing brother, continued to live. She was obviously distressed because she was separated from them, but the distress was compounded, she explained, because she felt emotionally constricted and isolated in America. Back in Italy, I learned, it is much more acceptable to discuss one's emotional distress with others. But here, she felt it was inappropriate, like she was asking too much. It makes me so sad to even type that.

And, as usual, we don't have to contemplate the extreme circumstances of death and funerals to see how suffering is shunned here. An acquaintance of mine, Joanna Barbera, is a charismatic and talented songstress here in Austin. We were chatting recently after one of her shows, and she seemed a little uncomfortable because of recent comments—that apparently felt, at least a little, like criticism—that her music is "sad." At some point, I tried to comfort her: It's not your responsibility to make the world feel good. In fact, if people get sad at your music, you didn't *do* that to them; you just catalyzed their contact with a sadness they brought to your show. Same goes for books like this one. I suspect many people would feel sad at times while reading it. But I'm not *making* you sad. Don't blame me or Joanna; blame the cosmos. We're just describing the way things seem to us. If it makes you sad, then you probably agree, on some level.

And again, when did feeling sad become so wrong? Paradoxically, if we just give ourselves permission to be sad, it eventually feels better than when we try to cope by suppressing the sadness. Otherwise, we psychologists believe that the *meta-emotions*, that is, the sadness and/or anxiety—if not shame—that we feel *about* our primary sadness or anxiety makes matters even worse. And the irony is that these emotions-about-emotions are not even necessary. Western culture forces them upon us, not Nature. We should just be sad sometimes, as God intended, without having to feel guilty for feeling that way.

Notes

THE NOTES BELOW include elaborations and more complete citations in reference to the epigraphs throughout this book (that is, the quotations that introduce each chapter, as well as those in the introductory text of the book).

INTRODUCTION

Neider, C. (Ed.). (2000). *The autobiography of Mark Twain* (pp. 326-327). New York: Perennial Classics. Twain's autobiography was published posthumously, by his design: "The very reason that I speak from the grave is that I want the satisfaction of sometimes saying everything that is in me instead of bottling the pleasantest of it up for home consumption" (ibid., p. 326).

Rawlings, G. B. (Ed. & Trans.). (2009). *Pascal's pensées; or, thoughts on religion* (p. 36 and p. 7). Charleston, SC: Bibliolife. (Original work published 1670). The *Pensées* is an unfinished, somewhat unorganized collection of notes that Pascal wrote towards the end of his life "in the intervals of painful and prostrating illness" (ibid., p.4). I've taken the liberty to combine two non-adjacent pensées, but I feel this is appropriate, given the disorganized nature of the work and the apparent congruence between the two.

CHAPTER 1

Becker, E. (1973). *The denial of death* (p. 50). New York: The Free Press.

CHAPTER 2

The quote is popularly attributed to Alfred Hitchcock, but I haven't been able to find the precise source. Also note that a popular variation states "the bang" instead of "a bang." See, for example, the Academy's Facebook post on August 13, 2014, celebrating his birthday. I don't know which way it's supposed to be, but I prefer "a."

CHAPTER 3

All Bible quotes in this book are from the *New American Standard Bible, Reference Edition.* (1975). Chicago: Moody Press. I still own the very same Bible I read growing up, and it still gets a lot of use.

CHAPTER 4

Meyers, J. (2000). *Edgar Allen Poe: His life and legacy* (p. 89). New York: Cooper Square Press.

Maugham, S. (2004). *The painted veil* (p. 172). New York: Vintage International.

Of course, the title of this chapter is the famous line from: Hendrix, J. (1967). Are you experienced? [Recorded by The Jimi Hendrix Experience]. On *Are you experienced?* [Vinyl record]. London: Track Records.

CHAPTER 5

Washington, H. A. (Ed.). (1854). *The writings of Thomas Jefferson* (v. 7, book 2, p. 284). Washington, DC: Taylor & Maury. Retrieved via Google books, http://books.google.com

CHAPTER 6

Muir, M. & George, R. (Writers). (1990). You can't bring me down. [Suicidal Tendencies]. On *Lights . . . Camera . . . Revolution!* US: Epic.

CHAPTER 7

The Denial of Death, p. 282-283.

CHAPTER 8
Lucretius. (2007). Lucretius, from de rerum natura (On the nature of things). (W. H. Brown, Trans.). In C. Hitchens (Ed.), *The portable atheist: Essential readings for the nonbeliever* (p. 2). US: Da Capo Press.

CHAPTER 9
Camus, A. (1989). *The stranger* (M. Ward, Trans.; p. 69). New York: Vintage International. (Original work published 1942).

CHAPTER 10
Harris, S. (2004). *The end of faith* (p. 78-79). New York: W. W. Norton.

CHAPTER 11
de Mello, A. (1988). *One minute wisdom* (p. 103). New York: Image Books.

APPENDIX
Watts, A. (2000). *Still the mind* (p. 43). Novato, CA: New World Library.

Acknowledgements

THANKS SO MUCH, FRIENDS, for reading drafts or portions of my book and being gentle but compelling with your criticisms: Madison "Smeller" Lowry, Lewis "Pops" Hussing, Matthew D. Arnold, Lee E. Davis, his excellent parents "Izzy" and Walt Davis, Aaron "Wally" Wallace, Steve Ilardi, Lance Myers, Jessieca Melendez, and "Battlestar Gailactica" Gresham.

And you too, Donald "Grumpa" Skrabanek, now resting in peace. After you were done, you told me that you believe in more of a "cycle of life." You were vague but passed away soon thereafter, before we had a chance to talk about it, just a few days before your youngest daughter's wedding. We had the wedding anyway; I like to think that's what you were talking about.

Spencer and Brittan: You are my family. If it wasn't for you, your sanctuaries, and your camaraderie, I really may have stepped off some sort of deep end.

Thanks, too, Mom and Dad. It's obviously been rough at times but, all said and done, I'm glad y'all made me happen.

Hook 'em!

About the Author

David is a licensed clinical psychologist in Austin, Texas specializing in forensic evaluation (juvenile probation, competency to stand trial, and the insanity defense). His formal education is from the University of Texas at Austin (B.A., Psychology; M.A., Neuroscience) and the University of Kansas (Ph.D., Clinical Psychology). While at Kansas, David earned the Irving-Handelsman Graduate Student Award for teaching introductory psychology courses and statistics. More recently, he has taught forensic psychology at St. Edward's University in Austin. When not working, he likes being outdoors, spending time with friends, barbecuing, cycling/jogging, spectating sports, and watching boring foreign movies.

Made in the USA
San Bernardino, CA
16 July 2016